SAX2

SAX2

David Brownell

O'REILLY®

Beijing · Cambridge · Farnham · Köln · Paris · Sebastopol · Taipei · Tokyo

SAX2

by David Brownell

Copyright © 2002 O'Reilly & Associates, Inc. All rights reserved.
Printed in the United States of America.

Published by O'Reilly & Associates, Inc., 1005 Gravenstein Highway North, Sebastopol, CA 95472.

O'Reilly & Associates books may be purchased for educational, business, or sales promotional use. Online editions are also available for most titles (*safari.oreilly.com*). For more information, contact our corporate/institutional sales department: (800) 998-9938 or *corporate@oreilly.com*.

Editor: Simon St.Laurent

Production Editor: Mary Brady

Cover Designer: Ellie Volckhausen

Printing History:

January 2002:   First Edition.

Nutshell Handbook, the Nutshell Handbook logo, and the O'Reilly logo are registered trademarks of O'Reilly & Associates, Inc. The association between the image of a pampas cat and the topic of SAX2 is a trademark of O'Reilly & Associates, Inc.

Many of the designations used by manufacturers and sellers to distinguish their products are claimed as trademarks. Where those designations appear in this book, and O'Reilly & Associates, Inc. was aware of a trademark claim, the designations have been printed in caps or initial caps.

While every precaution has been taken in the preparation of this book, the author and publisher assume no responsibility for errors or omissions, or for damages resulting from the use of the information contained herein.

ISBN: 0-596-00237-8
[M]

Table of Contents

Preface .... *vii*

1. *The Simple API for XML* *1*
   Types of XML APIs 2
   Why Choose SAX? 3
   Why Not to Choose SAX? 8
   A Short History of SAX 9
   Packages in the SAX2 API 14
   Some Popular SAX2 Parser Distributions 14
   Installing a SAX2 Parser 17
   What XML Are We Talking About? 19

2. *Introducing SAX2* *23*
   Producers and Consumers 24
   Beginning SAX 25
   Basic ContentHandler Events 33
   Producer-Side Validation 44
   Exception Handling 49
   Namespaces and SAX2 56

3. *Producing SAX2 Events* *67*
   Pull Mode Event Production with XMLReader 67
   Bootstrapping an XMLReader 76
   Configuring XMLReader Behavior 81

v

The EntityResolver Interface 88
Other Kinds of SAX2 Event Producers 91

4. **Consuming SAX2 Events** *103*
More About ContentHandler *103*
The LexicalHandler Interface *111*
Exposing DTD Information *115*
Turning SAX Events into Data Structures *122*
XML Pipelines *129*

5. **Other SAX Classes** *140*
Helper Classes *140*
SAX1 Support *147*

6. **Putting It All Together** *150*
Rich Site Summary: RSS *150*
XML and Messaging *165*
Including Subdocuments *174*

A. *SAX2 API Summary* *181*

B. *SAX2 and the XML Infoset* *201*

Index *219*

Preface

Think of this book as if it were really called *Everything You Wanted to Know About SAX*. It provides a quick tutorial, while also serving as a complete reference that explains how to use this popular XML API effectively and efficiently. You'll find motivations for every programming interface and see how to build components for your application (or specialized environment) on top of SAX.

The information in this book is based on the current version of the Java™ language support for SAX2. For any further updates to SAX2, see the SAX web site at *http://www.saxproject.org*.

Who Should Read This Book?

If you are programming with XML in Java, or starting to do that, and you want to learn how to use SAX2 to its fullest, this book is for you. It assumes that you are familiar with Java programming and have a basic understanding of XML, including DTDs. You may have some exposure to DOM, an alternative parser API, but you need more efficient, or more complete, access to XML than you can get with such a generic tree structure API. Although there's a lot of interest in XML from server-side programmers, and this book includes some examples targeted at servlet-based systems, SAX2 is addressed to Java developers working on all scales, from embedded systems to enterprise applications.

Although versions of the SAX API have been provided for developers who use C/C++, Pascal, Perl, and Python, this book is not addressed to such developers except in the broad sense that good SAX programming idioms transcend the particular language used to express them.

This book is for Java programmers working with XML who need an efficient way of reading or generating XML documents. The simple API for XML (SAX)'s event-based approach provides an extremely streamlined set of tools for Java programmers.

Organization of This Book

This book is divided into six chapters and two appendixes.

Chapter 1, *The Simple API for XML*, orients you in terms of API alternatives, SAX history, software choices, and basic SAX functionality.

Chapter 2, *Introducing SAX2*, introduces the core technical details of SAX, showing the basic event producer and consumer APIs needed by almost all code that uses SAX.

Chapter 3, *Producing SAX2 Events*, focuses on producing SAX events, showing the rest of the parser APIs as well as several nonparser models for using SAX.

Chapter 4, *Consuming SAX2 Events*, concentrates on consuming SAX events, showing the other event consumer interfaces (both core and extension), and exploring the SAX pipeline model in a bit more detail.

Chapter 5 *Other SAX Classes*, presents SAX helper classes that weren't yet presented, including legacy SAX1 support.

Chapter 6 *Putting It All Together*, provides more extensive examples than the earlier chapters.

The two appendixes are reference material. Appendix A, *SAX2 API Summary*, summarizes every class or interface in the API and should be a useful quick reference. Appendix B, *SAX2 and the XML Infoset*, shows how the XML Infoset concepts map to SAX APIs and should be a useful reference when you need to determine which APIs to use to access particular structural data.

Conventions Used in This Book

method()
: Method names sometimes include their interfaces or classes.

method parameter or *variable*
: Values bound to parameter or variable names are presented in the same way.

class, interface, or package.name
> Names identifying interfaces and classes are identified in the same way as package names.

`XML attribute` *or* `element`
> All XML markup in the body of the text is presented consistently.

How to Contact Us

Please address any comments and questions concerning this book to the publisher:

> O'Reilly & Associates, Inc.
> 1005 Gravenstein Highway North
> Sebastopol, CA 95472
> (800) 998-9938 (in the United States or Canada)
> (707) 829-0515 (international/local)
> (707) 829-0104 (fax)

We have a web page for this book, where we list errata, examples, or any additional information. You can access this page at:

> *http://www.oreilly.com/catalog/sax2/*

To comment or ask technical questions about this book, send email to:

> *bookquestions@oreilly.com*

For more information about our books, conferences, software, Resource Centers, and the O'Reilly Network, see our web site at:

> *http://www.oreilly.com*

Acknowledgments

This book would not have been possible without the contribution and support of many individuals. David Megginson, who led the original SAX and SAX2 development processes, deserves particular thanks from everyone who uses SAX. Numerous other people have contributed to SAX through the *xml-dev* mailing list, far too many to mention here by name. Simon St.Laurent at O'Reilly provided good feedback and regular encouragement during the creation of this book. Along with review comments from Murray Altheim and David Megginson, he helped identify rough spots and improve the content of this book in many ways.

In this chapter:
- *Types of XML APIs*
- *Why Choose SAX?*
- *Why Not to Choose SAX?*
- *A Short History of SAX*
- *Packages in the SAX2 API*
- *Some Popular SAX2 Parser Distributions*
- *Installing a SAX2 Parser*
- *What XML Are We Talking About?*

1
The Simple API for XML

When XML started, Java was best known as a fun new language that made developing programs for the World Wide Web easy. XML was intended to be the data foundation for the next generation of web infrastructure tools, and it clearly needed the same kind of support that Java offered. The Java programming environment included ways to fetch data over the Web with URLs, which was a novel notion at that. It even had support for Unicode, so working with languages used anywhere on the Web would be easy. Since both those capabilities were important for working with XML, there was already a very active community of XML developers using Java when the XML 1.0 Recommendation was finalized in early 1998. More XML parsers were available at that time for Java than for the more widely adopted C programming language!

Those parsers quickly came to share one feature: applications weren't restricted to some particular product's API. The *Simple API for XML*, SAX, was well under way; it was the first API usable with all the popular Java parsers. SAX helped make Java a premiere language for developing XML-based applications.

Since then the adoption of XML has exploded, as has the use of Java in web-oriented (and other) applications. Today's Java programmer has an embarrassingly large selection of XML-related APIs to choose from, and SAX has retained its role as a premier XML API. In this chapter we look at why this is true, and learn more about where SAX came from and its current state.

Types of XML APIs

An *Application Programming Interface* (API) is a set of interfaces and classes used to expose particular functionality to a variety of applications. Some APIs are specific to particular products. Better Java APIs, like SAX, use the `interface` facility to work with multiple products: they are defined so that multiple implementations can coexist. Such implementations behave the same except for differences allowed by the API. For example, one might be faster, while another might leverage private interfaces to some subsystem. (In that case an application could use the fast implementation most of the time and the slower one only when those added features are needed.) APIs differ in how they expose functionality, which affects how well applications work.

For the purposes of this book, there are two kinds of APIs to XML. We'll call one a "parser API" and the other a "high-level API." *Parser-level APIs* model documents in terms of XML notions such as elements, attributes, and character data, and hide all the details of actually turning XML text into information that applications can use. *High-level APIs* generally focus on non-XML notions, usually to make XML itself seem only an implementation artifact that might be easily replaced by other data interchange technology, or more rarely, by another document technology. This spectrum is not as wide as you might expect. Parser-level APIs are well-suited for working with XML-centric applications, higher-level APIs try to focus on particular visions of the data being encoded with XML, and some APIs "hop" between levels.

SAX is a parser-level API that is rather unique in flavor because it leaves all data structure choices up to higher levels. This feature helps scale XML applications, since it lets SAX be an unobtrusive and extremely effective building block. SAX models documents in terms of a stream of event callbacks; this has been called an "active" API. The events are more structured than the stream of mouse and keyboard events you may know from AWT or Swing. Events are sent to application handlers for basic XML content (such as elements and characters) in exactly the order they're found in the document, as shown in Figure 1-1. That's the same order in which you'd traverse a tree model of that markup: you'd start an element, look at its children, and then end the element.

Most other parser-level APIs provide a generic, object tree data structure mirroring the parse tree; these have been called "passive" APIs. Figure 1-2 shows some XML text, and its transformation to such a data structure.

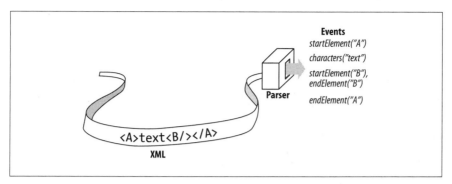

Figure 1-1. A streaming parser API

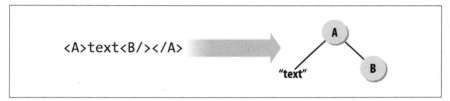

Figure 1-2. An object tree parser API

Examples of such generic data structures include W3C's DOM and more Java-friendly variants such as DOM4J and jDOM. Such generic tree structures are usually built with the output of an underlying SAX parser, and so are slightly higher level than SAX. However, these generic structures place significant constraints on application structure and scalability. A popular alternative approach involves building custom data structures from that same SAX output, instead of generic ones, larger than some fraction of available virtual memory. Because the data structures are custom built, they tend to be faster and more task-appropriate than structures built by generic APIs.

Why Choose SAX?

SAX gives you the flexibility to approach application design with your own trade-offs and goals in mind. High-level APIs often make many of those trade-offs for you, but not necessarily in ways that are best for your problems. In particular, SAX lets you design lightweight, task-oriented XML solutions, which can fit into small systems or scale up to large ones. Just having such options can be an important reason to choose SAX over generic APIs that work only at a high level. While initial deployment platforms might be richly featured, this won't necessarily be true for all the systems you need to support, or for the ones your customers want you to support.

Compared to other parser-level APIs, SAX has two unique structural features: its efficient event-stream processing model and its data structure flexibility. These give you more control over the results of your parse.

Stream-Based Processing

SAX is the API to use when you need to stream-process XML to conserve memory and, in most cases, CPU time. In SAX, handler interfaces call application (or library) code for each significant chunk of XML information as it's parsed. These chunks include character data, elements, and attributes. Each event passes information to your code, which can save it or ignore it as appropriate. These handlers see document information as a stream of such event calls, in "document order." Applications can process data incrementally, rather than in one big chunk, and they can discard information as soon as it's not needed.

SAX parsers have several key advantages:

- SAX parsers can be small and fast because they are minimal. SAX provides the most essential XML data, and no more.

  SAX parsers are well suited for use in resource-constrained environments. This includes not just small systems or classic embedded ones (where cost prevents using of much memory or fast CPUs), but also inside servers (which may have huge amounts of memory and fast CPUs, but need good scaling properties to share them with many clients) such as security gateways. Good security practice avoids large bodies of code, since assurance is so hard to achieve.

- Because SAX is a streaming API, it promotes pipelined processing, where I/O occurs while you use the CPU to do work. You will naturally structure applications (or at least their SAX components) to use efficient single-pass algorithms and incremental processing.

  As soon as XML data starts to become available (perhaps over a network), SAX parsers start to provide it to applications. While processing element or character data, the network or the filesystem prefetches the next data. Such overlapped processing lowers latencies and makes good use of limited CPU cycles. With most other APIs, your application won't even see data until the whole document has been fetched and parsed; you can't process documents larger than available memory. This causes major trouble when you work with large documents, as discussed in the next section.

- SAX gives you flexible control over how you handle errors and faults. Fatal errors aren't the only kind of reportable fault, and diagnostic information is readily accessible.

  You easily provide application-specific error reports with the standard mechanism. It's also easy to terminate parsing early: just throw an appropriate exception when you find the `<great:widget>` element you need, or when some unrecoverable error turns up.

- It's easy to define custom SAX event producers.

  That is, you can use SAX when your inputs aren't literal XML text. This is a powerful technique that helps you work with data at the level of parsed XML information (the XML "Infoset"), and postprocess SAX events or late-bind data into XML text format. Such early/late-binding flexibility is a powerful architectural tool.

You may be fortunate enough to be able to design the XML representations of your application tasks to facilitate such work-flow streams. When you do this, you may see substantial performance and scalability gains over alternative design approaches. You might even be able to pull the SAX event stream model up into higher-level work flows in your system so that more processing can be stream-based.

For example, you could structure your XML as a sequential list of reasonably sized tasks. Several kinds of data import/export problems are well suited to this approach, although you may find you need to be aware of the I/O costs of random access as you transform data to and from interchange formats.

Data Structure Flexibility

In contrast to higher-level APIs, or most design tools, SAX allows you to populate whatever data structures you choose. It lets you use custom data APIs, optimized for your application, or more general-purpose APIs. This flexibility operates at two broad system levels: architecture and design. Suchs flexibility is required to scale applications up (or down) and to update applications as systems evolve.

Application architecture components affect how systems interact with each other and with external systems. SAX doesn't constrain these components, which include data interchange formats and messaging paradigms, because it lets you use XML in any way you (or your systems partners) need. In contrast, settling early on higher-level XML APIs will constrain application architectures in many ways, often affecting XML structures used for interoperability. For example, many SOAP toolkits expect an RPC paradigm using W3C-style XML schemas, and many data-binding approaches demand a particular schema system and API toolset. The hope is that if you accept those system constraints, you win more than they cost. When that doesn't work, perhaps because the constraints don't suit your application, you'll appreciate the flexibility of SAX.

The design level affects application internals rather than the broader interfaces, which relate to architecture. Design constraints affect runtime and implementation costs. If you're adding XML support to an existing system, design-level concerns may dominate your planning. SAX lets you use your current optimized data structures or define new ones. Since such design issues will often dominate performance measurements (given reasonable architectures), preserving flexibility can be very important.

With SAX, you don't need to use generic (and largely untyped) data structures. You will normally store data directly into specialized data structures as SAX delivers it from its XML representation. This facilitates important architecture-level optimizations. Being able to use custom data structures means you can leverage the strong data-typing facilities in Java and detect many kinds of bugs early, while recovery is possible and cheap. Custom data decisions are the ideal way to work with large documents, for other cases where scale is a major concern, and anywhere that data structure decisions need to be driven by application issues rather than "one size fits all" generic tools.

Memory Consumption with SAX and DOM

To illustrate this design impact, we'll pick on DOM as a representative design choice for an API with a generic XML data structure. You'll often have reasons to use both SAX and DOM, even in the same application, so you'll need to know when to use each API. The strength of DOM is that it's a widely understood and available generic model; it can be good for "proof of concept" solutions. However, it has a high price in terms of flexibility and resource consumption. Later, we look at ways to reduce those DOM costs with help from SAX and ways that DOM and SAX representations of XML data can be interconverted.

For documents with a "typical" markup density, many DOM implementations in Java use about 10 bytes of memory to represent each byte of XML text. (Few take less, some take more.) Yes, that midsize three-megabyte document can easily balloon up to 30 megabytes of memory on your server!* When using DOM with large documents, memory shortages are common, both for virtual memory and for space in the Java heap. Shortages are made worse if you then need to convert data from a generic DOM representation into custom structures, because you need an extra copy of the data while you build the more appropriate data structure. This clearly limits application scalability.

On the other hand, with SAX you don't pay for any memory unless you choose to do so. You can ignore most of that three-megabyte document right up front; the API structure makes it natural to capture only significant data (whatever that may be in your application). This reduces memory allocation pressure, as well as overhead from garbage collection. Best, SAX parsers let you use data structures that are appropriate for *your* application from the very beginning. In fact, they all but require you to do that!

Other Reasons to Prefer SAX

SAX has always defined its concurrency behaviors, making it safe to use SAX in multithreaded applications. Since DOM does not specify those behaviors, multithreaded applications (such as most web services) accept implementation dependencies if they choose to use DOM.

SAX2 provides almost complete support for the XML Infoset, exposing the logical structure of XML data. (See Appendix B.) This means it's substantially more complete than most other XML APIs, and certainly more complete than any other widely available API. You are unlikely to need important information from an XML document that SAX can't provide. This contrasts with DOM, which doesn't have standard APIs to expose much of this information. SAX is great way to turn a stream of such Infoset data into other kinds of data.

At its core, SAX is indeed a very simple API for XML processing; such simplicity is a key virtue. You can write useful XML applications code with only a handful of method calls and still know that the rest of the XML Infoset data is available when you need it. It's not like DOM, in which syntax artifacts that mask the core data model of XML are common. DOM takes a more monolithic approach than SAX. A book that covers DOM as

---

* Some applications certainly revolve around large documents. One translation of the Old Testament is over 3 megabytes in size; one dictionary is over 50 megabytes. Dumps of databases can be gigabytes in size.

completely as this book covers SAX would need to be several times larger even if it didn't cover the latest version (Level 3).

On top of that, because SAX makes you actually think about the best way to represent your data, it's more fun to work with than tools that claim to solve those issues for you! (They usually can't.) It's also a great way to learn your way around XML and Java.

Why Not to Choose SAX?

No API solves problems by itself, and SAX avoided the kitchen sink syndrome better than many others. So there are times it will be clear SAX isn't the whole answer for some particular application-processing stage, even when you have the option to choose it. It will often still be the right way to get data into or out of another processing stage, particularly since many other APIs can interface with SAX. Also, building custom data import/export tools with SAX is fairly easy.

Probably the biggest single issue with SAX is that by itself it doesn't provide random access to XML data. Its event stream is "forward-only": you can't go backwards or reorder it without your own record of the events. Such data structure policy would be handled by application layers on top of SAX, and you'll need such layers if you use random access models such as XPath. Typically, applications use SAX to construct data structures that are either customized for their particular random access requirements or generic (typically DOM-like). You might create *Person* objects and index them by name, perhaps in some sort of hash table or using some kind of database as a backing store. In some applications it's acceptable to just rescan small to midsize XML documents on demand; it can be inexpensive when modern operating systems have already cached the data.

If you're looking for an API that helps you write a low-level XML text editor and lets you work with malformed XML while it preserves semantically meaningless information,* then SAX isn't what you want. Similarly, parsing less than an entire XML document isn't standardized by SAX (or by the XML specification). Such processing requires an API that works at the level of potentially malformed tokens. SAX (and any other application programming interface not targeted at text editors) makes hiding such

---

* For example, whitespace outside element content, attribute order, or singly versus doubly quoted strings.

details a primary goal. SAX works well for "structural" editors, which prevent creation of malformed XML and hide semantically meaningless information.

It's important to note that SAX is intentionally limited. It's the core of a library of XML support, and that "S" in its name really does mean "simple"; complex functionality is for layers on top of SAX and is not part of SAX itself. Even basic facilities like XML text output (printing) are layered over SAX. While open source code to handle such functions is often available on the Internet, you may still need to find and choose between such libraries. SAX is somewhat of a "close to the metal" low-level API, though it's more flexible than most such APIs.

A Short History of SAX

The official SAX web site is at *http://www.saxproject.org*. You will find a more complete history there, with updates for anything that happened after this book went to print, as well as the current software release and its documentation.

SAX1

SAX 1.0 development started in late December 1997, shortly after publication of the last review draft of the XML 1.0 specification. The initial impetus was to permit Java applications to be independent of which parser they used, and to promote uniformity in the data models available to applications without imposing some particular data representation. At that time, several such Java parsers existed (notably Ælfred, Lark, MSXML, and XP), each with their own APIs and feature sets. That approach would clearly be counterproductive and had already caused complications for one early XML browser, Jumbo, used with a Chemical Markup Language built with XML. (See *http://www.xml-cml.org* for more information about CML and Jumbo.)

Discussion proceeded quickly. The development primarily took place on the open Internet *xml-dev* mailing list. There was no bureaucracy since it was organized and run by one person, David Megginson, the original author of Ælfred. Essential contributions were made by developers of other Java XML parsers, including Tim Bray, editor of the XML 1.0 Recommendation and author of Lark, and James Clark, Technical Lead of the XML 1.0 Recommendation and author of XP. In terms of openness, the process was similar to those used historically by the Internet Engineering Task Force (IETF) and by many current open source development projects. Unlike the process for most recent Java/XML API standards, helping to define SAX required no nondisclosure agreements, or reassignment of intellectual property rights, and had a transparent process. Public list archives are available, if you want to see how (or why!) some things turned out the way that they did

The initial draft API was published in January 1998, less than a month after initial discussions started. It featured key characteristics still seen today: it was event based, and distinguished interface and implementation without insisting that implementations commit to the overhead of a "provider" glue layer. To improve its coolness factor, it used the *org.xml.sax* package name, since Jon Bosak owned the "xml.org" DNS domain name and gave approval for that use.* Best, it was indeed a *Simple API for XML*. Discussions continued fast and furious. More developers helped improve these early proposals, including the author of this book.

The SAX1 API was finalized in May 1998, just three months after XML itself was finalized, and was generally well received. Most Java XML parsers quickly adapted to it, and new ones quickly adopted it. At one point, it was possible to find no less than a dozen open source SAX1 parsers. Today, new XML projects tend to build on top of the standard APIs such as SAX, rather than underneath them, since most widely used parsers do support SAX.

SAX2

When SAX1 was finished, there were features it did not address. That was to be expected because of the 80/20 rule. Satisfying the 80% of application requirements that involved only simple functionality meant that only a small handful of applications needed more complex functionality; that handful was much less than 20% of the application space. Notably, anyone who tried to use SAX to *round-trip* XML data found that important parts were omitted. (Round-tripping a SAX event stream means turning it back into XML text and parsing the result, without losing any data.) Similarly, anyone using SAX to construct a DOM tree found that there was a mismatch: DOM also expected more information to be provided. Although many applications were happy not to see that additional data, it was still a

---

* This domain was subsequently transferred to the OASIS group, which later took over operations for the *xml-dev* mailing list. However, SAX still remains independent of OASIS. SAX is currently maintained using SourceForge.net project resources.

conformance issue. Moreover, since DTD declarations were not available, it wasn't practical to maintain arbitrary valid documents with a SAX1-only parser. On top of all that, it wasn't possible to tell if a parser could validate, nor could you change whether or not it was validating; this all but prevented parser-neutral application configuration and setup. As developers learned their way around XML, the 80/20 line shifted so more functionality was needed.

So discussions continued, but at a much slower pace. In late 1998 some draft interfaces were posted, which later became the basis of the two standard SAX2 extensions. (Not many parsers worked with those interfaces until they were fleshed out later in the SAX2 process.) Discussions later in the next year focused on ways to let such additional extension handlers and other new features be added without changing "core" APIs, by supporting parser configurability.

The final catalyst for SAX2 was probably the realization that without parser-level API support, the XML Namespaces specification would probably not be adopted soon with any really standard semantics. Application-specific implementations tended to have bugs in their interpretation of the namespaces specification. (That specification has turned out to cause a surprising amount of confusion.) To make a long story short, further discussions happened, and SAX2 was finalized in May 2000. SAX1 parsers were initially wrapped in adapters that layered the namespace processing, making it easy to convert to use the core SAX2 APIs. The first parser to natively support the full set of SAX2 APIs, including the extension interfaces, was Ælfred2, in the second half of 1999. By the second half of 2000, such support was available in the current releases of most other widely used parsers.

This book focuses on the current SAX2 release, which includes minor bug fixes as well as more robust bootstrapping and clarifications, and explanations for the API documentation.

SAX2 Extensions

As mentioned earlier, one of the original reasons to extend SAX1 was that the SAX core didn't expose information needed by various applications and, of course, DOM. Not everyone needs or wants that information. A cautionary example is exposing comments, which were never intended to be used (or seen) by applications; they were grandfathered into XML APIs through horrible accidents involving old HTML browsers and DOM. However, lack of such such data was a problem for some applications. That

80/20 rule kept such features at a relatively low priority. The fact that exposing this information called for changes to parser internals ensured that it couldn't be part of the SAX2 core. (Because information such as a comment was discarded in SAX1, this information couldn't be layered, in the same way that *org.xml.sax.helpers.ParserAdapter* does for namespace support.)

The resolution was to decouple development of the SAX2 declaration and lexical handlers from the SAX core and to make them optional. The "SAX-extension" interfaces were not finalized until December 2000, well after the SAX2 core was finalized; at this writing, many of the deployed SAX2 parsers still only support the beta test versions of those interfaces. In practice, most SAX2 parsers do support these two handlers, which are mostly used to develop infrastructure tools. Applications value the "simple" nature of SAX, which lets them focus primarily on a single event handler interface included in the core of SAX.

In the future, most SAX2 extensions will be able to be layered independently of SAX2 parsers. Only very few additional kinds of information appear to need standardized support from inside such parsers.* Today, most new XML technologies are defined as layers above the XML Infoset, so they can (and should!) be implemented as layers above SAX2-based parsers rather than within them.

Is SAX2 a "Standard"?

In a word, yes: SAX is a shining example of a de facto standard API. You will have a hard time finding an XML parser written in Java that doesn't support SAX. In contrast to the recent spate of standards originated by a formal de jure standards body (notably the International Standards Organization, or the ISO), or to specifications pushed by vendors or a vendor-dominated consortium, SAX2 is a standard in the more classic sense. It was hammered into shape by users, quenched in the fire of real-world use, and adopted as a tool *after* it proved its worth. This partially motivates its small size and clear focus: it had a clear mission, and little of the "mission creep" pressure often caused by standards organization politics. This also explains why its legal status may seem to be unique; SAX is in the public domain, not copyrighted or controlled by any corporation or consortium.

---

* See the SAX we site for more information about these. Also, some probable new extensions are noted in Appendix B.

You may be familiar with other examples of technology standards that were developed similarly. For example, the *sockets* network API widely used for TCP was popularized at the University of California at Berkeley; from there it migrated into other Unix systems and then into Microsoft Windows. Similar processes occured for other core Unix APIs and the standard C Library functions. (Some have entered de jure standardization processes through the ANSI or IEEE POSIX processes, or have been adopted by vendor consortiums like the one that produced the UNIX98 API set.)

The same sort of process has been happening with SAX. From its initial base in Java, it's been imported into many XML-programming tool sets in Python, Perl, Pascal, and JavaScript. There are several different C/C++ versions, and Microsoft has even provided SAX-like COM interfaces. Each new environment has made changes and adaptations. Some have remained truer to the original API (in Java) than others, but it looks as if this growth will only continue. In the best and most classic sense, SAX is a standard.

Sun's Java API for XML Processing (JAXP)

As of JDK 1.4, SAX2 has been incorporated into the Java2 Standard Edition (J2SE) through Sun's Java Community Process. It's part of Version 1.1 of Sun's *Java API for XML Processing* (JAXP). A JAXP implementation is bundled with JDK 1.4 releases, and is available separately for use with other Java-compliant platforms (JDK 1.1 and later). The Java2 Enterprise Edition (J2EE) has recognized JAXP for some time, and web applications that use servlets have long been using XML and SAX.

From the perspective of this book, JAXP is just a vehicle to get SAX2 interfaces (and the Crimson parser) into the hands of more Java developers. Sun incorporated these standard APIs directly into their API set, exactly as one would desire. In this case, the real community process had completed before Sun's own process started. The stamp of recognition provided by Sun facilitated further adoption; some organizations are uncomfortable with software that has no such recognition.

JAXP 1.1 also incorporates DOM Level 2 and some other APIs, including TRAX, a wrapper for XSLT-based transformations. TRAX offers limited SAX support; it supports producing partial SAX event streams as output or sometimes inputs. It's worth noting that if you use DOM, JAXP solves a critical portability problem for you. JAXP has the first "standard" Java solution for vendor-independent bootstrapping with DOM. DOM Level 3 plans to address that problem, but JAXP will have solved it years before Level 3 becomes widely available. If you don't use JAXP's DOM bootstrap APIs, you must use vendor-specific APIs to get a document object that's populated with the content of any XML text. Starting down the path of such vendor-specific APIs quickly leads to nonportable code. SAX has never had that problem, because it has always included vendor-neutral bootstrapping APIs. (Although JAXP defines additional SAX bootstrapping APIs, this book discourages their use.)

Packages in the SAX2 API

SAX2 consists of three packages:

org.xml.sax
    This package contains the core SAX interfaces and exceptions, plus two concrete classes. The package has SAX1 as well as SAX2 support.

org.xml.sax.helpers
    As suggested by its name, this package exists to help applications use the SAX core. Most of its classes are utility implementations of core interfaces (except the parser interfaces), but the portable bootstrap APIs are also part of this package. SAX2 added to what SAX1 started.

org.xml.sax.ext
    This package holds the SAX2 extension handlers, described earlier, and will probably grow to hold other SAX2 extensions in the future.

Only the *org.xml.sax* package is guaranteed to be part of every SAX distribution. The helpers don't depend on the extensions, to preserve this notion of "core plus options." In practice, it's a rare distribution that doesn't include all of these packages, and SAX2 parsers without support for the extension handlers are likely to support only XML subsets. JAXP 1.1 (and hence JDK 1.4) includes all three packages.

Some Popular SAX2 Parser Distributions

Today a variety of high-quality SAX2 parsers are available. Increasingly, they are packaged with Java programming environments, so you may not need to fetch one yourself unless you need upgrades (or bug fixes), or are constructing such a programming environment yourself (perhaps packaging an embedded system or a standalone application). You should be able to bootstrap any SAX parser. As a rule, if an XML parser is part of your Java programming environment, it already supports SAX and probably

SAX2. The documentation should say whether SAX2 is supported. If it only mentions SAX1, you can upgrade to get most of the core SAX2 features; see the section "SAX1 Support," in Chapter 5, for more information.

If your programming environment doesn't include a SAX parser, you'll need to get and install one. This section provides a brief summary of some of the most widely available open source SAX2 parsers.* These packages all include SAX2, DOM Level 2, and JAXP 1.1 support, and can validate XML for you. They also have full support for the standard SAX2 extensions. If you don't happen to download documentation that includes the SAX2 documentation, it'll be available from the same site as the parser. All of these perform well in most applications, as long as you avoid the memory penalties of DOM.

Current versions of all these parsers do quite well on the open source SAX/XML conformance tests, available at *http://xmlconf.sourceforge.net/java/*. Those tests verify that these processors report essential information required of a SAX1 processor, and evaluate how well they support the XML 1.0 specification. SAX2 conformance testing isn't yet as well advanced, though some tests are now available.

In addition to a SAX2 parser, you will likely want to have some SAX2/XML utilities that are layered on top of that parser. The packages described here include a DOM implementation, which is normally provided as a clean layer over SAX2. You might also consider other more Java-friendly packages such as DOM4J (*http://www.dom4j.org*) or JDOM (*http://www.jdom.org*), both of which are layered over SAX2, as well as other APIs that provide more data-structure options. When you're learning SAX, having access to the source code of tools and applications built with SAX can help you learn the API, at least if it's high-quality source that uses the SAX APIs correctly.

Ælfred2

One of the original XML parsers mentioned earlier, Ælfred, has long been recognized for its simplicity, small size, and good performance. As XML parsers go, it is easy to read and understand. With a different maintainer (your humble author), this parser was updated to be the first with full native SAX2 support, and to substantially improve its conformance to the XML specification. This updated version is called Ælfred2, and versions

---

* Proprietary SAX2 parsers exist, such as one from Oracle that is commonly used in Oracle-hosted server-side applications. More information is available on the Oracle web site, *http://www.oracle.com/xml/*.

have been incorporated in a variety of applications where its simplicity, size, and conformance are compelling features. It is now part of the GNU Classpath Extensions project and forms the core of the GNU JAXP library.

The updated version has taken SAX2 further than most other parsers. It has a highly modular structure; the reference distribution is able to use an optional "stream validator" that uses the SAX2 events. The model of an XML pipeline of such events is a natural and powerful way to think about SAX; the SAX2 pipeline package in this distribution lets applications compose arbitrary processing modules in series or parallel. This style of SAX2 processing is emphasized in this book, and some of the examples show how to use these advanced components. Validation and DOM support remain completely modular, and use SAX event pipelines, so Ælfred can still be distributed as a lightweight nonvalidating parser without those components. Likewise, the validation and DOM support don't need Ælfred to work.

The current version of Ælfred is licensed under the GNU General Public License (GPL), with the "library exception" clause to ensure that it can be used in proprietary applications (notably, embedded systems) that aren't themselves licensed under the GPL. That license is used with many GNU libraries, such as the GCC Java (GCJ) runtime libraries. Ælfred includes a *gnujaxp.jar* file that needs installation.

See *http://www.gnu.org/software/classpathx/jaxp/* for information about the current distribution of Ælfred.

Crimson

Sun, through *Java Project X* in its Java division, was one of the earliest major Java vendors to support SAX and XML namespaces. This parser was the first to demonstrate that XML could be validated without a significant penalty. It was dozens of times faster than its competitors and offered more XML conformance. History buffs may like to know that its validation was based on some of the SGML/HTML validation code from the HotJava web browser, the original Java-and-the-Web showpiece software package. This XML code ties directly to some of the earliest Java software seen outside of JavaSoft.

Crimson is a version of the Java Project X software, updated to support SAX2, DOM Level 2, and JAXP 1.1 (for which it is the reference implementation). It was submitted to the Apache XML project to help trigger a "best of breed" XML parser.

Crimson is licensed under the Apache Software License. The Crimson parser has been incorporated into Sun's JDK 1.4 release as its standard XML parser. It is separately distributed as the reference parser for JAXP, so most JAXP distributions include it. This book describes Crimson Version 1.1.3 (matching JDK 1.4), dated October 2001, which includes *jaxp.jar* and *crimson.jar* files that need installation.

See *http://java.sun.com/xml/* for information about this distribution.

Xerces

Xerces is a family of XML parsers in the Apache XML project; in this book, we refer only to the Java version, not the C/C++ version. It has evolved from the second generation of IBM's XML for Java (XML4J) parser, and much of its development and maintenance is still handled by IBM. It is relatively large, and is monolithic rather than modular. It also supports many nonstandard extensions. For example, validation against W3C's XML schemas is part of the parser, rather than a layered feature.

Xerces v2 is a third-generation project. Goals of that project include a more maintainable and modular design. It includes an internal XML event pipeline model, which is strikingly similar to that used in Ælfred to layer validation and DOM support, except that it doesn't use SAX2 to represent the XML Infoset data.

Xerces is licensed under the Apache Software License. This book describes Xerces Version 1.4.3, dated August 2001, which includes a *xerces.jar* file that needs installation.

See *http://xml.apache.org/xerces* for information about this distribution.

Installing a SAX2 Parser

Unless you use JDK 1.4 (which bundles SAX2 and the Crimson parser) or some other environment that's already set up with SAX2 support (such as any up-to-date web application server), you will need to update your Java programming environment so that you can use SAX. Consult the documentation that comes with your parser and Java Virtual Machine for specific details. Assuming the SAX interfaces and your SAX parser are distributed in a single JAR file called *xml.jar* (you'll need to know and use the correct full pathname, including the directory), you'll probably use one of these approaches shown in the following list.

Add to extensions directory
   If you use JDK 1.2 or later for your runtime environment,* you can install the JAR file into the *jre/lib/ext* subdirectory of your Java distribution. This is the preferred solution during development, since it's the simplest and least error-prone.

   On Windows, you may need to add this to two different locations: one for the development environment as well as one for the runtime environment.

Update class path on command line
   This solution works with JDK 1.2 and later. Whenever you invoke a program that needs the SAX support (such as *java*, *javac*, or *javadoc*) pass the *–cp xml.jar* parameter to add SAX to the class path.

Add to CLASSPATH in environment
   This is the original way to add software to your Java environment, and it works on a JDK 1.1–based system and on many Java implementations that aren't derived from Sun's JDK. You may prefer this technique if you have to make several different Java execution environments cooperate—perhaps one for each IDE and test environment used for application development. You could also have your application use its bundled JVM when it's deployed, rather than whatever the end user happened to have around.

   The details vary from operating system to operating system, and from installation to installation, because you may need to ensure that your CLASSPATH includes libraries internal to the JVM. Put the CLASSPATH assignment into your login script (*autoexec.bat* or your environment variables, *.profile*, *.login*, or other file). On Windows, you'll likely need to reboot after you modify *autoexec.bat*, to ensure that all new JVM instances see the new configuration.

You may end up with a variety of SAX2 parsers in your environment. Sometimes which parser you use will be important, but you should avoid creating such problems. See the section "Bootstrapping an XMLReader" in Chapter 3 for information about making sure you're using a particular parser; there are several mechanisms, including setting system properties and adding *META-INF/services/* resources to your class path. If you work within some application environment (perhaps a web server), you may want to look for specialized configuration mechanisms. Also, if you have

---

* Most current graphical development tools, called IDEs, bundle this software for Java.

SAX1 support in your environment, you can easily upgrade it; see the section "SAX1 Support" in Chapter 5.

Note that because SAX lets applications hand character streams to parsers with *java.io.Reader*, you can't use JDK 1.0 with SAX. You need JDK 1.1, which is a more complete and stable release in any case. Since the Java environments that aren't based on Sun's code generally treat JDK 1.1 as the conformance target,* that should cause no real trouble. SAX itself doesn't require more recent APIs, but some of the tools you use with SAX might have such requirements. For portability, the example code in this book avoids use of APIs added in JDK 1.2 and later. The main impact of this restriction is that in a few cases you'll be able to get minor performance improvements by using the collections APIs.

What XML Are We Talking About?

Over the past years, there has been an explosive growth in the number of XML-related standards. Talking about XML has become confusing, because those three letters can mean so many different things. Some people actually mean what I've called "Greater XML." Think of it this way: Boston is significant city, but people who don't live there may often name Boston to refer to other nearby towns (Arlington, Cambridge, and so on). What they're really talking about is the "Greater Boston Metropolitan Area," or sometimes even just "Eastern Massachusetts."

In much the same way, many people now talk about "XML" when they really mean one of dozens of related technologies built around the nucleus of XML. Some of these may even be part of the original XML vision as "SGML for the Web." Using XML to develop documents using a DTD like DocBook (*http://www.docbook.org*) is clearly part of that original open systems vision. However, it's also been trendy to market "new and improved!" software as based on XML. Such ambiguities can be confusing and can even implicitly promote vendor lock-in, rather than liberate customer data from vendor control. The simplicity at the core of XML isn't friendly to lock-in strategies, but complex application layers on top of XML can certainly cause closed systems.

So when someone says that SAX is a great API for XML processing, exactly what part of Greater XML does that mean? Briefly, parts built with the

---

* Many Macintosh developers can't use JDK 1.2 yet. The Microsoft JVM also does not support JDK 1.2 APIs.

"core" XML specifications. The following lists shows the parts that this book uses in most of its examples.

XML 1.0 (Second Edition)
http://www.w3.org/TR/REC-xml

This text document format is the core of XML. SAX2 parsers work with this format and turn it into a stream of events that present the XML Infoset. However, as we'll see, SAX can be quite useful without even parsing XML text. (The second edition incorporates a variety of bug fixes and a few functional changes, which were previously published as a separate list of errata.)

XML includes *Document Type Declarations*, or DTDs. These provide several processing facilities, most of which you can rely on even when you don't use a validating parser. All XML parsers must support DTDs; they're what "schema" technologies attempt to improve on.

Unicode support has been part of XML from the earliest days. Java programmers may tend to overlook the significance of that fact, since it's always been part of Java too. But it's actually a big deal that XML moves web technologies firmly away from ASCII toward Unicode, in all programming environments (not just Java)—not everyone needs to be a native English speaker to make best use of Internet technologies. XML has even been called a "virus for Unicode."

XML Infoset
http://www.w3.org/TR/xml-infoset/

The Infoset is best explained as an abstract model for what XML represents: information like elements, attributes, and character data. The Infoset exposes XML structure, not meaningful data. Applications transform Infoset data into forms that are suited to their particular tasks, normally behind a veil of application objects, unless they manipulate the text like a text editor.

The SAX2 event APIs present Infoset-level data; the lower-level alternative is to work directly with text. (See Appendix B for details about Infoset support in SAX2.) Other XML infrastructure, such as *XInclude*, generally transforms or augments Infoset data. Higher-level APIs generally hide such XML structures.

XML Namespaces
http://www.w3.org/TR/REC-xml-names/

Namespaces are an optional convention for XML 1.0 documents. Namespaces distinguish elements and attributes so that names can be reused when necessary. For example, in document markup a `<table>`

probably refers to a tabular presentation of data, but in a furniture catalog it might also refer to something rather different. XML namespaces distinguish those cases with name prefixes; unlike "straight XML" with DTDs, those prefixes are expected to change in different contexts (such as different parts of that furniture catalog). This makes combining namespaces and DTDs complicated.

One of the most visible differences between SAX1 and SAX2 is that SAX2 has integrated support for XML namespaces to promote their widespread adoption.

Over time, some other simple layers (and conventions) may become appropriate to view as part of the core of XML. The XML Base specification (*http://www.w3.org/TR/xml-base/*) might be an example of such a facility; it explains how to use an xml:base attribute to augment normal processing of relative URIs found in text.* Various internationalization rules and policies are also likely to fit into that core. One example is W3C work on the Character Model for the World Wide Web (*http://www.w3.org/TR/charmod/*), which promotes uniform handling of sequences used to represent some non-ASCII characters. Another is currently called XML Blueberry, which will modify XML 1.0 to allow use of new Unicode characters in element and attribute names. Those characters support languages not previously supported (before Unicode 3.1) and also improve support for languages such as Japanese.

Many of the increasingly substantial layers over XML, such as schemas (there are many schema approaches, with one from W3C), schema APIs and tools (which may focus on non-XML data models, distant from "downtown XML"), Remote Procedure Calls ("RPCs"; again, many approaches including one from W3C), XPath (and its outgrowths), and XSLT are prime examples of technologies that deserve to be viewed as technology choices in their own right. They are other cities in the metropolis of Greater XML, satellites of the original village that leverage the original civic infrastructure. Some of those layers may even reflect different fundamental goals and requirements from those that originally drove the creation and adoption of XML. That doesn't mean that you won't put SAX interfaces on them (or at least SAX-friendly ones), but because they are data layers over the core of XML, they may involve API layers too.

---

* In fact, since this list includes the XML Infoset in the core, documents with the xml:base attribute implicitly need XML base in their core view of XML to augment normal interpretation of URIs in document content. Example 5-1 shows one way to implement such processing in SAX.

If you look at Java implementations of other technologies in Greater XML, you'll probably find SAX not far from the surface. This book identifies a number of such SAX-based tools and shows SAX events used as a framework to efficiently integrate these different technologies.

In this chapter:
- *Producers and Consumers*
- *Beginning SAX*
- *Basic ContentHandler Events*
- *Producer-Side Validation*
- *Exception Handling*
- *Namespaces and SAX2*

2
Introducing SAX2

SAX gets its power from the unifying notion that sequences of event callbacks are powerful and lightweight ways to represent the information in XML documents. Building on that notion, you can create many powerful tools. Most of the essential SAX calls use interfaces, so the interesting behavior comes from how you combine implementations of those interfaces to assemble tools and what those implementations do.

This chapter shows the basic structure of SAX and of several classic SAX applications using an XML parser, the "simple" core of SAX. It starts by showing the essential components and the framework through which they relate. Then it shows how to customize the most important features and concepts in that framework and how to work with the core XML data model of elements, attributes, and text. You'll also see how to handle errors and learn how SAX exposes XML namespaces.

This chapter focuses on the parts of SAX that essentially every application needs to know. It doesn't provide full information about every interface. Later chapters elaborate on these structures and concepts, showing additional parts of these APIs, ways to combine SAX components, and how to work with additional parts of the XML data model. Depending on what your application needs to do, you may not need to know much more of SAX than is explained in this chapter.

Producers and Consumers

The first thing to learn is that there are really two kinds of roles in this API—or three, if you include your role as director, configuring sets of components to serve those roles and provide your application's functionality. Complete SAX applications integrate all these roles.

The first role is an event *producer*, which is typically an XML parser packaged as an instance of some library class. The producer is in charge of pushing parsing events to objects that serve the second role: an event *consumer*. Most SAX applications will only have one event producer, though we'll look at some cases where you need more than one. This chapter touches on several of the ways to configure (or customize) event producers.

Consumers normally do most of the "real" work for any given SAX-based application: they make sense of the parsing events and often create some specialized data structures. Without a consumer to handle events, nothing happens! SAX2 defines several kinds of *handlers* to consume different parts of the XML content. Later chapters look at each kind of handler in detail, but in this chapter we look only at the most important methods and handlers.

When we show SAX components connecting, we'll use diagrams like Figure 2-1, with the dashed lines indicating individual event handlers. There are four of them because there are four handlers used to deliver content to consumers. The producer uses a big arrow, which should remind you in which direction it pushes events.

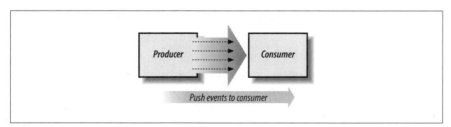

Figure 2-1. Producer and consumer

When you're using SAX, any or all of these components can be provided by your application or can be library components. Often you'll use an XML parser from a library to produce events, but in other cases applications produce such events directly.

Beginning SAX

This chapter explores SAX through some progressively more functional examples, which build on each other to present the key concepts that are discussed later in more detail. Essential producer and consumer interfaces are presented together to show how they interact, and you'll see how to customize classic SAX configurations. We'll focus first on the producer side, saving most details about consumer-side APIs for a bit later.

How Do the Parts Fit Together?

In the simplest possible example, you (in your role as director) will get an XML parser, which will later produce parsing events. Then you will get a consumer and connect it to the producer for processing the most important events. Finally, you'll ask that parser to produce events, pushing them through to the consumer.

To start, focus on what the different parts are, and how they relate to each other. Example 2-1 is a simple SAX program, which you can compile and run if you like.

Example 2-1. SAX2 application skeleton

```
import java.io.IOException;
import org.xml.sax.*;
import org.xml.sax.helpers.DefaultHandler;
import org.xml.sax.helpers.XMLReaderFactory;

public class Skeleton {

    // argv[0] must be the absolute URL of an XML document
    public static void main (String argv [])
    {
        XMLReader       producer;
        DefaultHandler  consumer;

        // Get an instance of the default XML parser class
        try {
            producer = XMLReaderFactory.createXMLReader ();
        } catch (SAXException e) {
            System.err.println (
                "Can't get parser, check configuration: "
                + e.getMessage ());
            return;
        }

        // Set up the consumer
```

Example 2-1. SAX2 application skeleton (continued)

```
        try {

            // Get a consumer for all the parser events
            consumer = new DefaultHandler ();

            // Connect the most important standard handler
            producer.setContentHandler (consumer);

            // Arrange error handling
            producer.setErrorHandler (consumer);
        } catch (Exception e) {
            // Consumer setup can uncover errors,
            // though this simple one shouldn't
            System.err.println (
                    "Can't set up consumers:"
                  + e.getMessage ());
            return;
        }

        // Do the parse!
        try {
            producer.parse (argv [0]);
        } catch (IOException e) {
            System.err.println ("I/O error: ");
            e.printStackTrace ();
        } catch (SAXException e) {
            System.err.println ("Parsing error: ");
            e.printStackTrace ();
        }
    }
}
```

This is a complete SAX application, though it's sort of boring since it throws away all the data the parser delivers. The only reason this program would print anything at all is if you didn't pass it an argument that was the URL for a well-formed XML file. Other than that, it's fairly typical of how you'll be using SAX2, at least in terms of the basic structure. You can make real programs from this skeleton if you substitute smarter components for the simple ones shown here.

We introduced a few SAX classes and interfaces, so we can add some details to our earlier producer/consumer picture to get Figure 2-2. This producer is an *XMLReader*, and we're listening to one consumer interface and the *ErrorHandler*. The whole thing is driven by an application which is pulling the whole document through the reader.

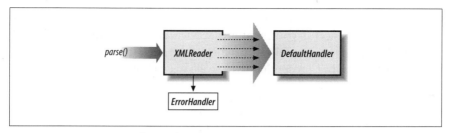

Figure 2-2. Basic SAX roles and components

`XMLReader producer;`

The most common type of SAX2 event producer is an XML parser. Like most parsers, XML parsers implement the *XMLReader* interface. Whether or not they parse actual XML (instead of HTML or something else), they are required to produce events as if they did.

Don't confuse this class with the *java.io.Reader* from which you can pull a stream of character data. SAX parsers produce streams of SAX events, which they push to event consumers. Those are rather different models for how to deliver data.

`producer = XMLReaderFactory.createXMLReader ();`

This is the best all-around SAX2 bootstrap API when you need an XML parser. The only time it should produce any kind of exception is when your environment is misconfigured. For example, you might need to set the *org.xml.sax.driver* system property to the class name for your parser (see the section "The XMLReaderFactory Class" in Chapter 3).

You can (and should!) keep reusing this *XMLReader*, but you should only have one thread touch a parser at a time. That is, parsing is not *re-entrant*. Parsers are perfectly safe to use with multiple threads, except that two threads can't use the same parser at the same time. (That's a good rule of thumb for most objects in multithreaded code, in all programming languages; it should feel natural to apply that rule to SAX parsers.)

`consumer = new DefaultHandler ();`

The *DefaultHandler* class is particularly handy when you're just starting to use SAX. It implements most of the event consumer interfaces, providing stubbed out (no-op) implementations for each method that's not part of an extension handler. That means it's easy to subclass this method if you need a place to start: just override each stub method to provide real code when you need it. We'll use *DefaultHandler* to avoid presenting extra callback methods.

`producer.setContentHandler (consumer);`
In this chapter, we're only showing the most commonly used consumer interfaces. *ContentHandler* is used to report elements, attributes, and characters; that's enough to get almost all serious XML work done.

`producer.setErrorHandler (consumer);`
ErrorHandler lets applications control handling of various kinds of errors, and we'll need it in later examples. We'll usually look at error handling as a specialized kind of task, different from other consumer roles. Even though "handler" is part of its name, it's a different kind of object.

`producer.parse (argv [0]);`
This call tells a parser to read the XML text found at a particular fully qualified URL. There's another call you'll use when you don't have a URL for that text, but most of the time this is the call you ought to use. *If you're tempted to pass filenames or relative URIs, just say no!* Filenames need to be converted to URLs first (see the section "Filenames Versus URIs" in Chapter 3), and relative URIs must be converted to absolute ones.

Parsing can report exceptions. This is important, and not just because it's the only way that a chunk of code like this (using just an *XMLReader*) could seem to "do" anything. Normally, those exceptions will be thrown only for fatal errors, such as well-formedness errors in an XML document, or for document I/O problems.

The application thread is "pulling" the XML text through the *XMLReader*-style producer: the `parse()` call won't return until the whole document is parsed, or until parsing is aborted by throwing an exception. Until it returns, the thread that called the *XMLReader* is either blocking on I/O, parsing data that it just read, or "pushing" data into one of the consumer interfaces. That is, from the perspective of event consumers SAX2 is a "push" API: handlers do nothing until they're asked.

What Are the SAX2 Event Handlers?

SAX2 events are grouped into several interfaces, which we explore later in more detail. All except two are implemented by *DefaultHandler*. Each interface encapsulates a set of events; to see those events, applications give parsers objects that implement the handler interfaces they're interested in.

org.xml.sax.ContentHandler
> Essentially every significant use of SAX2 involves this handler. The element and character data callbacks (discussed later in this chapter) are defined in this interface, as are callbacks for most other SAX2 events for general-purpose data. Many SAX2 applications will focus primarily on this interface. If you only need the core XML data model (elements, attributes, and text), this could be the only handler you use.

org.xml.sax.ext.DeclHandler
> This handler reports DTD declarations that aren't exposed through *DTDHandler* (or in one case *LexicalHandler*) callbacks: declarations for elements, attributes, and parsed entities.
>
> Because it is an extension handler, it won't necessarily be recognized by all SAX2 parsers, and *DefaultHandler* doesn't provide no-op implementations for its callbacks.

org.xml.sax.DTDHandler
> This handler reports DTD declarations that the XML 1.0 specification requires all processors to expose: declarations for notations and for unparsed entities. Most applications won't use this interface unless they're connected to SGML-based infrastructure that depends on such tools. This is probably the most exotic SAX handler interface; web-oriented XML applications will use MIME types instead of notations and URIs instead of unparsed entities.

org.xml.sax.ErrorHandler
> The events reported by this class are errors and warnings. These behaviors are part of XML, but not part of the data model so they don't show up in the Infoset. Grouping these events in one interface lets application code centralize treatment of XML or application data errors. After *ContentHandler*, it's probably the most important SAX2 handler. It's also usefully managed apart from other handlers, so in this book it's usually not lumped with "real" handlers. (This interface is discussed later in this chapter.)

org.xml.sax.ext.LexicalHandler

This interface mostly exposes information that is intended to be semantically meaningless, such as comments and CDATA section boundaries, as well as entity and DTD boundaries.

Because it is an extension handler, it won't necessarily be recognized by all SAX2 parsers, and *DefaultHandler* doesn't provide no-op implementations for its callbacks.

With the exception of *ErrorHandler*, you'll normally want to work with all of these interfaces as a single group: four interfaces, two for content in the document body and two for DTD content. That way, you will work with all the XML data from a document (its Infoset) as part of a cohesive whole. There are SAX2 helper classes (like *DefaultHandler* and *XMLFilterImpl*) that group most of these interfaces into classes, but they ignore the two extension handlers (Decl and Lexical handlers in the *org.xml.sax.ext* package). SAX2 application layers often handle such grouping; for example, you can subclass those helper classes in a different package, adding extension interface support.

The logic behind keeping these interfaces separate, rather than merging all of their methods into one huge interface, is that it's more appropriate for simple applications. You must explicitly ask for bells and whistles; they aren't thrust upon you by default. You can easily prune out certain data by ignoring the interfaces that report it. Most code only uses *ContentHandler* and *ErrorHandler* implementations, so the methods in other interfaces are easy to ignore. Plus, from the application perspective, parser recognition of the extension handlers isn't guaranteed. There's a slight awkwardness associated with needing to bind each type of handler separately, but that's a small trade-off for the benefit of having a modular API extension model already in place.

SAX2 defines another important interface beyond these handlers and the *XMLReader*: parsers use *EntityResolver* to retrieve external entity text they must parse. That interface is also stubbed out by *DefaultHandler*. If you want the parser to use local copies of DTDs rather than DTDs accessed from a server that might not be available, you'll want to become familiar with *EntityResolver*. However, it isn't really a consumer API since it doesn't deal directly with parsed XML data (the Infoset); it deals with accessing raw unparsed text, the same stuff that's given to `XMLReader.parse()` methods. This book presents it as a producer-side helper for parsers, in the section "The EntityResolver Interface" in Chapter 3.

XMLWriter: an Event Consumer

The next part of SAX we show in this overview is really not a part of SAX, except that it uses SAX to do something you'll likely need to do fairly often. (Pretty much everyone does!) As you've seen, SAX2 includes an *XMLReader* interface, used to turn XML text into a stream of SAX events. But it does not include the corresponding *XMLWriter* to reverse the process: turning such events back into text and supporting XML for program outputs as well as inputs. SAX isn't only for reading XML. The same APIs are used to write XML too.

It's almost a tradition to show how to write most of such a class as an example when explaining SAX. We avoid that in this book because getting all the XML details right is tricky, and because this class is a clear example of something that should be treated as a reusable SAX library component. There are lots of ways the data needs to be escaped, and sometimes you need to use output encodings (like ASCII) that have problems representing some XML characters.

There's a better solution: use one of several such classes, which are widely available. This book uses the *gnu.xml.util.XMLWriter* class (bundled with *gnujaxp.jar* and Ælfred) when it needs XML generation functionality, because it doesn't force applications to discard as much of the XML data. It supports all of the SAX2 handlers, including the extension handlers *LexicalHandler* and *DeclHandler*, so it can round-trip almost all XML data. To use such classes, at least in their simple low-fidelity modes, you can modify the skeleton program shown earlier to something like this:

```
import java.io.FileOutputStream;
import gnu.xml.util.XMLWriter;

public class ... {
    ...
        setContentHandler (
            new XMLWriter (new FileOutputStream ("out.xml"))
            );
    ...
}
```

In addition to the GNU class used in this book, other versions are available. One is provided with DOM4J *org.dom4j.io.XMLWriter*, which supports Content and Lexical handlers and evolved from the *com.megginson.sax.XMLWriter* class, which supports only *ContentHandler*. Curiously, neither Crimson nor Xerces include such SAX-to-text functionality at this time.

Event pipelines

Of course, just parsing and echoing data is not very useful. Such classes are best used to output XML data that you've massaged a bit. We'll look at two ways to do this later. One way is to use an *XML pipeline*, where consumers produce data for other consumers, as illustrated in Figure 2-3. For example, one stage could filter the event stream from a parser to remove various uninteresting elements, or otherwise transform the data, and then feed the result to an *XMLWriter*. You can combine several such stages into a "pipeline" and debug them using an *XMLWriter* to watch data as it flows through particular stages. Remember that *XMLReader* isn't the only kind of SAX event producer: programs can write events and feed the result to an XMLWriter. Also, the consumer doesn't need to be an XMLWriter; it could construct any kind of useful data structure. In fact we'll look later at doing this with DOM.

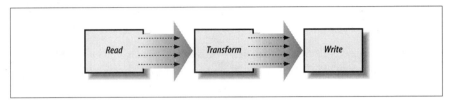

Figure 2-3. Simple SAX2 event pipeline

This kind of processing pipeline is a fundamental model for more advanced uses of SAX and for structuring components that are SAX-aware. We look at pipelines again in the section "XML Pipelines" in Chapter 4. For now, keep in mind that sometimes event consumers will be producing events for later processing components.

Concerns when writing XML text

There are several important issues to consider when writing XML output, which should be mentioned in the documentation for the *XMLWriter* you use. You may even be able to use your *XMLWriter* to canonicalize output, so you can safely compare processor output or create digital signatures. The GNU class shown earlier handles most of these directly, but that's not true for all such classes.

- You need the flexibility to choose different line endings, such as Macintosh style (CR only), DOS style (CRLF), and Unix style (LF only). The default should be right for the host Operating System, but sometimes that's not right for the destination.

- The SAX2 event stream might discard essential namespace prefix information. If you're using documents with namespaces, you need to provide a sanitized event stream, making sure either that such data is not discarded (using the "mixed mode" namespace handling discussed later in this chapter) or that corresponding data gets synthesized (maybe in some pipeline stage).

- You might be sending XML to applications that don't handle DTDs or external entities very well. For example, many web browsers won't read DTDs. To talk robustly to such applications, you might need to send standalone documents.

- If your application just uses *ContentHandler* events, you'll have discarded information needed to re-create "high-fidelity" output reflecting DTD content, comments, entity references, and CDATA section boundaries. More handlers are detailed in Chapter 4 as well as and briefly summarized later in this section; most of the writers implement many such interfaces.

- If you don't want to use UTF-8 as your character encoding (or UTF-16), you'll have to be sure the names used by your markup can be expressed using that character encoding. That's because while numeric character references can be used inside text, they can't be used inside markup components like element and attribute names. ASCII, for example, is hopeless at handling element names that use Japanese ideographic characters, but it can handle Japanese text if you don't mind that every character in the document text is cryptically expressed as a numeric character reference.

- The first time you try to debug XML output where a single line is even just a few kilobytes in length, you'll want your *XMLWriter* to be "pretty printing." Minimally it should add line breaks; ideally it should be able to indent to show document structure.

Such an *XMLWriter* is part of almost every developer's SAX toolkit, even though it isn't part of SAX itself. As you work with SAX, you'll probably start to collect and develop your own library of such reusable event consumer code.

Basic ContentHandler Events

You've just seen how the parts of a SAX2 application fit together, so now you're ready to see how the data is actually handled as it arrives. Here we focus on the events that deal with the core XML data model of elements, attributes, and text. To work with that model, you need to use only a handful of methods from the *ContentHandler* interface.

The DefaultHandler Class

As mentioned earlier, this class is a convenient way to start using SAX2 because it provides stubs for many of the handler methods. You can just override those stubs with methods to do real work. Using *DefaultHandler* as a base class is just an implementation option. It's often just as convenient not to use such a base class. The class is used in this chapter to avoid explaining handler methods that you don't really need.

In some scenarios, Sun's JAXP requires you to use *DefaultHandler* as a base class. That's much more of a restriction than SAX itself makes. If you stick to using the SAX *XMLReader* API, as recommended in this book, you'll still have the option of using *DefaultHandler* as a base class, but this policy won't be imposed on your application code. For example, you can have separate objects to encapsulate policies such as error handling, so you won't need to hardwire all such policies into a single class.

Example: Elements and Text

Let's use this simple XML document to learn the most essential SAX callbacks:

```
<stanza>
    <line>In a cavern, in a canyon,</line>
    <line>Excavating for a mine,</line>
    <line>Dwelt a miner, forty-niner,</line>
    <line>And his daughter Clementine.</line>
</stanza>
```

This is a simple document, only elements and text, with no attributes, DTD, or namespaces to complicate the code we're going to write. When SAX2 parses the document, our *ContentHandler* implementation will see events reported for those elements and for the text. The calls will be more or less as follows; they're indented here to correspond to the XML text, and the characters() calls show strings since slices of character arrays are awkward:

```
startElement ("", "", "stanza", empty)
    characters ("\n     ")
    startElement ("", "", "line", empty)
        characters ("In a cavern, i");
        characters ("n a canyon,");
```

```
        endElement ("", "", "line")
        characters ("\n    ")
        startElement ("", "", "line", empty)
            characters ("Excavating for a mine,");
        endElement ("", "", "line")
        characters ("\n    ")
        startElement ("", "", "line", empty)
            characters ("Dwelt a miner, forty-niner,");
        endElement ("", "", "line")
        characters ("\n    ")
        startElement ("", "", "line", empty)
            characters ("And his daughter");
            characters (" Clementine.");
        endElement ("", "", "line")
        characters ("\n")
    endElement ("", "", "stanza")
```

Notice that SAX does not guarantee that all logically consecutive characters will appear in a single `characters()` event callback. With this simple text, most parsers would deliver it in one chunk, but your application code can't rely on that always being done. Also, notice that the first two parameters of `startElement()` are empty strings; they hold namespace information, which we explain toward the end of this chapter. For now, ignore them and the last parameter, which is for the element's attributes.

For our first real work with XML, let's write code that prints only the lyrics of that song, stripping out the element markup. We'll start with the `characters()` method, which delivers characters in part of a character buffer with a method signature like the analogous `java.io.Reader.read()` method. This looks like Example 2-2.

Example 2-2. Printing only character content (a simple example)

```
public class Example extends DefaultHandler {
    public void characters (char buf [], int offset, int length)
    throws SAXException
    {
        System.out.write (new String (buf, offset, length));
    }
}
```

If you create an instance of this *Example* class instead of *DefaultHandler* in Example 2-1 and then run the resulting program[*] with a URL for the XML text shown earlier, you'll see the output.

---

[*] On some systems, the user will need to provide system property on the command line, passing *-Dorg.xml.sax.driver=...*, as shown in the section "Bootstrapping an XMLReader" in Chapter 3.

```
$ java Skeleton file:///db/sax2/verse.xml
```

    In a cavern, in a canyon,
    Excavating for a mine,
    Dwelt a miner, forty-niner,
    And his daughter Clementine.
$

You'll notice some extra space. It came from the whitespace used to indent the markup! If we had a DTD, the SAX parser might well report this as "ignorable whitespace." (See the section "Other ContentHandler Methods" in Chapter 4 for information about this callback.) But we don't have one, so to get rid of that markup we should really print only text that's found inside of <line> elements. In this case, we can use code like Example 2-3 to avoid printing that extra whitespace; however, we'll have to add our own line ends since the input lines won't have any.

Example 2-3. Printing only character content (a better example)

```
public class Example extends DefaultHandler {
    private boolean     ignore = true;

    public void startElement (String uri, String local, String qName,
            Attributes atts)
    throws SAXException
    {
        if ("line".equals (qName))
            ignore = false;
    }

    public void endElement (String uri, String local, String qName)
    throws SAXException
    {
        if ("line".equals (qName)) {
            System.out.println ();
            ignore = true;
        }
    }

    public void characters (char buf [], int offset, int length)
    throws SAXException
    {
        if (ignore)
            return;
        System.out.write (new String (buf, offset, length));
    }
}
```

With a more complicated content model, this particular algorithm probably wouldn't work. SAX content handlers are often written to understand particular content models and to carefully track application state within

Basic ContentHandler Events

parses. They often keep a stack of open element names and attributes, along with other state that's specific to the particular task the content handler performs (such as the "ignored" flag in this example). A full example of an element/attribute stack is shown later, in Example 5-1.*

In simple cases like this, where namespaces aren't involved, you could use a particularly simple stack, as shown in Example 2-4. You can use such an element stack for many purposes. The depth of the stack corresponds to the depth of element nesting. This feature can help you debug by allowing you to structurally indent diagnostics. You can also use the stack contents to make decisions: maybe you want to print line elements that are from some stanza of a song, but not lines spoken by a character in a play. To do that, you might verify that the parent element of the line was a stanza. Make sure you understand how this example works; once you understand how startElement() and endElement() always match, as well as how they represent the document structure, you'll understand an essential part of how SAX works.

Example 2-4. Printing only character content (element stack)

```
public class Example extends DefaultHandler {
    private Stack stack = new Stack ();

    public void startElement (String uri, String local, String qName,
        Attributes atts)
    throws SAXException
    {
        stack.push (qName);
    }

    public void endElement (String uri, String local, String qName)
    throws SAXException
    {
        if ("line".equals (qName))
            System.out.println ();
        stack.pop ();
    }

    public void characters (char buf [], int offset, int length)
    throws SAXException
    {
        if (!"line".equals (stack.peek ()))
```

---

* Whitespace handling in text can get quite messy. XML defines an xml:space attribute that may have either of two values in a document: default, signifying that whatever your application wants to do with whitespace is fine, and preserve, which suggests that whitespace such as line breaks and indentation should be preserved. W3C XML Schemas replace default with two other options to provide a partial match for the whitespace normalization rules that apply to attribute values.

Example 2-4. Printing only character content (element stack) (continued)

```
            return;
        System.out.write (new String (buf, offset, length));
    }
}
```

Although they didn't appear in this simple scenario, most `startElement()` callbacks will have if/then/else decision trees that compare element names. Or if you're the kind of developer who likes to generalize such techniques, you can store per-element handlers in some sort of table and look them up by name. In both cases, you need to have some way to handle unexpected elements, and because of XML namespaces, the *qName* parameter isn't always what you should check first. One policy is just to ignore unexpected elements, which is what most HTML browsers do with unexpected tags. Another policy is to treat them as some kind of document validity error.

The Attributes Interface

In the previous section, we skipped over the attributes provided with each element. Let's look at them in a bit more detail.

SAX2 wraps the attributes of an element into a single *Attributes* object. For any attribute, there are three things to know: its *name*, its *value*, and its *type*. There are two basic ways to get at the attributes: by an integer index (think "array") or by names. The only real complication is there are two kinds of attribute name, courtesy of the XML Namespaces specification.

Attribute lookup by name

You often need to write handler code that uses the value of a specific attribute. To do this, use code that accesses attribute values directly, using the appropriate type of name as arguments to a `getValue()` call. If the attribute name has a namespace URI, you'll pass the URI and the local name (as discussed later in this chapter). Otherwise you'll just pass a single argument. A value that is an empty string would be a real attribute value, but if a null value is returned, no value was known. In such a case, your application might need to infer some nonempty attribute value. (This is common for `#IMPLIED` attributes.)

Consider this XML element:

```
<billable label='finance'
        xmlns:units="http://www.example.com/ns/units"
```

```
            units:currency="NLG"
    >
    25000
</billable>
```

Application code might need to enforce a policy that it won't present documents with such data to users that aren't permitted to see "finance" labeled data. That might be a meaningful policy for code running in application servers where users could only access data through the server. Code to enforce that policy might look like this:

```
public void
startElement (String uri, String local, String qName, Attributes atts)
throws SAXException
{
    String    value;

    value = atts.getValue ("label");

    if ("finance".equals (value) && !userClearedForFinanceData
        getUser ()))
        throw new SAXException ("you can't see this data");

    ... process the element
}
```

Other application code might need to know the currency in which the billable amount was expressed. In this example, this information is provided using namespace-style naming, so you would use the other kind of accessor to ensure that you see the data no matter what prefix is used to identify that namespace:

```
    String       currency;
    currency = atts.getValue ("http://www.example.com/ns/units",
        "currency");

    // what's the best exchange rate today?
```

There are corresponding getType() accessors, which accept both types of attribute names, but you shouldn't want to use those. After all, if you know enough about the attribute to access it by name and to process it, you should certainly know its type already!

Accessing attribute values or types using an index is faster than looking up their names. If you need to access attribute values or types more than once, consider using the appropriate one of the two getIndex() calls to get and save the index, as well as using the third syntax of the getValue() or getType() calls (shown in the next section).

Attribute lookup by index

You might need to look at all the attributes provided with an element, particularly when you're building infrastructure components. Here's how you might use an index to iterate over all the attributes you were given in a `startElement()` callback and print all the important information. This code uses a few methods that we'll explain later when we discuss namespace support. `getLength()` works like the "length" attribute on an array.

```
Attribute       atts = ...;
int             length = atts.getLength ();

for (int i = 0; i < length; i++) {
    String uri = atts.getURI (i);

    // Does this have a namespace-style name?
    if (uri.length () > 0) {
        System.out.print ("{ " + uri);
        System.out.print (" " + atts.getLocalName (i) + " }");

    // no namespace
    } else
        System.out.println (atts.getQName (i));

    // value comes from document, or is defaulted from DTD
    System.out.print (", value = " + atts.getValue (i));

    // type is CDATA unless it comes from <!ATTLIST ...> in DTD
    System.out.print (", type = " + atts.getType (i));
}
```

You'll notice that accomodating input documents that use XML namespaces has complicated this code. It's important to remember that from the SAX perspective, attributes can have either of two kinds of names, and you must not use the wrong kind of name. (The same is true for elements.) Application code that handles arbitrary input documents will usually needs to handle both types of names, using the logic shown earlier. It's rarely safe to assume your input documents will only use one kind of name.

It's often good practice to scan through all the attributes for an element and report some kind of validity error if a document has unexpected attributes. (These might include `xmlns` or `xmlns:*` attributes, but often it's best to just ignore those.) This can serve as a sanity check or a kind of procedural validation. For example, if you validated the input against its own DTD, that DTD might have been modified (using the internal subset or some other mechanism) so that it no longer meets your program's expectations. Such a scan over attribute values can be a good time to make sure your application does the right thing with any attributes that need to be `#IMPLIED`, or have type ID.

Other attributes issues

Attribute values will always be whitespace-normalized as required by the XML specification. This means that the only whitespace in an attribute will be space characters or whitespace provided by character references to a tab, newline, or carriage return. If the type isn't reported as CDATA, additional normalization is done: leading and trailing spaces are stripped, and consecutive space characters are replaced by a single space.

If the parser read the DTD, you are able to see the XML attribute type it declared. The best way to see this type is to use the `DeclHandler.attributeDecl()` event, which needs a bit of advance planning. (This callback is discussed later in the section "The DeclHandler Interface" in Chapter 4.) Or you can use the `Attributes.getType()` methods if you can deal with incomplete reporting for enumerated types. (You won't see the possible values, and the type will either be `NOTATION` or `NMTOKEN`.)

The *Attributes* object passed to `startElement()` is only usable during that callback. If you need access to information found there, you must copy it. A utility *AttributesImpl* class is available, with a copy constructor, and is discussed in Chapter 5 in the section "The AttributesImpl Class.".

The methods in the *Attributes* interface are summarized in Appendix A. For more information, consult the SAX javadoc.

Essential ContentHandler Callbacks

In the earlier code example, we used some callbacks without really explaining what they did and what their parameters were. This section provides more details.

In the summaries of handler callbacks presented in this book, the event signatures are omitted. This is just for simplicity: with a single exception (`ContentHandler.setDocumentLocator()`), the event signature is always the same. Every handler can throw a *SAXException* to terminate parsing, as well as *java.lang.RuntimeException*s and *java.lang.Error*, which any Java method can throw. Handlers can throw such exceptions directly, or as a slightly more advanced technique, they can delegate the error-handling policies to an *ErrorHandler* and recover cleanly if those calls return instead of throwing exceptions. (*ErrorHandler* is discussed later in this chapter.)

The *ContentHandler* callbacks include:

```
void startElement(uri,local,qName,Attributes atts)
void endElement(uri,local,qName)
```
> These two callbacks bracket element content, starting with `startElement()` to identify the element and provide its attributes. Typically, `startElement()` will be followed by a series of other event callbacks to report child content, such as character data and other elements. After all children of the element have been reported, `endElement()` reports the end of the element.
>
> String uri
>> For elements associated with a namespace URI, this is the URI. For other kinds of elements, this is the empty string.
>
> String local
>> For elements associated with a namespace URI, this is the element name with any prefix removed. For other kinds of elements, this is the empty string.
>
> String qName
>> This is the element name as found in the XML text, but for elements associated with a namespace URI, this might be the empty string. (Don't rely on it being nonempty unless the URI is empty, or you've configured the parser in "mixed" namespace reporting mode as described later in this chapter, in the section "Namespace Feature Flags.")
>
> Attributes atts
>> An element's attributes are only provided in the `startElement()` call. The *atts* object is owned by the parser and is only on short-term loan to the event callback. If your application code needs to save attribute data, it must make a copy. (The *AttributesImpl* helper class may help.)
>
> These callbacks appear in pairs unless an exception is thrown to abort parsing. Even empty elements (like `<this/>`) cause two calls.
>
> Most applications do a lot of work in `startElement()` callbacks to set up further processing, but `endElement()` work varies. Sometimes `endElement()` does nothing, sometimes it's just a quick state cleanup (popping stacks), and sometimes it's where all the work queued during an element's processing is finally performed.

Basic ContentHandler Events

`void characters (buf, offset, length)`
> Text content is provided as a range from a character array. Applications will often need to make a copy of this data, appending it either to another character array or to a *StringBuffer*. (Use strings if their extra cost is not a problem.) Then the "real action" to process character data would be taken when this callback learns that all the relevant characters have been provided, often because of a `startElement()` or `endElement()` call.
>
> `char buf[]`
>> A character array holding the text being provided. You must ignore characters in this buffer that are outside of the specified range.
>
> `int offset`
>> The index of the first character from the buffer that is in range.
>
> `int len`
>> The number of text characters that are in the range's buffer, beginning at the specified offset.
>
> Application code must expect multiple sequential calls to this method. For example, it would be legal (but slow) for a parser to issue one callback per character. Content found in different external entities will be reported in different `characters()` invocations so location information is reported correctly. (This is described in the section "The Locator Interface" in Chapter 4.) Most parsers have only a limited amount of buffer space and will flush characters whenever the buffer fills; flushing can improve performance because it eliminates a need for extra buffer copies. Excess buffer copying is a classic performance killer in all I/O-intensive software.
>
> The XML specification guarantees that you won't see CRLF- or CR-style line ends here. All the line ends from the document will use single newline characters ("\n"). However, some perverse documents might have placed character references to carriage returns into their text; if you see them, be aware that they're not real line ends!

There are many other methods in the *ContentHandler* interface, discussed later in the section "Other ContentHandler Methods" in Chapter 4.

Producer-Side Validation

All uses of SAX2 parsers will involve extending and customizing the basic scenario we saw earlier. Our next example illustrates two basic configuration mechanisms: *error handling* options, which lets you use the appropriate policy when you see errors, and *parser configuration* through feature flags, which let you control some details of how the parser works. (Some event handlers are managed with a configuration mechanism that is quite similar to the feature flag mechanism.) The example also shows how SAX2 parsers expose the core XML notion of *DTD-based validation*.

You will often tell XML parsers to validate XML as they produce events. Because SAX2 provides access to most of the data in XML documents, including declarations from DTDs, it also supports performing such validation on the event consumer side, possibly with a cached DTD or schema. (The consumer side is the only place to perform procedural validation.) Such consumer-side validation can be important when you're trying to make your program output meet the constraints of a particular information interchange agreement; just add a streaming validation stage to your output processing. This approach can also be used for DOM revalidation and similar purposes. Here, we look at how to validate data that is already in the form of XML text.

Keep in mind that some important DTD-related processing does not involve validation. Documents with DTDs can use entity substitution for document modularity and text portability, and can have attributes defaulted and normalized. Validation with DTDs only involves checking a set of rules. Disabling DTD validation turns off only the rule checks, not the processing for entities and attributes.

SAX2 Feature Flags

SAX2 exposes many parser behaviors, including DTD validation, using a "feature flag" mechanism. These flags are Boolean settings, which may have values or be unspecified. Parsers can have up to four different modes for any feature flag. For example, with the validation flag SAX2 implies four kinds of XML parsers:

Optionally validating parsers
    The feature flag is read/write and can be either true or false. If it's set to false, few nonfatal errors will be reported and parsing will be a bit faster (maybe 5 or 10 percent of the cost of parsing XML, which is usually negligible to start with).

Validity and XML

Validation is particularly important when you are interchanging documents that have been wholly or partially authored by hand, but it can also be helpful when working with XML that's generated by custom code. When you validate an XML document, you ensure that it meets certain rules needed to process them—such as requiring a `<title>` element as the first child of every `<chapter>` element or prohibiting dangling internal cross-references.

Validation is done at several levels in most applications. Lower levels tend to use *rule-based logic*, such as the DTD validation that's defined by XML 1.0. The various types of XML schema provide different kinds of rule-based sanity checks, which are usually done before applications see the data. (W3C's schemas also extract additional information items, beyond the XML data model of elements, attributes, and text. This information is called the "Post-Schema-Validation Infoset" or PSVI.) Higher-level validation processes tend to involve richer notions of data validity and tend to be expressed as *procedural logic.* For example, "business logic" often involves ad hoc relationships, policies, and heuristics; it relies on information not normally expressible by DTD or schema-style rules. Such logic is often captured in application-level methods. As a rule, no single data validation technology is sufficient for all purposes.

Your development process should try to ensure that you create only valid documents; you will likely send XML to applications that don't handle invalid data very well. Safe operational practice involves validating all documents received from other parties and accepting the small costs involved. (Use local copies of DTDs, or schemas, to avoid depending on remote files that might disappear. Techniques to achieve this are discussed in the section "The EntityResolver Interface" in Chapter 3.) The cost of rule-based validation is usually smaller than routine system load variations for real applications; even in parsing speed benchmarks it's rarely high. It's usually worth the cost since it can prevent someone else's data from accidentally breaking your software. Validation against a good DTD (or schema) provides a useful base level of input data checking, but it will rarely be sufficient.

Nonvalidating parsers
   The feature flag is read-only and always false. Some nonfatal errors might be reported (the XML specification demands them in some cases).

Always validating parsers
   The feature flag is read-only and always true. Validity errors are always reported as nonfatal. (By default, such errors are ignored; see the section "Handling Validity Errors" later in this chapter.)

Unknown validation behavior
   The feature flag is not recognized, so its value can't be determined. (This mode is uncommon for the SAX2 validation flag, but you'll see it with other feature flags.)

Later in this chapter, look at the feature flags used to characterize namespace processing. Those flags are not optional, so fewer potential parser modes are possible. All the standardized feature flags are detailed in the section "XMLReader Feature Flags" in Chapter 3.

In SAX, URIs identify feature flags. These are used purely as unique identifiers. This is the same approach used in XML namespaces: don't use these URIs to retrieve data, even if they do look like URLs you could type into a browser. The URI *http://xml.org/sax/features/validation* identifies the flag-controlling validation.

To check how a given XML parser handles validation, use code similar to Example 2-5. Code for any other kind of parser feature will look much the same, as long as you use the correct ID for the feature flag; you'll see the same exception types working in the same way. (The same is true for parser "properties," which you'll see in the section "XMLReader Properties" in Chapter 3.)

Example 2-5. Checking for validation support

```
XMLReader      producer;
String         uri = "http://xml.org/sax/features/validation";

// ... get the parser

// Try getting and setting the flag
try {
    System.out.println ("Initial validation setting: "
        + producer.getFeature (uri));
    // if we get here, validation behavior is known

    producer.setFeature (uri, true);
    // if we get here, the parser either validates by
```

URIs = URLs + URNs

The use of URIs in XML namespaces has been confusing, and since SAX2 also uses URIs to identify parser feature flags and properties, the same sort of confusion can show up. Think of URIs as names: you can talk about "Fred" even if he's not there, or about "Godot" even if he may not exist, and "the third house on the left" probably makes sense to someone standing at your side.

Classically, a *Universal Resource Identifier* (URI), is either a *Universal Resource Locator* (URL) or a *Universal Resource Name* (URN). Both types of URIs are represented as strings. You're used to seeing URLs in web browsers; they serve as detailed addresses. They often look like *http://www.example.com/* but they may use other *URI schemes*—for example, they may use *https:*, *ftp:* and *file:*. The scheme indicates the way to access the resource. URNs use URI schemes that start with *urn:*. You probably have not seen many URNs; one example is *urn:uuid:221ffe10-ae3c-11d1-b66c-00805f8a2676*. URN schemes (like *uuid* in this example) describe what the resource is, more than how to access it.

Filenames are never URIs, but you can convert a filename into a URL (hence URI) that works on systems where the original filename was legal. Just to be confusing, there are also "relative URIs," which often look like POSIX-style filenames. Like filenames, relative URIs should never be handed directly to a SAX parser or be used as namespace identifiers.

With XML namespaces and SAX2, the term URI is used to emphasize that the string is being used as a pure identifier: it's more like a URN than a URL, even when the URI is syntactically a URL. It's explicitly irrelevant whether any resource is actually associated with the URI. Don't assume you can fetch resources using those URIs.

Example 2-5. Checking for validation support (continued)

```
    // default or is optionally validating

} catch (SAXNotSupportedException e) {
    // value not supported; parser is nonvalidating
    System.out.println ("Can't enable validation: "
        + e.getMessage ());
    System.exit (1);

} catch (SAXNotRecognizedException e) {
```

Example 2-5. Checking for validation support (continued)

```
    // feature not understood; parser has weak SAX2 support.
    // maybe it's a SAX1 parser inside a ParserAdapter
    System.out.println ("Doesn't understand validation: "
        + e.getMessage ());
    System.exit (1);
}
```

As a rule, programs will probably set the validation flag to true only when they really need reports of validity errors. (Why? As we'll see in a moment, it's natural to ignore reports of validity errors when they're not important, so it doesn't much matter if you validate when you don't need to.) The skeleton program in Example 2-1 really just needs a `setFeature()` call and a small update to the diagnostic message, to be sure it's always validating. (The diagnostics could be more precise using some more-specialized exceptions that we haven't discussed yet.)

```
// Get an instance of the default XML parser class
try {
    producer = XMLReaderFactory.createXMLReader ();
    producer.setFeature (
            "http://xml.org/sax/features/validation",
            true);
} catch (SAXException e) {
    System.err.println (
            "Can't get validating parser, check configuration: "
        + e.getMessage ());
    return;
}
```

The validation feature flag is probably the most widely used, with the possible exception of the flags controlling namespace handling. Most parsers leave validation off by default to save some minor parsing overhead.

Handling Validity Errors

If you modify the skeleton program to set the parser's validation flag and then run it on a well-formed but invalid document (perhaps one without a DTD), you will probably be surprised to discover that it doesn't seem to report any errors. That's exactly what should happen since it's the default behavior specified by SAX. To make validity errors cause anything interesting to happen, you have to change how they're handled. *If you don't change this handling, you won't be able tell a validating parser apart from a nonvalidating one!*

The simplest way to change the handling of validity errors is to make them work just like well-formedness errors: by aborting the parse. This uses the *ErrorHandler* interface that we look at later in this chapter, in the section "ErrorHandler Interface," but for now it's simpler to focus on one method. In terms of the skeleton program shown earlier, such a change can be an update to just one line, using an anonymous inner class to make the code look simple. (Of course, avoid using anonymous classes for anything complex; they can make code hard to maintain.)

```
// Get a consumer for all the parser events
consumer = new DefaultHandler () {
    public void error (SAXParseException e)
    throws SAXException
        { throw e; }
};
```

XML parsers call `ErrorHandler.error()` whenever they find a validity error, or when they see certain other nonfatal errors. In this case, our custom handler adopts a policy that whenever it sees such an error, it will abort the parse by throwing the exception reported to it. Later in this chapter we look at some alternative policies.

When your callback detects serious application-level errors, you can throw a *SAXException* from any SAX event handler callback to abort parsing. That doesn't have be done only from an *ErrorHandler*. For example, when input data is valid XML but doesn't meet essential semantic requirements of the application, report it using some kind of *SAXException*. If your code only knows how to process shipping invoices, then greeting cards should be rejected immediately.

Exception Handling

Exceptions are the primary way that SAX event consumers communicate to event producers; this is the reverse of the typical communication pattern (from producer to consumer). We'll look at SAX exceptions before we delve more deeply into either producers or consumers. We'll look at the several types of exceptions that might be thrown, the error handler interface that lets your code decide how to handle errors, and then how these normally fit together.

Keep this rule of thumb in mind: when a SAX handler throws any exception—including a *java.lang.RuntimeException* or a *java.lang.Error*—parsing stops immediately. The exception passes through the parser and is thrown by `XMLReader.parse()`. Beyond some possible additional error reports, the only additional event callback should be `ContentHandler.endDocument()`. This method is always called before parsing finishes, even after errors, to ensure it can be used for cleaning up. (That callback is presented in Chapter 4, in the section "Other ContentHandler Methods.")

SAX2 Exception Classes

There are four standard exception classes, with a common base class used in the signature for all handler methods. The `parse()` methods, as well as the *EntityResolver* class presented in the section "The EntityResolver Interface" in Chapter 3, can also throw *java.io.IOException* to indicate problems unrelated to XML text content. You will find that many XML APIs are declared the same way; for example, JAXP parser methods may throw such exceptions even if they don't expose SAX events directly. See Appendix A for method summaries for these exception classes.

org.xml.sax.SAXException
> This is the base exception class. Typically you will see its subclasses. These exceptions have messages and may wrap other exceptions for diagnostic purposes. When an application's event callback catches an exception it's not permitted to throw, it can wrap it in one of these exceptions and then throw that exception. *Every SAX2 event callback can throw a SAXException,* although most callback examples in this book won't demonstrate this.

org.xml.sax.SAXNotRecognizedException
> This exception is thrown when the parser does not understand the URI identifying a feature or property you tried to access. Most processors recognize the standard IDs, so if you're trying to use those and you get this exception, make sure you're using the correct URI.

org.xml.sax.SAXNotSupportedException
> These exceptions are typically used to indicate that an *XMLReader* property or feature value you tried to change was recognized, but the value you requested isn't supported. Reasons this might be reported include setting a property to an illegal value (such as the wrong type of handler) and trying to set a feature or property that is read-only in a given implementation (or when the request is made). For instance, it's not possible to ask a parser to stop validating in mid-parse, but for some parsers it's reasonable to do so before starting to parse a document.

org.xml.sax.SAXParseException
> This is the most commonly seen exception class; instances provide detailed diagnostic information, such as the base URI of a file with bad XML content, and the line and column number of such content.

XML parsers provide such exceptions when the report sends errors to *ErrorHandler* implementations.

Applications can also construct this information when reporting application-level errors through SAX callbacks. In fact, they probably *should* do so, providing a *Locator* object to the constructor (and perhaps wrapping an exception to identify a root cause) in order to provide good diagnostics. (See the section "The Locator Interface" in Chapter 4 for information about *Locator* objects.)

The "wrapped" exception is a powerful tool. You might be familiar with this mechanism from the new JDK 1.4 "Chained Exception" facility or the older *java.lang.reflect.InvocationTargetException* exception mechanism. (The JDK 1.4 getCause() method exposes essentially the same functionality as the SAX getException(), though it builds on new JVM features to add intelligence to exception printing.) While parsers may use it internally, you'll likely want to use it to ensure higher-level software will see the root cause of some *SAXException* your handler reported:

```
// in some SAX event handler:
try {
    ... application specific stuff ...
} catch (MyApplicationException cause) {
    throw new SAXException ("it broke!", cause);
    // or better yet: throw new SAXParseException
    //    ("broke", locator, cause)
}
```

If you print the stack backtrace of such a *SAXException*, you'll see two stacks, starting with the root cause. Being able to see that root cause information can be a real lifesaver when debugging. And some application error recovery strategies will use the SAXException.getException() method to find the root cause and then determine how to recover from it. For example, if the application exception identified some resource that was unavailable, higher levels in the application might be able to use that information to choose an alternative resource and restart processing.

ErrorHandler Interface

Normally, you will configure SAX event-processing code to use a specialized implementation of *ErrorHandler* to process faults that are uncovered during parsing. This is done with the XMLReader.setErrorHandler() call. This interface has three methods; you saw one of them in an earlier example. The interface is used to encapsulate an error-handling strategy. The primary choices you have to make are whether to ignore an error or to abort parsing, and whether to emit diagnostics. Those strategies are driven by the severity of the problem, as exposed by which method is used to report it, though sometimes exception-typing may give programs information about exactly what error was detected.

`void error (SAXParseException e)`
> This method is used to report errors that aren't expected to be fatal. The best-known example is violation of XML validity constraints, but some other XML errors are nonfatal too. Many kinds of application-level errors (as reported by event-consumer logic, not XML parsers) will fall into this category, and most parsers use this callback to report violations of namespace constraints (such as referring to an undeclared namespace prefix).
>
> When validating, applications often adopt a policy of treating these errors as if they were fatal, or generating a diagnostic for every such error. By default, all nonfatal errors are ignored. That default will be a big surprise, if you expect a validating parser to stop parsing when it sees validation errors. You have to override the default error-handling policy if you want such behavior.

`void fatalError (SAXParseException e)`
> This method is used to report errors, typically violations of well formedness, that are fatal. Some XML parsers may be able to continue processing after reporting such errors, but only to report additional errors. The XML specification itself requires that no more data will be reported after a fatal error.
>
> By default, fatal errors cause parsing to stop; the `parse()` method will return. This method is often used to provide a diagnostic or to log the exception. After it does that, it has two main choices: throw the parameter to terminate processing or return. Most parsers will treat a return as equivalent to throwing the parameter to terminate parsing. Some XML parsers continue checking for errors; in such cases, they aren't allowed to call any handlers other than the *ErrorHandler*.

`void warning (SAXParseException e)`
> This method is used to report problems that aren't errors. Such situations are specific to the software that reports the warning; unlike fatal and nonfatal errors, the XML specification doesn't place requirements on reporting such situations. XML infrastructure software may generate warnings for any reason at all (much like many pet dogs I have known) and yet be fully compliant with the XML specification.
>
> By default, warnings are ignored. Applications typically ignore them, or print low-priority diagnostics. Because there is such variability in

what generates a warning, it is probably not useful to put a "no warnings allowed" policy into software (by treating this like a fatal error); users have to decide on a warning-by-warning basis whether to ignore it or treat it as significant.

Event consumers can also use this API to provide a standard way to report faults uncovered in layers above pure XML, for instance, when data in element content or an attribute value is invalid or corrupt. When both the application and the SAX-related components use the same *ErrorHandler* instance to handle error-reporting policy issues, maintaining that policy is easier. For example, developers like being able to collect lots of error reports with one test run rather than getting only one error per run; it can be more effective to resolve problems in groups, with shorter test cycles. You can do that with SAX by saving the exceptions (or their associated diagnostics) as they're reported. The same flexibility can be important in production systems.

An *ErrorHandler* can throw any *SAXException* it wants; it doesn't have to be the *SAXParseException* passed as its argument. Don't throw a different exception unless you find a certifiably excellent reason to do so; to discard that original exception just makes problems become harder to troubleshoot. One such reason might be to report a "double fault," in which you triggered another exception while handling the first one. (Operating systems sometimes panic in such cases, so there's no reason applications shouldn't do so too!)

JAXP also uses this handler to report errors when building DOM documents; *SAXException* objects may be thrown to terminate parsing after a DOM parser finds a problem, if the application chooses to handle those errors. Most DOM implementations in Java use SAX parsers to populate their DOM tree, so this is natural behavior. (JAXP only specifies a SAX-compatible way to present and report such errors. They might be reported from a non-SAX parser.)

Errors and Diagnostics

When you see a *SAXException*, it'll normally have a message you'll use for diagnostics, like any exception. It'll also have stack backtrace, which will help when you're debugging, like any exception; in some cases you might even see a nested "root cause" exception. At this time, standard methods only tell an error's severity; there's no way to distinguish different validity errors from each other, for example.

You can get better diagnostics when the exception is really a *SAXParseException*, and give accurate information about exactly where the error appeared. SAX parsers normally provide such data when reporting parsing errors, and applications can do the same thing by avoiding the more generic *SAXException*. With non-GUI applications, I often use code like that shown in Example 2-6 to present the most important diagnostic data.

Example 2-6. Getting diagnostics from a SAXParseException

```
static private String printParseException (
    String              label,
    SAXParseException   e
) {
    StringBuffer        buf = new StringBuffer ();
    int                 temp;

    buf.append ("** ");
    buf.append (label);
    buf.append (": ");
    buf.append (e.getMessage ());
    buf.append ('\n');
    // most such exceptions include the (absolute) URI for the text
    if (e.getSystemId () != null) {
        buf.append ("    URI:  ");
        buf.append (e.getSystemId ());
        buf.append ('\n');
    }
    // many include approximate line and column numbers
    if ((temp = e.getLineNumber ()) != -1) {
        buf.append ("    line: ");
        buf.append (temp);
        buf.append ('\n');
    }
    if ((temp = e.getColumnNumber ()) != -1) {
        buf.append ("    char: ");
        buf.append (temp);
        buf.append ('\n');
    }
    // public ID might be available, but is seldom useful

    return buf.toString ();
}
```

It's natural to call such code in two places. One place is after you've caught an exception of this type, in a "try" block. That's a bit awkward and error prone; you'll need to have two different "catch" clauses, first for SAXParseException and then for *SAXException*, or else use a cast. The more natural place is centralized in an *ErrorHandler* that can treat generating diagnostics as one of several options for processing errors, as shown in Example 2-7. In fact, it's the only way to generate diagnostics for

Exception Handling

nonfatal errors, or for warnings, without treating them as fatal errors; or to centralize your error-handling policy to make it easily configurable.

Example 2-7. Customizable diagnostic error handler

```java
public class MyErrorHandler implements ErrorHandler
{
    int         flags;

    // bit mask values for flags
    public static final int ERR_PRINT = 1;
    public static final int ERR_IGNORE = 2;
    public static final int WARN_PRINT = 4;
    public static final int FATAL_PRINT = 8;
    public static final int FATAL_IGNORE = 16;

    MyErrorHandler () { flags = ~0; }
    MyErrorHandler (int flags) { this.flags = flags; }

    public void error (SAXParseException e)
    throws SAXParseException
    {
        if ((flags & ERR_PRINT) != 0)
            System.err.print (printParseException ("Error", e));
        if ((flags & ERR_IGNORE) == 0)
            throw e;
    }

    public void fatalError (SAXParseException e)
    throws SAXParseException
    {
        if ((flags & FATAL_PRINT) != 0)
            System.err.print (printParseException ("FATAL", e));
        if ((flags & FATAL_IGNORE) == 0)
            throw e;
    }

    public void warning (SAXParseException e)
    throws SAXParseException
    {
        if ((flags & WARN_PRINT) != 0)
            System.err.print (printParseException ("Warning", e));
        // always ignored
    }

    // printParseException() method (above) is part of this class
}
```

Such an error handler gives you flexibility about which errors to report and how to handle the various types that show up. A silent mode of operation might never print diagnostics, a verbose one might print all of them, and a different default could be somewhere in between. A defensive operational mode might terminate XML processing when it sees any error; a permissive one might try to continue after every error. The default shown is verbose and permissive.

To use such an error handler for handling application-specific *SAXExceptions*, you'll need to adopt the same classifications that SAX derives from XML: fatal errors, nonfatal errors, and warnings. That's usually pretty natural, particularly if application configuration flags control which potential error cases are tested.

Namespaces and SAX2

However you use XML namespaces with SAX, you need to understand the core concepts discussed in this section. Namespaces can be confusing; they're more complex than perhaps they ought to be. In part this is because of how they interact (or don't interact) with other parts of Greater XML; in part it's because everyone has different ways to a determine what words mean, and XML names are kinds of words. We'll look at some of those complexities first, and then at the mechanisms SAX2 has to help you deal with them.

But first, just what are namespaces supposed to do? Usually, they identify some particular technical vocabulary. People often reuse words rather than create new ones, and they acquire context-specific meanings and nuances that can be extremely important. A namespace can distinguish whether a word like "bill" refers to part of a bird, a now-archaic weapon, part of a hat, legislative acts, or a number of other things. So a <bill length='45cm'/> element might be associated with a namespace, which provides context that should help applications interpret the element. A processor for "Birder's Markup Language" could know to reject (or ignore) markup intended for legislative or financial uses, even if they all use "bill" elements.

XML defines a way to declare namespaces as needed, using attributes. Namespaces are usually indicated by a prefix, which can serve as a qualifying adjective: "the bird's bill" might be bird:bill while "the consultant's bill" might be consultant:bill. You can also set up a default element namespace so that an unadorned bill element might indicate, for example, a weapon.

What Namespaces Do to XML

XML namespaces are a convention for using attributes to associate URIs with some element and attribute names. Since not all legal XML documents follow this convention, the XML Namespaces specification effectively specifies a dialect of XML. SAX2 supports both dialects: strict XML and XML plus namespaces. By default, SAX2 parsers expect the namespaces dialect. In most cases you'll be able to ignore the difference between those two XML dialects, since documents that use XML in namespace-incompatible ways aren't common.

Even apart from the two-dialects issue, the use of namespaces with XML complicates XML programming. There are two models for using element and attribute names in XML:

- In one model, names have a single role (or "type," or "meaning") throughout the document. This is the model most XML DTDs use, except they allow different attributes to use the same name with different meanings if the attributes are attached to different element types. (But even for attributes, well-designed DTDs share attribute definitions between elements.) The `startElement()` callback parameters give you all the information you need, even when those names are "globalized" using namespace URIs.

- In the other model, a name's role is dependent on context. For example, the same name used in two different enclosing elements might mean two different things. It gets confusing, just like names in the real world. This model is used with elements in some schema systems, such as local elements in W3C-style XML schemas.

If you're working with or designing XML structures with context-dependent names, then namespaces add new kinds of context and hence new ways to cause confusion. SAX2 gives you the tools to track all the context, but you'll have to record it yourself (probably with some kind of stack) since `startElement()` parameters will no longer give all the context you need.

There are also some conflicts between the element-naming approach of the XML Namespaces specifications and DTD validity as defined in the XML specification. They may not affect your SAX2 programs, but can affect the systems you're implementing with XML and SAX2. The issue is basically that DTDs expect everything to be declared once up front (like `import` statements in Java), while the namespace mechanism provides a lexical scoping mechanism (like declaring variables that live on the execution stack) that's flexible about what a given prefix indicates. You can make namespace-correct documents that are DTD-valid, but then you can't change the prefixes bound to namespaces.* Namespace-aware DTDs will often define default element namespaces for element names.

If you are designing a namespace and want to use the URI to publish information describing the namespace, rather than just use it as a unique identifier, then RDDL (*http://www.rddl.org*) is probably a good resource. RDDL defines an XHTML-based document syntax that can be viewed or mechanically processed. It lets you find some of the resources that might be important when working with the namespaces—for example, different stylesheets and schemas and documentation in various languages. The RDDL web site includes SAX support for accessing this data.

Element and Attribute Naming with Namespaces

The direct impact of XML namespaces on your SAX2 application code is to give you a second way to identify elements and attributes. Documents will normally use only one identification style for a given element or attribute. These identification styles are distinct from the two models for using such names, described earlier:

Qualified names
> These are exactly as found in the XML text. Examples include `para` and, with a prefix, `xhtml:p`. (XML documents that don't use namespaces, and some namespace-style documents won't use colons.)

Universal names
> These consist of two separate strings: a "local name" from the XML text (removing any namespace prefix) and a "namespace name" (always a URI) from namespace declarations. For the qualified name `xhtml:p`, the local name is `p`, and the namespace name is the URI associated with the prefix `xhtml`, which is a function in the namespace declaration. Such names are in a sense "universalized" by addition of a suitable URI.

---

* If you want any flexibility in those prefixes, and have a deep understanding of how to use parameter entities, look at the approach to DTD modularization found in the XHTML 1.1 specification.

Note that the XML Namespaces specification only standardizes the "qualified name" (*qName*) terminology; it doesn't standardize terminology for universal names. Because of this, you will also see other terms, such as "expanded names" (the term used by XPath) or "namespace-style names" (used to talk about that style of naming).

Since `ContentHandler.startElement()` callbacks now have to deal with three different kinds of name strings, the code can get rather complicated. Plus, even if you're expecting only universal names, you'll need to notice when elements or attributes don't have universal names and use qualified names to work with them. Element names are identified in method parameters (the same as in `ContentHandler.endElement()`), while attribute names show up in accessor methods for *Attributes* objects. We'll use the following XML text to illustrate these different types of names:

```
<big:animals xmlns="http://www.example.com/dog">
             xmlns:big="http://www.example.com/big">
    <wolfhound cat='no' big:dog='yes' >
    <greyhound big:dog='yes' xmlns="">
</big:animals>
```

SAX2 calls names in XML text "Qualified Names." These are the same thing as "XML 1.0 names" except that XML 1.0 names have no restrictions on the use of colons. When you disable namespace processing in a SAX2 parser, it will deliver "qualified names" that are really XML 1.0 names, without those restrictions. With namespace processing enabled, many qualified names (including every name with a prefix) will correspond to a namespace-style name.

Element names without a prefix might not have a corresponding universal name. Unprefixed attribute names will never have a universal name. In those cases, applications must use the qualified name along with non-namespace context, such as the enclosing element, to figure out what the name is supposed to mean. There are no universally accepted policies for such cases. Yes, all that confuses other people as well.

Element naming

The identifiers for the element names are the first three parameters of void `startElement(String namespaceURI, String localName, String qName, Attributes atts)`. Table 2-1 shows the values of the element names for the previous example, as reported by a SAX2 parser in its default mode. Notice particularly that the namespace URI is empty except when a namespace declaration applies to that element name, and that if there's a nonempty namespace URI, there might not be a value for *qName*. That's not just for element names using namespace prefixes; for element names, a default element namespace declaration will apply if it's within scope. (Remember that empty strings aren't the same as nulls.)

Table 2-1. ContentHandler.startElement( ) parameters for element names

namespaceURI	localName	qName
http://www.example.com/big	animals	empty or big:animals
http://www.example.com/dog	wolfhound	empty or wolfhound
empty	empty	greyhound

You could end up with lots of code like this in your SAX event handlers. Or, you may prefer to factor it as a table lookup (maybe using application-specific types of handler objects) rather than as a tree of comparisons. Notice that for elements without a namespace URI, the qName is checked, but if there's a namespace URI, then localName is used. Also all unrecognized elements are reported as a kind of validity error. You may well need to have more context-dependent logic too, if elements may only show up in appropriate contexts. Such contexts often need different decision trees. See Example 2-8 for a decision tree for startElement().

Example 2-8. Decision tree in startElement( )

```
public void
startElement (String uri, String localName, String qName, Attributes atts)
throws SAXException
{
    // elements outside of any namespace?
    if ("".equals (uri)) {
        if ("greyhound".equals (qName)) {
            ... handle
            return;
        }
        ... else handle N other elements; return on success

        // no recognized element: a validity error
        errorHandler.error (new SAXParseException (
                "Unrecognized element: " + qName,
                locator
                ));
        // if that doesn't abort the parse:
        return;

    // in the "big" namespace?
    } else if ("http://www.example.com/big".equals (uri)) {
        if ("animals".equals (localName)) {
            ... handle
            return;
```

Example 2-8. Decision tree in startElement( ) (continued)

```
    }
    ... handle "islands" and N other big things; return on success
    // FALLTHROUGH for unrecognized elements

// in the "dog" namespace?
} else if ("http://www.example.com/dog".equals (uri)) {
    if ("wolfhound".equals (localName)) {
        ... handle
        return;
    }
    ... handle "terrier", "collie" and so on; return on success
    // FALLTHROUGH for unrecognized elements
}

... and so on for other namespaces

// element not in a namespace we recognize: a validity error
errorHandler.error (new SAXParseException (
        "Unrecognized element: " + uri + " (" + localName + ")",
        locator
        ));
// returns if that doesn't abort the parse
}
```

Most SAX2 parsers provide qualified names in all cases, but you shouldn't rely on their availablity unless the parser is configured to provide namespace prefix information (which also causes namespace-declaration attributes to be "un-hidden"). You should probably avoid using the *qName*, even for diagnostics, when there's a nonempty *namespaceURI*.

Attribute naming

The identifiers for the attribute names are accessed using *Attributes* methods such as getQName(), getLocalName(), and getURI() when you iterate over an element's attributes with a "for" loop. You can access attribute values directly if you use either XML 1.0–style names (*qName*) or XML Namespace–style names (*namespaceURI* and *localName*).

SAX2 parsers handle attribute names from the example text as shown in Table 2-2. This table shows the "mixed mode" behavior, described later; in the default SAX2 parser mode, the xmlns and xmlns:big attributes won't appear. You'd have to set the *namespace-prefixes* feature flag (as described later in this chapter, in the section "Namespace Feature Flags") to see these attributes. Note that according to the namespaces specification there is no such thing as a default namespace for attribute names, so that namespace declaration attributes don't go into any namespace.

Table 2-2. Attributes methods to access attribute names

getURI()	getLocalName()	getQName()
empty	empty	xmlns
empty	empty	xmlns:big
empty	empty	cat
http://www.example.com/big	dog	empty or big:dog

So if you wanted to write some code that ignored elements without a big:dog attribute (that is, the URI is *http://www.example.com/big/* and the local name is dog) with value "yes", it might look like this:

```
public void startElement (String uri, String local, String qName,
        Attributes atts)
throws SAXException
{
    String    value;

    value = atts.getValue ("http://www.example.com/big", "dog");
    if (!"yes".equals (value)) {
        // arrange to ignore text and elements until this finishes
        return;
    }

    ... process the element
}
```

Things to keep in mind

To avoid confusing things, the previous code didn't illustrate two somewhat perverse cases. First, if the big prefix were redefined for some element, the same qualified name could correspond to a different universal name, with the same local name but different namespace URIs. That's one reason the previous code doesn't check for a *qName* of big:dog. Using a *qName* of big:dog might make sense if you were working with XML 1.0 without using XML namespaces. Second, if the URI used with the big prefix were associated with a second prefix, different qualified names could correspond to the same universal names. That's another reason the previous code doesn't check for a *qName* of big:dog. If you are writing namespace-aware code, use only namespace-style name testing in your code to avoid such problems. That makes your code work correctly even when it deals with documents that use namespace declarations in ways you didn't expect.

By default, SAX2 XML parsers provide universal names for elements and attributes that have namespaces (they'll have nonempty **localName** and *namespaceURI* strings) or qualified names for elements and attributes that don't, and will remove the namespace declaration attributes from the *Attributes* object provided in the `ContentHandler.startElement()` event. Unless a default element namespace declaration is in scope, an element whose XML 1.0–style name has no prefix won't have a namespace-style identifier. Attributes with unprefixed names work differently, since default element namespace declarations never apply to attribute names.

If you work with both SAX2 and DOM Level 2, you need to be aware of the differences in how these APIs expose namespaces. The terminology is similar but not identical; SAX2 talks about "URI" while DOM Level 2 talks about "NamespaceURI," and SAX2 uses "QName" not "Name"; but both APIs talk about the "LocalName." When using element or attribute construction methods in the *org.w3c.dom.Document* class, you will notice that DOM uses two different APIs in places in which SAX2 provides just one callback (in three different modes, as discussed in the next section). You are most likely to trip over different ways to tell whether an element or attribute has no namespace URI: SAX2 uses an empty string (length zero), while DOM Level 2 uses a null string. You may also notice that while SAX2 follows the XML Namespaces specification with regards to the attributes that define namespaces, DOM does not. In SAX2, those attributes have no URIs, but DOM assigns *http://www.w3.org/2000/xmlns/* as their namespace URI.

Namespace Feature Flags

SAX2 controls its namespace-processing support through two feature flags, which can be tested and changed using the `setFeature()` and `getFeature()` methods described earlier in this chapter in the section "SAX2 Feature Flags." The two flags are *http://xml.org/sax/features/namespaces* (*namespaces*), which controls whether parsers handle namespace declarations, and *http://xml.org/sax/features/namespace-prefixes* (*namespace-prefixes*), which controls whether applications can see the underlying XML syntax. All SAX2 parsers support both flags, although their values might be read-only.

Given two flags, there are four possible combinations. Only three are legal. It's easiest to understand what the flags do by considering them as each controlling a small processing task layered over a core that just parses XML text. The SAX2 defaults are set so both tasks are performed.

XML 1.0 mode
　Only XML 1.0–style names are reported for elements and attributes, using the *qName*. The *namespaces* flag is false, and the *namespace-prefixes* flag is true; those values are exactly the opposite of the SAX2 defaults.

　This mode passes xmlns and xmlns:* attributes without looking at them. Namespace-style names (with URIs) *might* be provided with element or attribute names, but you must not rely on this; few parsers will do the extra work of processing the namespace declarations. If you enable this mode, your SAX2 parser will be doing what a SAX1 parser did, but the information will flow through APIs with slots for holding namespace-style names.

Mixed mode
　Both XML 1.0– and XML plus Namespaces–style names are reported for elements and attributes. The *namespaces* flag is true (like the default SAX2 mode), and the *namespace-prefixes* flag is true (like XML 1.0 mode).

　This mode is much like XML 1.0 mode, but setting the *namespaces* flag causes startPrefixMapping() and endPrefixMapping() events (discussed in the next section) to match xmlns and xmlns:* attributes, and processes those declarations so the parser always provides namespace URIs for element and attribute names when they're defined. The *qName* is always provided, even when a namespace URI is defined.

　Parsers running in this mode should generate some kind of error report for legal XML 1.0 documents that don't meet all the rules of the "XML plus namespaces" dialect. (Most parsers use ErrorHandler.error() although the namespace specification doesn't say what class of error to report.) One example is to use colons in names for things that aren't elements or attributes, and not declare namespace prefixes. Similarly, you might get warnings about using relative URIs in namespace declarations. There is a performance impact to this additional processing, often five percent of the usually negligible overhead for XML parsing.

XML plus namespaces mode (SAX2 default)
　The difference between this and mixed mode is that some information is discarded. The *namespaces* flag is true, and the *namespace-prefixes* flag is false.

　Clearing the *namespace-prefixes* flag tells parsers they must filter out xmlns and xmlns:* attributes, and they *may* report empty strings instead of providing the *qName* (as found in the document) whenever a namespace URI is reported. In practice, most current SAX2 parsers always report qualified names, since there's little benefit to filtering them out.

The fourth combination of flags, disabling both namespace support and namespace prefix reporting, would be meaningless, and so it is an illegal parser state. Don't set this mode; parsers might not detect that you've put them into an illegal mode and may react unintelligently (such as by entering "XML 1.0 mode"). Unfortunately it's easy to set this mode if you just set the *namespaces* flag to false without first setting the *namespaces-prefix* flag to true (entering mixed mode).

I tend to prefer the mixed mode over the SAX2 default mode. Enabling it is simple: just set the *namespaces-prefix* flag to true, after setting up a parser for the SAX2 defaults. This mode provides better support for the XML Infoset, since it doesn't discard information about the prefixes. You won't see implementation-dependent behaviors in exposing either type of name. Certain kinds of XML processing will work better. In particular, algorithms working near the XML syntax level—such as writing out XML text or performing consumer-side DTD validation—will then work without needing to guard against discarded prefixes and without re-creating namespace declaration attributes. Discarding or changing prefixes, in particular, can cause confusion when people need to look at the XML output. The only real impact on applications is having to ignore `xmlns` and `xmlns:*` attributes, which isn't hard.

Few, if any, applications really need to work with documents that use colons in ways other than the XML namespaces specification, leaving a small performance impact as the primary reason to care about the pure XML 1.0 mode. Even applications that don't use namespaces usually won't see colons used in interesting ways (like `nested:contexts:for:names`). While most SAX2 XML parsers support all three of these modes, they are only required to support the SAX2 default mode.

ContentHandler and Prefix Mappings

Sometimes XML needs to handle "meta-level" processing, in which XML talks about XML. In such processing, namespace URIs are sometimes implicitly called by prefixes found in places no XML parser will look: CDATA attributes (which can contain anything) and character content found within elements. For example, XPath expressions include prefixes, and they are found in XSLT template attributes. The W3C XML Schema

Datatypes (XSD) defines a QName datatype that formalizes such usage.

When you need to work with those types of XML text, you'll find two particular *ContentHandler* event callbacks helpful. They provide the same information found in xmlns and xmlns:* attributes, relieving your application code of the responsibility of correctly applying the XML Namespaces specification. For example, your code won't need to know how a default element namespace declaration can be explicitly undone by xmlns="" attributes or by ending the lexical scope of that attribute.

void startPrefixMapping(String prefix, String uri)
> Each namespace declaration causes one of these calls. Each call corresponds to an attribute in the next startElement() callback to be made; you probably won't see other callbacks intervening. (This method has to appear before the element; the mapping will be used to interpret names of the element or its attributes.) If the prefix is the empty string, then the declaration is for the default element namespace. This is the only time the URI may be specified as the empty string (indicating that there is no longer a default element namespace in effect).

void endPrefixMapping(String prefix)
> Each call to startPrefixMapping() is paired with a matching event to declare that the mapping has gone out of scope. These calls correspond to the most recent endElement() callback. However, the mapping "start" calls and the mapping "end" calls won't necessarily be perfectly nested. For example, two prefix mappings found in one element might be started in the order xlink then MyApp, but either mapping could end first.

You'd normally ignore these two calls, unless you use them to maintain some data structure that tracks active namespace prefixes. It would have to be a stacklike data structure, since one mapping for a prefix only temporarily hides a previous mapping for the same prefix. This is the notion of lexical scope, which you are familiar with from most programming languages. SAX2 includes a helper class to handle this for you: *NamespaceSupport*, discussed in the section "The NamespaceSupport Class" in Chapter 5. Then when you parse the meta-level content, you can use those data structures to interpret prefix references and handle other namespace-related work.

In this chapter:
- Pull Mode Event Production with XMLReader
- Bootstrapping an XMLReader
- Configuring XMLReader Behavior
- The EntityResolver Interface
- Other Kinds of SAX2 Event Producers

3
Producing SAX2 Events

The preceding chapter provided an overview of the most widely used SAX classes and showed how they relate to each other. This chapter drills more deeply into how to produce XML events with SAX, including further customization of SAX parsers.

Pull Mode Event Production with XMLReader

Most of the time you work with SAX2, you'll be using some kind of *org.xml.sax.XMLReader* implementation that turns XML text into a SAX event stream. Such a class is loosely called a "SAX parser." Don't confuse this with the older SAX1 *org.xml.sax.Parser* class. New code should not be using that class!

This interface works in a kind of "pull" mode: when a thread makes an `XMLReader.parse()` request, it blocks until the XML document has been fully read and processed. Inside the parser there's a lot of work going on, including a "pull-to-push" adapter: the parser pulls data out of the input source provided to `parse()` and converts it to events that it pushes to event consumers. This model is different from the model of a *java.io.Reader*, from which applications can only get individual buffers of character data, but it's also similar because in both cases the calling thread is pulling data from a stream.

You can also have pure "push" mode event producers. The most common kind writes events directly to event handlers and doesn't use any kind of input abstraction to indicate the data's source; it's not parsing XML text.

We discuss several types of such producers later in this chapter. Using threads, you could also create a producer that lets you write raw XML text, a buffer at a time, to an *XMLReader* that parses the text; that's another kind of "push" mode producer.

The XMLReader Interface

The SAX overview presented the most important parts of the *XMLReader* interface. Here we discuss the whole thing, in functional groups. Most of the handlers are presented in more detail in the next chapter, which focuses on the consumption side of the SAX event streaming process. Each handler has get and set accessor methods, and has a default value of null.

XMLReader has the following functional groups:

```
void parse(String uri)
void parse(InputSource in)
```
> There are two methods to parse documents. In most cases, the Java environment is able to resolve the document's URI; the form with the absolute URI should be used when possible. (You may need to convert filenames to URIs before passing them to SAX. SAX specifically disallows passing relative URIs.) The second form is discussed in more detail along with the *InputSource* class. Both of these methods can throw a *SAXException* or *java.io.IOException*, as presented earlier. A *SAXException* is normally thrown only when an event handler throws it to terminate parsing. That policy is best encapsulated in an *ErrorHandler*, but handler methods can make such decisions themselves.
>
> Only one thread may call a given parser's `parse()` method at a time; applications are responsible for ensuring that threads don't share parsers that are in active use. (SAX parsers aren't necessarily going to report applications that break that rule, though!) The thread doing the parsing will normally block only while it's waiting for data to be delivered to it, or if a handler's processing causes it to block.

```
void setContentHandler(ContentHandler handler)
ContentHandler getContentHandler()
```
> Key parts of the *ContentHandler* interface were presented as part of the SAX overview; *ContentHandler* packages the fundamental parsing callbacks used by SAX event consumers. This interface is presented in more detail in Chapter 4, in the section "Other ContentHandler Methods."

```
void setDTDHandler(DTDHandler handler)
DTDHandler getDTDHandler()
```
   The *DTDHandler* is presented in detail later, in Chapter 4 in the section "The DTDHandler Interface."

```
void setEntityResolver(EntityResolver handler)
EntityResolver getEntityResolver()
```
   The *EntityResolver* is presented later in this chapter, in the section "The EntityResolver Interface." It is used by the parser to help locate the content for external entities (general or parameter) to be parsed.

```
void setErrorHandler(ErrorHandler handler)
ErrorHandler getErrorHandler()
```
   The *ErrorHandler* was presented in the section "ErrorHandler Interface" in Chapter 2. It is often used by consumer code that interprets events reported through other handlers, since they may need to report errors detected at higher levels than XML syntax.

```
void setFeature(String uri, boolean value)
boolean getFeature(String uri)
```
   Parser feature flags were discussed in Chapter 2, and are presented in more detail later in this chapter in the section "XMLReader Feature Flags."

```
void setProperty(String uri, Object value)
Object getProperty(String uri)
```
   Parser properties are used for data such as additional event handlers, and are presented in more detail later in this chapter in the section "XMLReader Properties."

All the event handlers and the entity resolver may be reassigned inside event callbacks. At this level, SAX guarantees "late binding" of handlers. Layers built on top of SAX might use earlier binding, which can optimize event processing.

Many SAX parsers let you set handlers to null as a way to ignore the events reported by that type of handler. Strictly speaking, they don't need to do that; they're allowed to throw a *NullPointerException* when you use null. So if you need to restore the default behavior of a parser, you should use a *DefaultHandler* (or something implementing the appropriate extension interface) just in case, rather than use the more natural idiom of setting the handler to its default value, null.

If for any reason you need a push mode XML parser, which takes blocks of character or byte data (encapsulating XML text) that you write to a parser, you can easily create one from a standard pull mode parser. The cost is one helper thread and some API glue. The helper thread will call parse() on an *InputSource* that uses a *java.io.PipedInputStream* to read text. The push thread will write such data blocks to an associated *java.io.PipedOutputStream* when it becomes available. Most SAX parsers will in turn push the event data out incrementally, but there's no guarantee (at least from SAX) that they won't buffer megabytes of data before they start to parse.

The InputSource Class

The *InputSource* class shows up in both places where SAX needs to parse data: for the document itself, through parse(), and for the external parsed entities it might reference through the *EntityResolver* interface.

In almost all cases you should simply pass an absolute URI to the XMLReader.parse() method. (If you have a relative URI or a filename, turn it into an absolute URI first.) However, there are cases when you may need to parse data that has no URI. It might be in unnamed storage like a *String*; or it might need to be read using a specialized access scheme (maybe a *java.io.PipedInputStream*, or POST input to a servlet, or something named by a URN). The web server for the URI might misidentify the document's character encoding, so you'd need to work around that server bug. In such cases, you must use the alternative XMLReader.parse() method and pass an *InputSource* object to the parser.

InputSource objects are fundamentally holders for one or two things: an entity's URI and the entity text. (There can be a "public ID" too, but it's rarely useful.) When only one of those is needed, an application's work for setting up the *InputSource* might end with choosing the right constructor. Whenever you provide the entity text, you need to pay attention to some character encoding issues. Because character encoding is easy to get wrong, avoid directly providing entity text when you can.

Always provide absolute URIs

You should try to *always* provide the fully qualified (absolute) URI of the entity as its systemId, even if you also provide the entity text. That URI will often be the only data you need to provide. You must convert filenames to URIs (as described later in this chapter in the section "Filenames Versus URIs"), and turn relative URIs into absolute ones. Some parsers have bugs and will attempt to turn relative URIs into absolute ones, guessing at an appropriate base URI. Do not rely on such behavior.

If you don't provide that absolute URI, then diagnostics may be useless. More significantly, relative URIs within the document can't be correctly resolved by the parser if the base URI is forgotten. XML parsers need to handle relative URIs within DTDs. To do that they need the absolute document (or entity) base URIs to be provided in *InputSource* (or `parse()` methods) by the application. Parsers use those base URIs to absolutize relative URIs, and then use *EntityResolver* to map the URIs (or their public identifiers) to entity text. Applications sometimes need to do similar things to relative URIs in document content. The `xml:base` attribute may provide an alternative solution for applications to determine the base URI, but it is normally needed only when relative URIs are broken. This can happen when someone moves the base document without moving its associated resources, or when you send the document through DOM (which doesn't record base URIs). Moreover, relative URIs in an `xml:base` attribute still need to be resolved with respect to the real base URI of the document.

The following methods are used to provide absolute URIs:

`InputSource(String uri)`
> Use this constructor when you are creating an *InputSource* consisting only of a fully qualified URI in a scheme understood by the JVM you are using. Such schemes commonly include *http://*, *file://*, *ftp://*, and increasingly *https://*.

`InputSource.setSystemId(String uri)`
> Use this method to record the URI associated with text you are providing directly.

For example, these three ways to parse a document are precisely equivalent:

```
String    uri = ...;
XMLReader parser = ...;

parser.parse (uri);
// or
parser.parse (new InputSource (uri));
```

Providing entity text

For data without a URI, or that uses a URI scheme not supported by your JVM, applications must provide entity text themselves. There are two ways to provide the text through an *InputSource*: as character data or as binary data, which needs to be decoded into character data before it can be parsed. In both cases your application will create an open data stream and give it to the parser. It will no longer be owned by your application; the parser should later close it as part of its end-of-input processing. If you provide binary data, you might know the character encoding used with it and can give that information to the parser rather than turning it to character data yourself using something like an *InputStreamReader*.

InputSource(java.io.Reader in)
> Use this constructor when you are providing predecoded data to the parser, which will then ignore what any XML or text declaration says about the character encoding. (Also, call setSystemId(uri) when possible.) This constructor is useful for parsing data from a *java.io.Reader* such as *java.io.CharArrayReader* and for working around configuration bugs in HTTP servers.
>
> Some HTTP servers will misidentify the text encoding used for XML documents, using the content type *text/xml* for non-ASCII data, instead of *text/xml;charset=...* or *application/xml*.* If you know a particular server does this, and that the encoding won't be autodetected, create an *InputSource* by using an *InputStreamReader* that uses the correct encoding. If the correct encoding will be autodetectable, you can use the *InputStream* constructor.

InputSource(java.io.InputStream in)
> Use this constructor when you are providing binary data to a parser and expect the parser to be able to detect the encoding from the binary data. (Also, call setSystemId(uri) when possible.)
>
> For example, UTF-16 text always includes a Byte Order Mark, a document beginning <?xml ... encoding="Big5"?> is understood by most parsers as a Big5 (traditional Chinese) document, and UTF-8 is the default for XML documents without a declaration identifying the actual encoding in use.

InputSource.setEncoding(String id)
> Use this method if you know the character encoding used with data you are providing as a *java.io.InputStream*. (Or provide a *java.io.Reader* if you can, though some parsers know more about

---

* *application/xml* is the safest MIME type to use for *.xml, *.dtd, and other XML files. See RFC 3023 for information about XML MIME types and character encodings.

encodings than the underlying JVM does.)* If you don't know the encoding, *don't guess*. XML parsers know how to use XML and text declarations to correctly determine the encoding in use. However, some parsers don't autodetect EBCDIC encodings, which are mostly used with IBM mainframes. You can use this method to help parsers handle documents using such encodings, if you can't provide the document in a fully interoperable encoding such as UTF-8.

All XML parsers support "UTF-8" and "UTF-16" values here, and most support other values, such as US-ASCII and ISO-8859-1. Consult your parser documentation for information about other encodings it supports. Typically, all encodings supported by the underlying JVM will be available, but they might be inconsistently named. (As one example, Sun's JDK supports many EBCDIC encodings, but gives them unusual names that don't suggest they're actually EBCDIC.) You should use standard Internet (IANA) encoding names, rather than Java names, where possible. In particular, don't use the name "UTF8"; use "UTF-8".

So if you want to parse some XML text you have lying around in a character array or String, the natural thing to do is package it as a *java.io.Reader* and wrap it up in something like this:

```
String      text = "<lichen color='red'/>";
Reader      reader = new StringReader (text);
XMLReader parser = ... ;

parser.setContentHandler (...);
parser.parse (new InputSource (reader));
```

In the same way, if you're implementing a servlet's POST handler and the servlet accepts XML text as its input, you'll create an *InputSource*. The *InputSource* will never have a URI, though you could support URIs for *multipart/related* content (sending a bundle of related components, such as external entities). Example 3-1 handles the MIME content type correctly, though it does so by waving a magic wand: it calls a routine that implements the rules in RFC 3023. That is, *text/** content is US-ASCII (seven-bit code) by default, and any charset=... attribute is authoritative. When parsing XML requests inside a servlet, you'd typically apply a number of

---

* JDK 1.4 includes public APIs through which applications can support new character encodings. Some applications may need to use those APIs to support encodings beyond those the JVM handles natively.

configuration techniques to speed up per-request processing and maintain security.*

Example 3-1. Parsing POST input to an HTTP Servlet

```
import gnu.xml.util.Resolver;

public void doPost (HttpServletRequest request, HttpServletResponse response)
throws IOException, ServletException
{
    String       type = req.getContentType ();
    InputSource  in;
    XMLReader    parser;

    if (!(type.startsWith ("text/xml")
            || type.startsWith ("application/xml"))  {
        response.sendError (response.SC_UNSUPPORTED_MEDIA_TYPE,
            "non-XML content type: " + type);
        return;
    }

    // there's no URI for this input data!
    in = new InputSource (req.getInputStream ());

    // use any encoding associated with the MIME type
    in.setEncoding (Resolver.getEncoding (req.getContentType ()));

    try {
        parser = XMLReaderFactory.createXMLReader ();
        ...
        parser.setContentHandler (...);
        parser.parse (in);
        // content handler expected to handle response generation

    } catch (SAXException e) {
        response.sendError (response.SC_BAD_REQUEST,
            "bad input: " + e.getMessage ());
        return;

    } catch (IOException e) {
```

---

* You might have a pool of parsers, to reduce bootstrap costs. You'd use an entity resolver to turn most entity accesses from remote ones into local ones. Depending on your application, you might even prevent all access to nonlocal entities so the servlet won't hang when remote network accesses get delayed.

Some security policies would also involve the entity resolver. Basically, every entity access "requested" by the client (through a reference in the document) is a potential attack. If it's not known to be safe (for example, access to standard DTD components), it may be important to prevent or nullify the access. (This does not always happen in the entity resolver; sometimes system security policies will be more centralized.) In a small trade-off against performance, security might require that the request data always be validated, and that validity errors be treated as fatal, because malformed input data is likely to affect system integrity.

Example 3-1. Parsing POST input to an HTTP Servlet (continued)

```
            // maybe a relative URI in the input couldn't be resolved
            response.sendError (response.SC_INTERNAL_SERVER_ERROR
                "i/o problem: " + e.getMessage ());
            return;
        }
    }
}
```

You might have some XML text in a database, stored as a binary large object (BLOB, accessed using java.sql.Blob) and potentially referring to other BLOBs in the database. Constructing input sources for such data should be slightly different because of those references. You'd want to be sure to provide a URI, so the references can be resolved:

```
String          key = "42";
byte            data [] = Storage.keyToBlob (key);
InputStream     stream = new ByteArrayInputStream (data);
InputSource     source = new InputSource (stream);
XMLReader       parser = ... ;

source.setSystemId ("blob:" + key);
parser.parse (source);
```

In such cases, where you are using a URI scheme that your JVM doesn't support directly, consider using an *EntityResolver* to create the *InputSource* objects you hand to `parse()`. Such schemes might be standard (such as members of a MIME *multipart/related* bundle), or they might be private to your application (like this *blob:* scheme). (Example 3-3 shows how to package handling for such nonstandard URI schemes so that you can use them in your application, even when your JVM does not understand them. You may need to pass such URIs using public IDs rather than system IDs, so that parsers won't report errors when they try to resolve them.)

Filenames Versus URIs

Filenames are not URIs, so you may not provide them as system identifiers where SAX expects a system identifier: in `parse()` or in an *InputSource* object. If you are depending on JDK 1.2 or later, you can rely on `new File(name).toURL().toString()` to turn a filename into a URI. To be most portable, you may prefer to use a routine as shown in Example 3-2, which handles key issues like mapping DOS or Mac OS filenames into legal URIs.

Example 3-2. File.toURL() analogue for JDK 1.1

```
public static String fileToURL (File f)
throws IOException
{
    String      temp;

    if (!f.exists ())
        throw new IOException ("no such file: " + f.getName ());

    temp = f.getAbsolutePath ();

    if (File.separatorChar != '/')
        temp = temp.replace (File.separatorChar, '/');
    if (!temp.startsWith ("/"))
        temp = "/" + temp;
    if (!temp.endsWith ("/") && f.isDirectory ())
        temp = temp + "/";
    return "file:" + temp;
}
```

If you're using the GNU software distribution that is described earlier, `gnu.xml.util.Resolver.fileToURL()` is available so you won't need to enter that code yourself.

Bootstrapping an XMLReader

There are several ways to obtain an *XMLReader*. Here we'll look at a few of them, focusing first on the most commonly available ones. These are the "pure SAX" solutions.

It's good policy to reuse parsers, rather than constantly discard and recreate them. Some parsers are more expensive to create than others, so such reuse can improve performance if you parse many documents. Similarly, factory approaches add some fixed costs to achieve vendor neutrality, and those costs can add up. In contexts like servlets, where any number of threads may need to parse XML concurrently, parsers are often pooled so those bootstrapping costs won't increase per-request service times.

The XMLReaderFactory Class

The simplest way to get a parser is to use the default parser for your environment, as we saw earlier:

```
import org.xml.sax.helpers.XMLReaderFactory;

...

XMLReader       parser = null;
```

Bootstrapping an XMLReader

```
try {
    parser = XMLReaderFactory.createXMLReader ();
    // success!

} catch (SAXException e) {
    System.err.println ("Can't get default parser: " + e.getMessage ());
}
```

Normally, the default parser is defined by setting the *org.xml.sax.driver* system property. Application startup should set that property, normally using JVM invocation flags. (In a very few cases `System.setProperty()` may be appropriate.)

```
$ java -Dorg.xml.sax.driver=gnu.xml.aelfred2.XMLReader
```

Unfortunately, in many cases the original reference implementation of that method is used. This is problematic in two situations: when the system property isn't set and when security permissions are set to prevent access to that system property; this is common for many applets. Good SAX2 distributions will ensure that this factory method succeeds in the face of such errors. The current release of the SAX2 helper classes makes this easy to do.*

Because of that problem, you may choose to code your application so parser choice is a configuration option encoded through some other mechanism than system properties. You can't keep it in your application's XML-format configuration file. Once you get that configuration data you'll probably use a different *XMLReaderFactory* call:

```
import org.xml.sax.helpers.XMLReaderFactory;

...

XMLReader    parser = null;
String       className = ...;

try {
    parser = XMLReaderFactory.createXMLReader (className);
    // success!
```

---

* The current version of *XMLReaderFactory* has more intelligence and supports additional configuration mechanisms. For example, your application or parser distribution can configure a *META-INF/services/org.xml.sax.driver* resource into its class path, holding a single string to be used if the system property hasn't been set. SAX2 parser distributions are expected to work even if the system property or class path resource hasn't been set.

```
    } catch (SAXException e) {
        System.err.println ("Can't get default parser: " + e.getMessage ());
    }
```

Using this factory call, the class name identifies the SAX parser you want to use. It may well be one of the entries in Table 3-1, though some frameworks bundle other parsers.

Table 3-1. SAX2 XMLReader implementation classes

Parser (and type)	Class name
Ælfred (nonvalidating)	*gnu.xml.aelfred2.SAXDriver*
Ælfred (optionally validating)	*gnu.xml.aelfred2.XmlReader*
Crimson (optionally validating)	*org.apache.crimson.XmlReaderImpl*
Xerces (optionally validating)	*org.apache.xerces.parsers.SAXParser*

If you're using a parser without a settable option for validation, you may want to let distinct parsers be configured for validating and nonvalidating usage, assuming that your application needs both. Parsers with validation support are significantly larger than ones without it, which is partly why Ælfred still has a nonvalidating class.

Calling Parser Constructors

If you need to force the use of some particular parser, you can invoke its constructor directly. Every SAX2 *XMLReader* must have a default constructor in order to work with the *XMLReaderFactory* class. Since it exists, you can invoke it directly using the same class names you may have passed to the *XMLReaderFactory*, if you used application-level configuration:

```
import org.xml.sax.XMLReader;
import gnu.xml.aelfred2.XmlReader;

...

    XMLReader      parser = new XmlReader ();
```

In some cases you may actually prefer to force use of some particular parser. In other cases, you may have no option, maybe because of class loader or security configuration. If you run into trouble with those mechanisms, you may not be able to use factory APIs to access parsers unless they are visible through the system class loader.

In general, avoid such nonportable coding decisions; use a factory API wherever you can.

Using JAXP

Sun's JAXP 1.1 supports yet another way to bootstrap SAX parsers. It's a more complex process, taking several steps instead of just one:

1. First, get a *javax.xml.parsers.SAXParserFactory*.
2. Tell it to return parsers that will do the kind of processing needed by your application.
3. Ask it to give you a JAXP parser of type *javax.xml.parsers.SAXParser*.
4. Finally, ask the JAXP parser to give you the *XMLReader* that is normally lurking inside of it.

Conceptually this is like the no-parameters XMLReaderFactory.createXML-Reader() method, except it's complicated by expecting the factory to return preconfigured parsers.* Configuring the parser using the SAX2 flags and properties directly is preferable; the API "surface area" is smaller. Other than having different default namespace-processing modes, the practical difference is primarily availability: many implementations ensure that a JAXP system default is always accessible, but they haven't paid the same attention to providing the default SAX2 parser. (Current versions of the SAX2 classes make that easier, but you might not be using such versions.)

The code to use the JAXP bootstrap API to get a SAX2 parser looks like this:

```
import org.xml.sax.*;
import javax.xml.parsers.*;

XMLReader        parser;

try {
    SAXParserFactory factory;

    factory = SAXParserFactory.newInstance ();
    factory.setNamespaceAware (true);
    parser = factory.newSAXParser ().getXMLReader ();
    // success!

} catch (FactoryConfigurationError err) {
    System.err.println ("can't create JAXP SAXParserFactory, "
        + err.getMessage ());
```

---

* You can also look at this as choosing between parsers. For example, JAXP 1.2 will probably say how to request that schema validation be done. That's most naturally done as a layer on top of SAX, with a parser filter postprocessing the output of some other SAX parser.

```
        } catch (ParserConfigurationException err) {
            System.err.println ("can't create XMLReader with namespaces, "
                + err.getMessage ());
        } catch (SAXException err) {
            System.err.println ("Hmm, SAXException, " + err.getMessage ());
        }
```

Rather than calling newInstance(), you can hardcode the constructor for a particular factory, probably using one of the classes listed in Table 3-2. It's better to keep implementation preferences as configuration issues though, and not hardwire them into source code. For situations where you may have several parsers in your class path (or a tree of class loaders, as found in many recent servlet engines), JAXP offers several methods to configure such preferences. You can associate the factory class name value with the key *javax.xml.parsers.SAXParserFactory* by using the key to name a system property (which sets the default parser for your JVM instance) or by putting it in the *$JAVA_HOME/jre/lib/jaxp.properties* property file (which sets the default policy for that JVM implementation). I prefer the *jaxp.properties* solution; with the other method the default parser is a function of your class path settings and even the names assigned to various JAR files. You can also embed this preference in your application's JAR files as a *META-INF/services/...* file, but that solution is similarly sensitive to class loader configuration issues.

Table 3-2. JAXP SAXParserFactory implementation classes

JAXP factory	Class name
Ælfred	gnu.xml.aelfred2.JAXPFactory
Crimson	org.apache.crimson.jaxp.SAXParserFactoryImpl
Xerces	org.apache.xerces.jaxp.SAXParserFactoryImpl

If you're using JAXP to bootstrap a SAX2 parser, rather than the SAX2 APIs, the default setting for namespace processing is different: JAXP parsers don't process namespaces by default, while SAX2 parsers do. SAX2 normally removes all xmlns* attributes, reports namespace scope events, and may hide the namespace prefixes actually used by element and attribute names. JAXP does none of that unless you make it; in fact, the default parser mode for some current implementations is the illegal SAX2 mode described in the previous chapter. The example code in this section made the JAXP factory follow SAX2 defaults.

This book encourages you to use SAX2 directly, rather than through the JAXP factory mechanism. Even if JAXP is available, it's more complex to use. Also, the resulting parser is configured differently, so many of the examples in this book would break.

Configuring XMLReader Behavior

A configuration mechanism was one of the key features added in the SAX2 release. Parsers can support extensible sets of named Boolean *feature* flags and *property* objects. These function in similar ways, including using URIs to identify any number of features and properties. The exception model, presented in Chapter 2 in the section "SAX2 Feature Flags" is used to distinguish the three basic types of feature or property: the current value may be read-only, read/write, or undefined. Some flags and properties may have rules about when they can be changed (typically not while parsing) or read.

Applications access property objects and feature flags through get*() and set*() methods and use URIs to identify the characteristic of interest. Since SAX does not provide a way to enumerate such URIs as supported by a parser, you will need to rely on parser documentation, or the tables in this section, to identify the legal identifiers. (Or consult the source code, if you have access to it.)

If you happen to be defining new handlers or features using the SAX2 framework, you don't have to ask for permission to define new property or feature flag IDs. Since they are identified using URIs, just start your ID with a base URI that you control. (Only the SAX maintainers would start with the *http://xml.org/sax/* URI, for example.) Typically, it will be easiest to make up some HTTP URL based on a fully qualified domain name that you control. As with namespace URIs, these are used purely as identifiers rather than as locations from which data would be retrieved. (The "I" in URI stands for "identifier.")

XMLReader Properties

SAX2 defines two *XMLReader* calls for accessing named property objects. One of the most common uses for such objects is to install non-core event handlers. Accessing properties is like accessing feature flags, except that the values associated with these names are objects rather than Booleans:

```
XMLReader      producer ...;
String         uri = ...;
Object         value = ...;
```

```
// Try getting and setting the property
try {
    System.out.println ("Initial property setting: "
        + producer.getProperty (uri);
    // if we get here, the property is supported

    producer.setProperty (uri, value);
    // if we get here, the parser set the property

} catch (SAXNotSupportedException e) {
    // bad value for property ... maybe wrong type, or parser state
    System.out.println ("Can't set property: "
        + e.getMessage ());
    System.exit (1);

} catch (SAXNotRecognizedException e) {
    // property not supported by this parser
    System.out.println ("Doesn't understand property: "
        + e.getMessage ());
    System.exit (1);
}
```

You'll notice the URIs for these standard properties happen to have a common prefix. This means that you can declare the prefix (*http://xml.org/sax/properties/*) as a constant string and construct the identifiers by string catenation.

Here are the standard properties:

http://xml.org/sax/properties/declaration-handler
> This property holds an implementation of *org.xml.sax.ext.DeclHandler*, used for reporting the DTD declarations that aren't reported through *org.xml.sax.DTDHandler* callbacks or for the root element name declaration, *org.xml.sax.ext.LexicalHandler* callbacks. This handler is presented in the section "The DeclHandler Interface."

> Ælfred, Crimson, and Xerces support this property. In fact, all JAXP-compliant processors must do so.

http://xml.org/sax/properties/dom-node
> Only specialized parsers will support this property: parsers that traverse DOM document nodes to produce streams of corresponding SAX events. (Typical SAX2 parsers parse XML text instead of DOM content.) When read, this property returns the DOM node corresponding to the current SAX2 callback. The property can only be written before a parse, to specify that the DOM node beginning and ending the SAX event stream need not be a *org.w3c.dom.Document*. This

type of parser is presented later in this chapter, in the section "DOM-to-SAX Event Production (and DOM4J, JDOM)."

One example of such a parser is *gnu.xml.util.DomParser*, which is currently packaged along with the Ælfred parser. At this time, neither Crimson nor Xerces include such functionality.

http://xml.org/sax/properties/lexical-handler
This property holds an implementation of *org.xml.sax.ext.LexicalHandler*, used for reporting various events mostly (but not exclusively) relating to details of XML text that have no semantic or structural meaning, such as comments. This handler is presented in Chapter 4 in the section "The LexicalHandler Interface."

Ælfred, Crimson, and Xerces support this property. In fact, all JAXP-compliant processors must do so.

http://xml.org/sax/properties/xml-string
This property returns a literal string of characters associated with the current parser callback event. Exactly which characters are returned isn't specified by SAX2. An example would be returning all the characters in the start tag of an element, including unexpanded entity and character references as well as excess whitespace and the exact type of quote characters (single, double) used to delimit attribute values. (This feature is intended to be of use when constructing certain kinds of XML editors, or DTD analyzers, that are willing to re-parse this data.)

No widely available open source SAX2 parser currently supports this property.

Applications may find it useful to define their own types of handler interfaces, assembling sequences of SAX event "atoms" into higher-level event "molecules" that incorporate essential application-level semantics (and probably some procedural validation). This is the same kind of process model used by W3C's XML schema processing model: the Post-Schema-Validation Infoset (PSVI) additions incorporate semantics suited to processing with that kind of schema. Most applications need to associate even more semantics with data than are easily captured by such simple rules (including DTDs and all types of schema). Those semantics would likely not be understood by any common *XMLReader*, but other kinds of SAX processing components can help manage such application-level handlers. You can see an example of this technique in Example 6-3.

XMLReader Feature Flags

The previous chapter showed how to access feature flags from SAX parsers and used the standard validation flag as the primary example. Accessing feature flags follows the same model as accessing properties, except the values are `boolean` not `Object`. There are a handful of standard SAX2 feature flags, which are all you normally need. The namespace for features is different from the namespace for properties. You can't set a property to a *java.lang.Boolean* value and expect to have the same effect as setting the feature flag that happens to use the same identifier.

As with properties, the URIs for these standard feature flags happen to have a common prefix: *http://xml.org/sax/features/*. It's good programming practice to declare the prefix as a constant and construct these feature identifiers by string catenation, helping reduce errors. Also, remember that flags aren't necessarily either settable (read/write)* or readable (supported); some parsers won't recognize all these flags, and in some cases these flags expose parser behaviors that don't change.

The standard flags are as follows:

http://xml.org/sax/features/external-general-entities
 The default value for this flag is parser-specific. When the parser is validating, and in most other cases, the flag is *true*, indicating that the parser reads all external entities used outside the DTD. When the flag is *false*, the XML parser won't expand references to external general entities, so applications won't see the entire body of documents using such entities. This value can't be changed during parsing.

 Crimson and Xerces only support *true* for this property. (For such parsers, you can get most of the effect of setting this flag to *false* by using an *EntityResolver* that returns zero-length entities after the first `startElement()` event.) Ælfred supports changing the value of this property.

http://xml.org/sax/features/external-parameter-entities
 The default value for this flag is parser-specific. When the parser is validating, and in most other cases, the flag is *true*, indicating the DTD will be completely processed. When the flag is *false*, the XML parser will skip any external DTD subset, as well as named external parameter entities, so it won't necessarily read the entire DTD for a document. This value can't be changed during parsing.

---

* SAX could support write-only flags too, but these are rarely a good idea.

Skipping these entities means attributes declared in them will not be defaulted or normalized as expected, and their types won't be known. As a result, default namespace declarations may get dropped. Parts of the internal subset after a reference to a skipped external parameter entity will be ignored. It also means some general entities might not be declared, making it impossible to correctly distinguish whether references to undefined entities are well-formedness errors.

Normally, you are better off providing an entity resolver that accesses locally cached copies of your DTD components, or not using DTDs, rather than disabling processing of external parameter entities. But don't assume all the XML you work with will have these DTD entities processed; the XML processors in some web browsers will not read these entities by default.

Xerces and Crimson only support *true* for this property. (For such parsers, you can get an effect similar to setting this to *false* by using an *EntityResolver* that returns zero-length entities before the first `startElement()` event. The parser won't correctly ignore declarations found later in the DTD.) Ælfred supports changing the value of this property.

http://xml.org/sax/features/is-standalone/

This feature flag derives its value from the document being parsed, so it is read-only and only available after the first part of the document has been parsed. When the flag is *true*, the document has been declared to be standalone. If that declaration is correct, then all external entities may be safely ignored. This feature is part of XML 1.0 and is intended to reduce the cost of parsing some documents.

This flag should be part of an upcoming SAX extensions release.

http://xml.org/sax/features/lexical-handler/parameter-entities

The default value for this flag is parser-specific and is implicitly false if the parser doesn't support the *LexicalHandler* through a parser property. When the flag is *true*, the parser will report the beginning and end of parameter entities through *LexicalHandler* calls. (Skipped parameter entities are always reported, through the appropriate *ContentHandler* call.) Parameter entities are distinguished from general entities because the first character of their entity name will be a percent sign (%). The value can't be changed during parsing.

Currently, only the Ælfred parser reports parameter entities.

http://xml.org/sax/features/namespaces
> This flag defaults to *true* in XML parsers, which indicates the parser performs namespace processing, reporting `xmlns` attributes by `startPrefixMapping()` and `endPrefixMapping()` calls and providing namespace URIs for each element or attribute. Otherwise no such processing is done at the parser level. This can't be changed during parsing.
>
> You will leave flag this at its default setting unless your XML documents aren't guaranteed to conform to the XML Namespaces specification. Setting this to *false* usually gives some degree of parsing speed improvement, although it will likely not provide a significant impact on overall application performance. If you disable namespaces, make sure you first enable the *namespace-prefixes* feature.
>
> This is supported by all SAX2 XML parsers. Ælfred, Crimson, and Xerces support changing the value of this property.

http://xml.org/sax/features/namespace-prefixes
> This flag defaults to *false* in XML parsers, indicating the parser will not present `xmlns*` attributes in its `startElement()` callbacks. Unless the flag is *true*, parsers won't portably present the qualified names (which include the prefix) used in an XML document for elements or attributes. The value can't be changed during parsing.
>
> If you want to see the namespace prefixes for any reason, including for generating output without further postprocessing or for performing layered DTD validation, make sure this flag is set. Also make sure this flag is set if you completely disable namespace processing (with the *namespaces* feature flag), because otherwise the behavior of a SAX2 parser is undefined.
>
> This is supported by all SAX2 parsers. Ælfred, Crimson, and Xerces support changing the value of this property.

http://xml.org/sax/features/string-interning
> The default value for this flag is parser-specific. When true, this indicates that all XML name strings (except those inside attribute values) and namespace URIs returned by this parser will have been interned using `String.intern()`. Some kind of interning is almost always done to improve the performance of parsers, and this flag exposes this work for the benefit of applications. This value can't be changed during parsing.
>
> When applications know interning has been done, they know they can rely on fast, identity-based tests for string equality (== or !=) rather than the more expensive `String.equals()` method. Using

equality testing for strings will always work, but it can be much slower than identity testing. Java automatically interns all string constants. Lots of startElement() processing needs to match element and attribute name strings (as sketched in Example 2-8), so this kind of optimization can often be a win.

Ælfred interns all strings. Some older versions of Crimson don't recognize this flag, but all versions should correctly intern those strings. Xerces reports that it does not intern these strings.

http://xml.org/sax/features/validation
   The default value for this flag is parser-specific; in most cases it is *false*. When the flag is *true*, the parser is performing XML validation (with a DTD, unless you've requested otherwise). When the flag is *false*, the parser isn't validating. The value can't be changed while parsing.

   Ælfred, when packaged with its optional validator, Crimson, and Xerces support both settings.

A few additional standard extension features will likely be defined, providing even more complete Infoset support from SAX2 XML parsers. Ælfred also includes a nonvalidating parser, which supports only *false* for this flag.

Of the widely available parsers, only Xerces has nonstandard feature flags. (The Xerces distribution includes full documentation for those flags.) As a rule, avoid most of these, because they are parser-specific and even version-specific. Some are used to disable warnings about extra definitions that aren't errors. (Most parsers don't bother reporting such nonerrors; Xerces reports them by default.) Others promote noncompliant XML validation semantics. Here are a few flags that you may want to use.

http://apache.org/xml/features/validation/schema
   This tells the parser to validate with W3C-style schemas. The document needs to identify a schema, and the parser must have namespaces and validation enabled. (Defaults to *false*.)

   W3C XML schema validation does not need to be built into XML parsers. In fact, most currently available schema validators are layered.

http://apache.org/xml/features/validation/schema-full-checking
   This flag controls whether W3C schema validation involves all the specified tests. By default, some of the more expensive checks are not performed; Xerces is not "fully conforming" by default.

http://apache.org/xml/features/allow-java-encodings
    This flag defaults to *false*, limiting the encodings that the parser accepts to a handful. When the flag is set to *true*, more encoding names are supported. Most other SAX2 parsers effectively have *true* as their default. A few of those additional encoding names are Java-specific (such as "UTF8"); most of them are standard encoding names, either the preferred version or recognized alternatives.

http://apache.org/xml/features/continue-after-fatal-error
    When set, this flag permits Xerces to continue parsing after it invokes `ErrorHandler.fatalError()` to report a nonrecoverable error. If the error handler doesn't abort parsing by throwing an exception, Xerces will continue. The XML specification requires that no more event data be reported after fatal errors, but it allows additional errors to be reported. (Of course, depending on the initial error, many of the subsequent reports might be nonsense.)

The EntityResolver Interface

As mentioned earlier, this interface is used when a parser needs to access and parse external entities in the DTD or document content. It is not used to access the document entity itself. Cases where an *EntityResolver* should be used include:

- When "more local" copies of entity data should be used. Such copies might be from a local filesystem or from a smart caching proxy. A normal web server may be unavailable or may only be accessible through a slow or congested network link; such remote access can cause application slowdowns and failures. This is generically called catalog or cache processing.

- When the entity's *systemId* uses a URI scheme that is not understood by the underlying JVM. Built-in schemes usually include *http://*, *file://*, *ftp://*, and increasingly *https://*. Schemes not supported by the JVM include *urn:* and application-specific schemes. (You may need to put such URI schemes into publicID values, in order to prevent problems resolving relative URIs.)

- When entities need to be constructed dynamically, or not through the standard URI resolution scheme. For example, entity text might be the result of a query through some user interface or another computation.

- When the XML source text doesn't provide usable URIs. SGML-style systems sometimes use system identifiers that aren't really URIs; they might be relative to some base URI other than the base URI of the appropriate entity (document or DTD). Avoid this practice for XML-based systems; it's not very interoperable because most XML processors strongly expect system IDs in XML documents to be valid URIs, relative to the actual base URI of their declaration.

Applications that handle documents with DTDs should plan to use an *EntityResolver* so they work robustly in the face of partial network failures, and so they avoid placing excessive loads on remote servers. That is, they should try to access local copies of DTD data even when the document specifies a remote one. There are many examples of sloppily written applications that broke when a remote system administrator moved a DTD file. Examples range from purely informative services like most RSS feeds to fee-based services like some news syndication protocols.

You can implement a useful resolver with a data structure as simple as a hash table that maps identifiers to URIs. There is normally no reason to have different parsers use different entity resolvers; documents shouldn't use the same public or (absolute) system identifiers to denote different entities. You'll normally just have one resolver, and it could adaptively cache entities if you like.

More complex catalog facilities may be used by applications that follow the SGML convention that public identifiers are Formal Public Identifiers (FPIs). FPIs serve the role that Universal Resource Names (URNs) serve for Internet-oriented systems. Such mappings can also be used with URIs, if the entity text associated with URIs is as stable as an FPI. (Such stability is one of the goals of URNs.)

Applications pass objects that implement the *EntityResolver* interface to the `XMLReader.setEntityResolver()` method. The parser will then use the resolver with all external parsed entities. The *EntityResolver* interface has only one method, which can throw a *java.io.IOException* as well as the *org.xml.sax.SAXException* most other callbacks throw.

`InputSource resolveEntity(String publicId, String systemId)`
: Parsers invoke this method to map entity identifiers either to other identifiers or to data that they will parse. See the discussion in the section "The InputSource Class," earlier in this chapter, for information about how the *InputSource* interface is used. If null is returned, then the parser will resolve the `systemId` without additional assistance. To avoid parsing an entity, return a value that encapsulates a zero-length text entity.

The *systemId* will always be present and will be a fully resolved URI. The *publicId* may be null. If it's not null, it will have been normalized by mapping sequences of consecutive whitespace characters to a single space character.

Example 3-3 is an example of a simple resolver that substitutes for a web-based time service running on the local machine by interpreting a private URI scheme and mapping public identifiers to alternative URIs using a dictionary that's externally maintained somehow. (For example, you might prime a hashtable with the public IDs for the XHTML 1.0, XHMTL 1.1, and DocBook 4.0 XML DTDs to point to local files.) It delegates to another resolver for other cases.

Example 3-3. Entity resolver, with chaining

```
public class MyResolver implements EntityResolver
{
    private EntityResolver next;
    private Dictionary     map;

    // n -- optional resolver to consult on failure
    // m -- mapping public ids to preferred URLs
    public MyResolver (EntityResolver n, Dictionary m)
        { next = n; map = m; }

    InputSource resolveEntity (String publicId, String systemId)
    throws SAXException, IOException
    {
        // magic URL?
        if ("http://localhost/xml/date".equals (systemId)) {
            InputSource retval = new InputSource (systemId);
            Reader      date;

            date = new InputStringReader (new Date().toString ());
            retval.setCharacterStream (date);
            return retval;
        }

        // nonstandard URI scheme?
        if (systemId.startsWith ("blob:") {
            InputSource retval = new InputSource (systemId);
            String      key = systemId.substring (5);
            byte        data [] = Storage.keyToBlob (key);

            retval.setInputSource (new ByteArrayInputStream (data));
            return retval;
        }

        // use table to map public id to local URL?
        if (map != null && publicId != null) {
            String url = (String) map.get (publicId);
```

Example 3-3. Entity resolver, with chaining (continued)

```
            if (url != null)
                return new InputSource (url);
        }

        // chain to next resolver?
        if (next != null)
            return next.resolveEntity (publicId, systemId);
        return null;
    }
}
```

Traditionally, public identifiers are mainly used as keys to find local copies of entities. In SGML, system identifiers were optional and system-specific, so public identifiers were sometimes the only ones available. (XML changed this: system identifiers are mandatory and are URIs.) In essence, public identifiers were used in SGML to serve the role that URNs serve in web-oriented architectures. An ISO standard for FPIs exists, and now RFC 3151 (available at *http://www.ietf.org/rfc/rfc3151.txt*) defines a mapping from FPIs to URNs. (The FPI is normalized and transformed, then gets a urn:publicid: prefix.) When public identifiers are used with XML systems, it's largely by adopting FPI policies to interoperate with such SGML systems; however, XML public identifiers don't need to be FPIs. You may prefer to use URN schemes in newer systems. If so, be aware that some XML processing engines support only URLs as system identifiers. By letting applications interpret public IDs as URNs, SAX offers more power than some other XML APIs do.

If you want richer catalog-style functionality than the table mapping shown earlier, look for open source implementations of the XML version of the OASIS SGML/Open Catalog (SOCAT). At this time, a specification for such a catalog is a stable draft, still in development; see *http://www.oasis.org/committees/entity/* for more information. This specification defines an XML text representation of mappings; the mappings can be significantly more complex than the tabular one shown earlier.

Other Kinds of SAX2 Event Producers

Normally, an *XMLReader* turns XML text into SAX event callbacks. This book encourages you to think of those event consumer callbacks as the most important part of the process, so using XML text as input is just one option for feeding those consumers.

For example, some SAX parsers have turned HTML text into SAX callbacks; there have even been SAX wrappers around the limited *javax.swing.text.html* parser. These wrappers can help migrate to XHTML, first by making sure tags are properly formed, paired, and nested, then by helping make the XHTML be valid so more tools can work with it. Malformed HTML is a huge problem; there's lots of brain-dead HTML text on the Web.* In practice, no generally available SAX HTML parser is quite good enough to substitute for tools like HTML Tidy (see *http://tidy.sourceforge.net*) combined with manual fixup for problem cases, but that could change.

DOM-to-SAX Event Production (and DOM4J, JDOM)

It's so typical to want to turn a DOM node into a series of SAX events that SAX2 defined a standard way to do this. Several of the projects that claim to improve on DOM by being more Java-friendly, such as DOM4J and JDOM, have similar functionality.

In conjunction with any sort of SAX text output API (such as an *XMLWriter*), this technique is an easy way to turn a DOM tree into text. Utilities to turn a DOM node into text all need to do more or less the same thing: traverse the tree and emit the right sort of text. Using SAX (and SAX utilities) you can do this without needing support for any optional DOM Level 3 modules and without relying on any vendor-specific DOM extensions. (It's also a fine technique to use when you need a debugging snapshot and can't afford the memory needed to deep-clone a DOM document.)

---

* One early browser development policy was that *there's no such thing as broken HTML*, so parsers needed to accept pretty much everything. The policy helped simplify content creation when there were few tools beyond text editors, but it also led to serious problems with browser incompatibility which are only now beginning to go away. It's also helped spread tools fostering malformed HTML (including flakey CGI scripts) and made it harder to present HTML on low-cost systems (it takes a fat parser to handle even a fraction of the different kinds of broken HTML).

  The draconian error-handling policy of the XML specification (if it's not well formed, it must be rejected) was a reaction to those problems: XML parsers don't need to compete on how well they can make sense of garbage input. It was added at the request of the main browser vendors, which were then Netscape and Microsoft. This policy makes it a lot easier to create tools to process XML text, including presentation tools (XHTML browsing) that can even work on limited resource systems (such as PDAs or cell phones), content management tools, and "screen scrapers" for mining XHTML presentation text (to repurpose the data shown there).

Of course, any other processing can be done too, such as validating the output. After initializing and connecting an appropriate event producer, consumer-side validator, and *ErrorHandler*, just produce the events and watch for reports of validity errors. In some cases (as with DOM-to-SAX converters), you can look at individual element subtrees; in other cases, you'll need to examine entire documents.

Turning DOM trees into SAX events

To turn a DOM node into SAX events, you'll need to use a special parser class; normal SAX parsers require text as input and won't know the first thing about DOM. If it's a Level 2 DOM and is using namespace support, you'll probably need to manually patch up the namespace data, since DOM isn't guaranteed to maintain it. Patching can be done before or after you generate SAX events; I prefer to use a single, generic SAX2 processing component to handle namespace fixups no matter where the problem arose, since DOM isn't the only culprit. Given such a parser class (the GNU version is used here), your code will look like this:

```
import gnu.xml.util.XMLWriter;
import org.w3c.dom.Node;
import gnu.xml.util.DomParser;

XMLReader       parser;
Node            node = ...;
ContentHandler  contentHandler = new XMLWriter (system.out);

parser = new DomParser ();
parser.setContentHandler (contentHandler);
// you may also set DTDHandler, LexicalHandler, and DeclHandler

parser.setProperty ("http://xml.org/sax/properties/dom-node", node);
parser.parse ("dom-node value gets parsed");
```

Neither Crimson nor Xerces currently include support for such DOM-to-SAX transformations.

Turning DOM4J trees into SAX events

In DOM4J (*http://www.dom4j.org*), it works like this. The current version of DOM4J isn't as flexible or complete as a DOM-to-SAX converter, though it has a few more options than JDOM. See the current release for more information.

```
import gnu.xml.util.XMLWriter;
import org.dom4j.io.SAXWriter;
import org.dom4j.Document;
```

```
SAXWriter        parser;
ContentHandler   contentHandler = new XMLWriter (system.out);
Document         doc = ...;

parser = new SAXWriter ();
parser.setContentHandler (contentHandler);
// you may also set DTDHandler and LexicalHandler

parser.write (doc);
```

Turning JDOM trees into SAX events

Here's how to do this conversion in JDOM (*http://www.jdom.org*). As this is being written, the current version of JDOM doesn't support the level of flexibility of a DOM-to-SAX parser; it only handles JDOM document nodes. It also doesn't support *LexicalHandler* or *DeclHandler* events. JDOM could support some of the *LexicalHandler* events, such as those for comments and CDATA section boundaries. See the current release for more information.

```
import gnu.xml.util.XMLWriter;
import org.jdom.Document;
import org.jdom.output.SAXOutputter;

SAXOutputter     parser;
ContentHandler   contentHandler = new XMLWriter (system.out);
Document         doc;

parser = new SAXOutputter (contentHandler);
// you may also set DTDHandler

parser.output (doc);
```

Push Mode Event Production

Since SAX event handlers are just objects, your application software can call their methods directly. This is a common technique for application code that needs to convert data structures to XML: turn them into SAX event streams for processing by other components. That component could be an *XMLWriter* sending data across the web to a partner, but you can do other kinds of processing too. Such application code normally has no reason to be wrapped as an implementation of *XMLReader*.

When used with in-memory data structures, this is part of what's sometimes called *serialization*. Be careful not to confuse this with the more specialized meaning in Java RMI, where serialization is a binary data format tied to individual Java classes. Other words used to describe this kind

Other Kinds of SAX2 Event Producers

of process include "marshaling," "encoding," and "pickling." Reversing the process is an important parallel problem, since most of the time applications must both produce and consume XML data. That is, most applications round-trip data, rather than just consuming it or producing it.

This event generation technique is not restricted to data structures that were originally stored in memory. You can use it with data from databases, stored on filesystems, and entered through user interfaces. The same general technique is used in all these cases.

Turning CSV files into SAX events

Comma Separated Values, or CSV, is a data format that is widely used for some data interchange problems. Many spreadsheets and databases can read and write it, and it can be used to publish fairly large databases. It's one of the more widely understood "flat file" text formats, and it's not uncommon to need to translate data CSV formats into XML. With luck, the meaning of each field will be documented or maybe obvious from context. A simple CSV list of some yoga classes might have five fields per record and look like this:

```
daniela,4:30-5:45pm,ashtanga,sun,mixed
(staff),10:30am-12:00m,sivanenda,daily,open
philippe,7-9:00pm,ashtanga,mon,mixed
larry,4:30-5:45pm,ashtanga,wed,rocket
mahadevi,6-8:00pm,sivanenda,wed,advanced
savonn,7-8:30pm,vinyasa,wed,2-3
kei,9:30-11am,vinyasa,thu,intermediate
patti,7:30-9pm,iyenegar,thur,1-2
regan,9:30-11am,bikram,fri,open
mark,12m-2pm,ashtanga,sat,mysore
```

The translation is easier than the parsing of CSV itself. Details like handling of empty or missing fields, quoted values, and inconsistent value syntax are messy, and critical when importing lots of data. In fact, it's so messy that Example 3-4 completely avoids such lexical issues for CSV input data. (Nonlexical issues should be delegated to XML processing layers.) The example shows one way to translate; it's packaged more simply than a real-world application would probably expect. (Making an *XML-Reader* that emits SAX events is possible and might be convenient.) This approach turns each CSV record into a single element by using attributes (with a sneak peek at a helper class we'll see later). It prints the output as XML text, which is probably not how you'd normally work with such data; the output is more naturally sent through a processing pipeline.

Example 3-4. Producing SAX2 events from CSV input

```java
import java.io.*;
import java.util.StringTokenizer;
import org.xml.sax.*;
import org.xml.sax.helpers.*;
import gnu.xml.util.XMLWriter;


public class csv
{
    // stdin = (simple) CSV, stdout = XML
    public static void main (String argv [])
    {
        BufferedReader    in;
        XMLWriter         out;
        ErrorHandler      errs;
        String            line;

        try {
            in = new BufferedReader (new InputStreamReader (System.in));
            out = new XMLWriter (System.out);
            errs = new DefaultHandler () {
                    public void fatalError (SAXParseException e) {
                        System.err.println ("** parse error: "
                            + e.getMessage ());
                    }
                };

            out.startElement ("", "", "yoga", new AttributesImpl ());
            while ((line = in.readLine ()) != null)
                parseLine (line, out, errs);
            out.endElement ("", "", "yoga");
            out.flush ();
        } catch (Exception e) {
            System.err.println ("** error: " + e.getMessage ());
            e.printStackTrace (System.err);
            System.exit (1);
        }
    }

    // this doesn't handle quoted strings (with commas inside),
    // empty fields, tabs used as delimiters, or column headers.
    private static void parseLine (
        String            line,
        ContentHandler    out,
        ErrorHandler      errs
    ) throws SAXException
    {
        StringTokenizer  tokens = new StringTokenizer (line.trim (), ",");
        String           values [] = new String [5];

        // if there aren't five values, it's malformed
        if (tokens.countTokens () != 5) {
```

Example 3-4. Producing SAX2 events from CSV input (continued)

```
            errs.fatalError (
                new SAXParseException ("not enough values", null));
            return;
        }
        for (int i = 0; i < 5; i++)
            values [i] = tokens.nextToken ();

        // now that we parsed the line safely, report its contents

        // the AttributesImpl class is shown later
        AttributesImpl    atts = new AttributesImpl ();

        atts.addAttribute ("", "", "teacher", "CDATA", values [0]);
        atts.addAttribute ("", "", "time", "CDATA", values [1]);
        atts.addAttribute ("", "", "type", "CDATA", values [2]);
        atts.addAttribute ("", "", "date", "CDATA", values [3]);
        atts.addAttribute ("", "", "level", "CDATA", values [4]);

        out.ignorableWhitespace ("\n  ".toCharArray (), 0, 3);
        out.startElement ("", "", "class", atts);
        out.endElement ("", "", "class");
    }
}
```

The output of that program looks somewhat like this:

```
<yoga>
  <class teacher="daniela" time="4:30-5:45pm" type="ashtanga"
        date="sun" level="mixed"></class>
  <class teacher="(staff)" time="10:30am-12:00m" type="sivanenda"
        date="daily" level="open"></class>
  <class teacher="philippe" time="7-9:00pm" type="ashtanga"
        date="mon" level="mixed"></class>
  <class teacher="larry" time="4:30-5:45pm" type="ashtanga"
        date="wed" level="rocket"></class>
  <class teacher="mahadevi" time="6-8:00pm" type="sivanenda"
        date="wed" level="advanced"></class>
  <class teacher="savonn" time="7-8:30pm" type="vinyasa"
        date="wed" level="2-3"></class>
  <class teacher="kei" time="9:30-11am" type="vinyasa"
        date="thu" level="intermediate"></class>
  <class teacher="patti" time="7:30-9pm" type="iyenegar"
        date="thur" level="1-2"></class>
  <class teacher="regan" time="9:30-11am" type="bikram"
        date="fri" level="open"></class>
  <class teacher="mark" time="12m-2pm" type="ashtanga"
        date="sat" level="mysore"></class></yoga>
```

This included some ignorable whitespace to prevent the output from appearing as one big line of text; enabling pretty printing would do as well. Notice that the output needed to be flushed, else the JVM would normally exit with data still buffered in memory. We haven't yet looked at the endDocument() callback that would normally flush the data. Finally, notice that handling of any CSV conversion errors is delegated to a SAX error handler, which in this case adopts a very permissive strategy.

Turning objects into SAX events

For simple objects, something like the following "Address" example works. For a more complex object, such as a purchase order with multiple addresses for shipping and billing, you'll likely have routines that encode other data and use routines like this one as subroutines. You won't need to use any other handler interfaces, though you might want to embed comments or create CDATA boundaries using a *LexicalHandler*. Notice that startElement() calls always have matching endElement() calls, just as if the text was generated by an XML parser. This example declares and uses namespaces; you don't need to do that on the producer side if you patch them up later, but it's a reasonable practice to adopt. As used here, the *AttributesImpl* class just creates an empty set of attributes to pass on because null values can't be used:

```
static final String nsURI = "http://example.com/xml/address";

void toXML (Address addr, ContentHandler stream)
{
    char            temp [];
    Attributes      atts;

    // create an empty set of attributes
    atts = new AttributesImpl ();

    // <address xmlns="http://example.com/xml/address">
    stream.startPrefixMapping ("", nsURI);
    stream.startElement (nsURI, "address", "address", atts);

    // <street>...</street>
    stream.startElement (nsURI, "street", "street", atts);
    temp = addr.getStreet ().toCharArray ();
    stream.characters (temp, 0, temp.length);
    stream.endElement (nsURI, "street", "street");

    // <city>...</city>
    stream.startElement (nsURI, "city", "city", atts);
    temp = addr.getCity ().toCharArray ();
    stream.characters (temp, 0, temp.length);
    stream.endElement (nsURI, "city", "city");

    // <country>...</country>
    stream.startElement (nsURI, "country", "country", atts);
    temp = addr.getCountry ().toCharArray ();
```

```
            stream.characters (temp, 0, temp.length);
            stream.endElement (nsURI, "country", "country");

            // ... there would probably be more elements,
            // but not all application data in the "Address"
            // would be shared with the recipient.

            // </address>
            stream.endElement (nsURI, "address", "address");
            stream.endPrefixMapping ("");
      }
```

If you're printing such output, you might want to add some ignorable whitespace to keep all the text from appearing on a single line. The resulting XML text will be easier to read, though having text without line breaks should not matter otherwise. (Better yet: use an XMLWriter with pretty-printing support.) If you are working with many namespaces, you may want to use the *NamespaceSupport* class (see the section "The NamespaceSupport Class" in Chapter 5) to track and select the prefixes used in the element and attribute names you write.

It may also be a good idea to write "unmarshaling" code (taking such events and recreating, or looking up, application objects) at the same time you write marshaling code (like the preceding code, creating SAX events from application objects). That helps test the code: when round-trip processing works for many different data items (save a lot of test cases), you know it's behaving. Unmarshaling code can also be an appropriate place to test for semantic validity of data: you might have reason to trust that your current marshaling code is correct, but changes made next year could break something, and it's not good to expect everyone else will marshal correctly.

Data modeling concerns

As a rule of thumb, avoid assuming that your XML data model ought to match your application's data structures. Such policies can sometimes be appropriate, but more often, your application's internal data structures were optimized for something unrelated to communicating with other applications. Most systems that automatically marshal and unmarshal data structures (maybe using "reflection" in Java) will make such assumptions; they lead to tightly coupled systems. Tight coupling tends to cause fragility in the face of system evolution, since upgrades normally occur incrementally on widely distributed systems (such as almost all web-based applications).

For example, when you interchange the results of a complex set of queries from your database (perhaps for a large purchase order), it is typically appropriate to mask the exact relational structure used in your application. The recipient of your XML may well have adopted a different relational normalization. The recipient might not even expect to perform database operations on such data. Data displays may need to address usability issues that are completely unrelated to how applications "think" about the same data. Similar logic applies when the application data isn't stored in a database or is only partially stored in one.

On the other hand, if you're using XML to transfer a relation from one database to another, encoding a *java.sql.ResultSet* (or CSV table) into a series of elements (one element per table row, without duplications) may be exactly the right model. (The reverse transformation would be unmarshaling—consuming XML to populate a database.) You won't always want to denormalize, even though the ability to easily do that is one of the great strengths of using XML to interchange data. Many common messaging scenarios involve the kind of data model that serves as input to normalization processes, and are oriented to individual cases not aggregates.

When you're encoding individual data items, such as integers, dates, or binary data encoded using BASE64, you should consider using the datatyping facilities in Part 2 of the W3C XML Schema specification (*http://www.w3.org/TR/xmlschema-2/*). Those "simple" datatypes are intended to be used in many specifications. Its association with the particular schema system described in other parts of the W3C XML Schema specification can be viewed as a historical accident; you don't need to use W3C schemas to use these datatypes.

Producing Well-Formed Event Streams

If you are generating SAX2 events from any event producer that's not an actual XML parser (maybe by using an HTML parser or code that traverses data structures), you may need to ensure the event stream is legal before passing it to other components (maybe by printing it as XML text). There are issues of well formedess to think about: startElement() calls need matching endElement() calls, other calls require similar start/end nesting, carriage returns are prohibited in line ends, and more. Correct reporting of namespace information is important: prefixes must be declared and correctly used. Validity will also be an issue in many contexts as a policy of eliminating data format errors as early as possible. (It's cheaper to fix bugs before you ship them in products than afterward, and validation tools make some bugs easy to find.)

The particular issues you may have depend on what kind of event producer you use and what kinds of events you generate. DOM streams can easily be namespace-invalid; for example, prefixes are often undeclared or missing. Code that generates events directly is particularly prone to violate element nesting and closure requirements and to omit namespace declarations. Few tools prevent all kinds of illegal content;]]> could appear in CDATA sections, and -- (two hyphens) within comments, both of which will prevent generation of legal XML text.

With high-quality producer-side code, you'll have fixed all those problems before the code is released. But you'll still probably want code that dynamically verifies that there's no problem to use when debugging or troubleshooting. If you adopt a good SAX2 event pipeline framework, it can easily support components that monitor event streams to ensure they meet those data integrity constraints or, in some cases (like namespaces), patch event streams so they are correct.

The XMLFilter Interface

SAX2 added the *XMLFilter* interface. *XMLFilter* is just an *XMLReader* that can be associated with a "parent" reader. What's interesting is the expectation that the parent is producing the events and the filter postprocesses them; the filter parses and modifies Infoset data, not XML text. From the perspective of your application code, a filter that you use as an *XMLReader* is doing some postprocessing of your parser requests, some processing on the XML data, then passing you the results; it's a preprocessor for infoset data.

The *XMLFilter* interface adds these methods to *XMLReader*:

void setParent(XMLReader parser)
XMLReader getParent()
> The parent of an *XMLFilter* is accessed using standard JavaBeans property-naming conventions. Use this property to control which parser (or filter) generates the events to be filtered.

The role of the *XMLFilter* implementation is primarily to intercept and process SAX content events. Because its real work is to process those events, the code in such a filter is acting as a consumer. Implementing the *XMLReader* interface is a facade to make that consumer code look like a pull API (*XMLReader*) and let it intercept requests to an underlying parser. That is, it supports one kind of XML pipeline model.

Since the interesting issues are all on the consumer side, *XMLFilter* is discussed later with other kinds of SAX event pipeline models, in the section "XML Pipelines," in Chapter 4, along with the *XMLFilterImpl* helper class.

If you're using these filters as event producers, you'll need to pay attention to a secondary role of an *XMLFilter*: intercepting and modifying parser requests. This kind of filter is a *compound object*. It consists of the filter, plus a reader (which might in turn be another filter), handler bindings, and settings for feature flags and properties. The interrelationships of these parts can get murky. In simple cases you can ignore the distinction, treating this type of SAX filter just like another reader. But in other cases you may need to remember that the filter and its parent are distinct objects with different behaviors.

For example, sometimes you'll find implementations of *XMLFilter* that don't use mechanisms such as the *EntityResolver* or *ErrorResolver*. When you need to use those mechanisms, you'd need to bind such objects to the parent parser. But most filters pass those objects on to the parent and may even need to use them internally, so you'd bind them to the filter instead. You'll need to know which kind of filter you have. In a similar way, if an underlying parser interns its strings, but the filter changes them (for example, swapping one namespace URI for another) and doesn't intern those strings, then code that talks to the filter can't use identity tests to replace the slower equality tests. The filter would have to expose a different setting for such feature flags than the parent parser.

In this chapter:
- *More About ContentHandler*
- *The LexicalHandler Interface*
- *Exposing DTD Information*
- *Turning SAX Events into Data Structures*
- *XML Pipelines*

4
Consuming SAX2 Events

Most of the power of SAX is exposed through event callbacks. In previous chapters you've seen some of the most widely used event callbacks as well as how to ensure that all the callbacks are generated and reported to application code.

This chapter presents the rest of the standard SAX event-handling interfaces (including the extension handlers), then talks about some of the common ways that event consumers use those interfaces. These interfaces are primarily implemented by application code that consumes events and needs to solve particular problems. You might also write custom event producers, which call these interfaces directly rather than expecting some type of *XMLReader* to issue them.

More About ContentHandler

In the section "Basic ContentHandler Events," in Chapter 2, we looked at the most important APIs used to handle XML document content. Some other APIs were deferred to this section because they aren't used as widely. Depending on what problems you're solving, you may rely heavily on some of these additional methods.

Other ContentHandler Methods

Five *ContentHandler* callbacks were discussed in Chapter 2: the section "Essential ContentHandler Callbacks" explained how characters and element boundaries were reported, and the section "ContentHandler and Prefix Mappings" explained how namespace-prefix scopes were reported. But the interface has five other methods. Here's what they do and when you'll want to use them:

`void setDocumentLocator (Locator l)`

This is normally the first callback from a parser; the single parameter is a *Locator*, discussed later. Strictly speaking, SAX parsers are not required to provide a locator or to make this callback; however, you'd want to avoid parsers that don't provide this information. Your implementation of this callback will normally just save the locator; it can't do much more since it's the only SAX event callback that can't throw a *SAXException*:

```
class MyHandler implements ContentHandler ... {
    private Locator    locator;
    ...
    public void setDocumentLocator (Locator l)
        { locator = l; }
    ...
}
```

Use this object as discussed later in this chapter, in the section "The Locator Interface." It is the standard way to report the base URI of the XML text currently being parsed; that information is essential for resolving relative URIs. It's also essential for diagnostics that tell you where application code detects errors in large quantities of XML text.

`void startDocument ()`
`void endDocument ()`

These two callbacks bracket processing for a document, and they are normally used to manage application state associated with the document being parsed. If you're parsing a document, these methods will always be called once each, even when parsing is cut short by a thrown exception. No other methods have such guarantees.

`startDocument()` is always called before any data is reported from the parser, and is normally used to initialize application data structures. It will usually be the second callback from the parser; parsers that provide a *Locator* will report that first. You can't rely on a `setDocumentLocator()` call before `startDocument()`; structure your initialization code to do the real work in the callback guaranteed to be available.

`endDocument()` is always called to report that no more document data will be provided. The normal application response is to clean up all state associated with the current parse. The parser closes any input data streams you gave it using an *InputSource* (discussed later), so the

More About ContentHandler

application doesn't need to do that. Cleanup would include forgetting any saved *Locator* since that object is no longer usable when the parse is complete. Also, you'd likely close other files or sockets that were opened while processing this document:

```
class MyHandler implements ContentHandler ... {
    ...
    public void startDocument ()
    throws SAXException
    {
        // initialize data structures for ALL handlers here
        ...
    }
    public void endDocument ()
    throws SAXException
    {
        // free those same data structures
        locator = null;
        elementStack = null;
        ...
    }
    ...
}
```

These two calls are widely used in robust SAX code because they provide such good hooks to control memory usage and manage associated file descriptors. However, some SAX2 parsers have a bug that reduces the robustness offered by SAX; they won't correctly call **end-Document()** when parsing is aborted by throwing exceptions.

void processingInstruction (target, data)

Processing Instructions (PIs) are used in XML for data that doesn't obey the rules of a DTD. They can be placed anywhere in a document, including within the DTD, except inside other markup constructs like tags. Unlike comments, PIs are designed for applications to use. They're part of the document structure that programmatic logic must understand; they can follow rules, just not ones found in a DTD or schema. This method has two parameters:

String *target*

XML applications use this parameter to determine how to handle the PI. You can rely on the fact that it'll never be the string **xml** (in any combination of upper- and lowercase characters) because XML and text declarations are not processing instructions.

Some documents follow the convention that the target of a PI names a notation (perhaps the fully qualified URI found in its system identifier) and the meaning is associated with the notation rather than the name. That's a fine practice to follow, but it isn't essential. Most code just compares target names as strings, rather than use data reported with DTDHandler.notationDecl() to figure out what a target name should mean.

String *data*
This parameter is data associated with the PI, and it may be the null string if no data was provided after the target name. Some applications use the syntax of an attribute here; others don't bother.

Processing instructions are natural to use in template systems and other document-oriented applications.*

Processing instructions are normally safe to ignore when your processing doesn't recognize them (passing them on to any subsequent processing stage), or to store. If the parser does recognize them, it normally acts on then immediately. For example, an <?xml-stylesheet ... ?> PI might select a particular XSLT stylesheet to use for generating a servlet's output. The processing instruction event is used later, in Example 6-9.

void ignorableWhitespace(buf,offset,len)
This is an optional callback, made by most parsers (including all that are validating) to report whitespace that separates elements in element content models, like those of the form (title,para*,sect1*) but not (#PCDATA|para|comment)*, ANY, or EMPTY. Whitespace before or after the document's root element is not treated as ignorable and is completely discarded. Providing this information is a requirement of the XML specification, since this kind of whitespace is defined to be markup rather than document content. If the parser doesn't see such a content model declaration for any reason, it can't use this callback; it'll use characters() instead, and applications will need to figure out if the whitespace is part of markup or part of content.

The parameters are exactly the same as those of the characters() callback, except that you know the characters in the specified range will all be spaces, tabs, or newlines. (Keep that in mind if you're directly producing ignorable whitespace to feed some event consumer. Using CRLF- or CR-style line ends here is a bug, though you

---

* For example, the syntax of PHP, the web page scripting tool, looks like a processing instruction, <?php ... ?>. For various reasons, PHP is not actually an XML document syntax.

might not see immediate consequences.) Like characters(), this method can be called several times in a row, to complete processing a single stretch of characters.

There are two popular ways to handle this callback. My favorite is to drop all the characters; they're only in the source document to make the elements lay out nicely, so they won't ever mean anything. There's rarely a reason to even look at the data, much less save it. The other option is to delegate handling and just call the characters() callback with the whitespace.

void skippedEntity (String name)
    The parameter is a *String* that identifies an internal or external parsed entity. General entity names are presented as found in their declarations (dudley). Parameter entity names begin with a percent sign (%nell). The external DTD subset is special; it's an unnamed parameter entity and is reported with the name [dtd]. You might not be able to tell if the skipped entity was an internal or external entity, even using *DeclHandler* events.

    You probably don't ever want to see this call, since it means that part of your document has been hidden. XML 1.0 processors are required to report this case; SAX 1.0 didn't, and most other parser-level APIs (such as DOM Level 2) still don't. This is a call that only nonvalidating parsers may issue, and even then only if they are not parsing all the external entities referred to in documents—that is, where one or both of the external entities feature flags is set to false, to disable reading external general or parameter entities. No widely used Java parsers clear those flags by default, so this is a rare call in Java. However some C parsers, such as Expat (used in Mozilla), won't normally parse external entities, so the notion isn't exotic in all languages.

The Locator Interface

This useful interface is sometimes overlooked. It gives information that is essential for providing location-sensitive diagnostics and is often given to *SAXParseException* constructors. That same information is also needed to resolve relative URIs in document content or attribute values (such as xml:base). Parsers provide one instance of this class, which can be used inside event callbacks to find what entity triggered the event and approximately where. Use that locator only during such callbacks. There are only a few methods in this class.

`String getSystemId ()`
> This is the most important method in this interface. It returns the base URI (system ID) for the entity being parsed; this is always an absolute URI. (However, versions of Xerces that are current at this writing have a bug here. They sometimes return nonabsolute URIs.) Use this method to identify the document or external entity in diagnostics or to resolve relative URIs (perhaps in conjunction with `xml:base` attributes).
>
> If the parser doesn't know this value, null is returned. This normally indicates that the parser was not given such a URI inside of a *Input-Source* encapsulating document text. That's bad practice except when it's unavoidable, such as parsing in-memory data or input to the POST method in a servlet.

`int getLineNumber ()`
`int getColumnNumber ()`
> These two functions approximate the current position of a parser within an entity. The position reflected is where the relevant event's data ended. It is only an approximation for diagnostics, but most parsers do try to be accurate about the line number.
>
> These numbers count up from 1 as appropriate for user-oriented diagnostics. Not all implementations will provide these values; the value -1 is returned to indicate that no value was provided.

`String getPublicId ()`
> A public identifier may be provided with this method. Otherwise null is returned. This may be useful for diagnostics in some cases.

One common use for a locator is to report an error detected while an application processes document content. The *SAXParseException* class has two constructors that take locator parameters. (The descriptive string is always first, the locator is second, and an optional "root cause" exception is third.) Once you create such an exception, it can be thrown directly, which always terminates a parse. Or you pass it to an *ErrorHandler* to centralize error handling-policy in your application:

```
// "locator" was saved when setDocumentLocator() was called earlier
// or was initialized to null; this is safe in both cases
try {
    ...
    engine.setWarpFactor (11);
    ...
} catch (DriveException e) {
    SAXParseException    spe = new SAXParseException (
        "The warp engine's gonna blow!",
```

More About ContentHandler

```
            locator,
            e);
    errHandler.error (e);
    // we'll get here whenever such problems are ignored
}
```

To resolve relative URIs in document content—for example, one found in an `<xhtml:a href="..."/>` reference in a link checker—you'd use code like this (ignoring `xml:base` complications):

```
public void startElement (String uri, String lname, String qname,
        Attributes atts) throws SAXException
{
    if (xhtmlURI.equals (uri)) {
        if ("a".equals (lname)) {
            String href = atts.getValue ("href");
            if (href != null) {
                // ASSUMES:  locator is nonnull
                System.out.println ("Found href to: " +
                    new URI (new URI(locator.getSystemId ()), href));
            }
            // else presumably <xhtml:a name="...">
        }
    } ...
}
```

Some of the *XMLReader* implementations cannot possibly call ContentHandler.setDocumentLocator() with a *Locator*. When parsing in-memory data structures, such as a DOM document, a locator will normally be meaningless. When parsing in-memory buffers like a *String* (with a *StringReader*), there won't usually be a URI in the locator.

If your application supports the layered `xml:base` convention (which lets documents "lie" about their true locations for purposes of resolving relative URIs), it will need to track those attributes itself, as part of a context stack mechanism. (An example of such a stack is shown later, in Example 5-1.) Such attributes can sometimes help make up for SAX event sources that can't provide locator information, such as DOM-to-SAX producers. But they can confuse things too: in the following example, `xml:base` would apply to the top element and its direct children, but nothing within the external entity reference. (Let's assume, for the sake of discussion, that no element has an `xml:base` attribute.)

```
<top xml:base="http://www.example.com/moved/doc2.xml">
    <xhtml:a href="abc.xml">
    <xhtml:div> &external; </xhtml:div>
    <xhtml:a href="xyz.xml">
</top>
```

When character content of an element is reported, characters from different external entities will get different callbacks, so the locator can be used to tell those different entities apart from each other.

Internationalization Concerns

One of the goals of XML was to bring Unicode into widespread use so that the Web could really become worldwide in terms of people, not just technology. This brings several concerns into text management. You may not need to worry about these if you're working only in ASCII or with just one character encoding. While you're just starting out with Java and XML you should certainly avoid worrying about these details. Some other users of SAX2 will need to understand these issues. Since they surface primarily with *ContentHandler* event callbacks, we briefly summarize them here.

If your application works with MathML, or in various languages whose character sets gained support in Unicode 3.1 through the so-called Astral Planes, you will need to know that what Java calls a char is not really the same thing as a Unicode character or an XML character. If you aren't using such languages, you'll probably be able to ignore this issue for a while. Still, you might want to read about Unicode 3.1 to learn more about this and minimize trouble later. By the time you read this, the W3C may even have completed its "Blueberry" XML update, intended to allow the use of some such characters within XML names.

In the case of such characters, whose Unicode code point is above the value U+FFFF (the maximum 16-bit code point), these characters are mapped to two Java char values, called a *surrogate pair*. The char values are in a range reserved for *surrogate* characters, with a *high surrogate* always immediately followed by a *low surrogate*. (This is called a *big-endian* sequence.) Surrogate pairs can show up in several places in XML, and hence in SAX2: in character content, processing instructions, attribute values (including defaults in the DTD), and comments.

At this time, Java does not have APIs to explicitly support characters using surrogate pairs, although character arrays and *java.lang.String* will hold them as if the char values weren't part of the same character. The *java.lang.Character* class doesn't recognize surrogate pairs. The best precaution seems to be to prefer APIs that talk in terms of slices of character arrays (or *Strings*), rather than in terms of individual Java char values. This approach also handles other situations where more than one `char` value is needed per character.

Depending on the character encodings you're using and the applications you're implementing, you may also need to pay attention to the W3C Character Model (*http://www.w3.org/TR/WD-charmod/* at this writing) and Unicode Normalization Form C. Briefly, these aim to eliminate undesirable representations of characters and to handle some other cases where Unicode characters aren't the same as XML characters or a Java `char`, such as composite characters. For example, many accented characters are represented by composing two or more Unicode characters. Systems work better when they only need to handle one way to represent such characters, and Form C addresses that problem.

The LexicalHandler Interface

This extension interface is new in SAX2. It's in the *org.xml.sax.ext* package, which means among other things that it is optional and isn't supported by all SAX APIs and layers, such as *DefaultHandler*. However, any SAX2 parser that can be bootstrapped with JAXP supports this interface. Parsers that support *LexicalHandler* expose comment text and the boundaries of CDATA sections, DTDs, and most parsed entities. There is no `setLexicalHandler()` method; bind these handlers to parsers like this:

```
XMLReader         producer = ...;
LexicalHandler    handler = ...;

producer.setProperty ("http://xml.org/sax/properties/lexical-handler",
        handler);
// throws SAXNotSupportedException if parameter isn't a LexicalHandler
// throws SAXNotRecognizedException if parser doesn't support it.
```

The information this exposes is needed for applications that need more in the way of "round-tripping" support than the SAX2 core allows. That is, less of the information read by parsers will be completely discarded. The application needs SAX to provide more complete support for the XML Infoset (or for the XPath data model). To completely support DOM, XPath, or XSLT on top of a SAX2 parser, this interface is as necessary as the namespaces exposed in the SAX2 *ContentHandler* and *Attributes* interfaces. The downside is that much of this information is in the category of information applications shouldn't want to deal with. Be careful how you use these callbacks; don't assume that just because the information is available, you should use it.

LexicalHandler has the following methods:

`void comment(buf,offset,len)`

    Reports characters inside a `<!-- ... -->` comment section (without the delimiting characters). For many applications, this event is the only reason to use this interface. This is *almost* the same convention *ContentHandler* uses to report character content or ignorable whitespace; the parameters are identical. Comments are always reported in a single callback. Two consecutive `comment()` calls means two consecutive comments, while two consecutive `characters()` calls just enlarge a given logical span of text.

`char buf []`

    A character array that holds the comment text. As with the `ContentHandler.characters()` callback, you must ignore characters in this buffer that are outside of the specified range.

`int offset`

    The index of the first comment character in the buffer.

`int len`

    How many comment characters are in the buffer, beginning at the specified offset.

Comments show up in the XPath data model, so they are reflected in layers (such as XSLT, XPointer, and XLink) that build on XPath. Strictly speaking, applications should ignore comments except when they round-trip data provided during authoring. Instead, they should use processing instructions when they need to work with annotations. You might need to use comment data with HTML processors because it doesn't support processing instructions. For example, HTML documents often use comments to wrap CSS data, JavaScript code, or server-side includes.

There are two good ways to handle comments. One is just to discard them and make the implementation of this method do nothing. (I like that one!) The other is to create a new *String* using the method parameters and save the string somewhere. Avoid parsing comment content; if you're tempted to do that in new applications, try to use PIs (which were designed for such purposes).

```
public void comment (String buf, int offset, int len)
throws SAXException
{
    String value = new String (buf, offset, len);
    ... now that you have it, what do you want to do?
}
```

The LexicalHandler Interface

```
void startDTD(name, publicId, systemId)
void endDTD()
```

The `startDTD()` event reports the beginning of a document's DTD, and `endDTD()` reports the end. These events can be useful when you save DTD information, such as the partial support in DOM Level 2. It is also important when you create SAX event streams that may need to print as documents that include a DTD.

String name
> The declared name of the root element for the document. It is never omitted, though for invalid documents it may not correspond to the name of the root element.

String publicId
> Normalized version of the public ID declared for the external subset, or null if no such subset was provided.

String systemId
> The system ID declared for the external subset, or null if no such ID was provided. Note that this URI is not absolutized.

When the end of the DTD is reported, all other declarations that should have been reported (with *DeclHandler* or *DTDHandler* callbacks) will have been reported. If any `ContentHandler.skippedEntity()` calls were made for external parameter entities, applications will normally infer that some declarations were not processed.

Parsers are not required to distinguish the internal and external subsets. There are two mechanisms applications can use, but both of them are optional. The natural method is to rely on external parameter entity boundary reports, using other methods in this interface. Not all parsers report those entities; you can check the *lexical-handler/parameter-entities* feature flag to see if this mechanism will work for you. The other mechanism compares base URIs as reported through the `Locator.getSystemId()` method; base URIs for external subset components will differ from those of the document itself. Most parsers support this method, but it's awkward to use for this purpose.

If you're saving DTD content, these methods will bracket a lot of work where you squirrel data away for later use. Otherwise, you'll probably arrange to ignore all the other DTD events and will only need to decide what to do with comments and processing instructions, if you don't just ignore them. Ignoring them within DTDs is a popular strategy even when they're not ignored elsewhere. This is because comments or PIs inside a DTD would seem to apply to DTD contents, while most applications are instead working with document contents.

void startCDATA()
void endCDATA()

These methods report the beginning and end of a <[CDATA[...]]> text section; the bracketing characters are not reported. Any content within a CDATA section is reported with characters() events; the < and & characters within CDATA sections are parsed like normal characters, not like delimiters for markup.

Most software has little reason to care whether character content is contained in CDATA sections. Unless you are trying to round-trip data while preserving those lexical artifacts (to simplify potential future work done with text editors), the right response to CDATA events is to ignore them.

void startEntity(String name)
void endEntity(String name)

These methods report the beginning and end of internal or external entity expansion. The entity is named using the same rules as the ContentHandler.skippedEntity() callback. If you need to indicate which kind of entity is being expanded, record information from the DeclHandler.externalEntityDecl() callback and consult it in these methods. (That means you'll likely really want an extended *DefaultHandler* or *XMLFilterImpl* that supports both of the standardized extension classes.)

Expansions of general entity references, like &dudley;, are reported everywhere except inside attribute values. Such expansions within entity values can't meaningfully be reported, since all markup within start tags is reported at the same time.

Not all parsers report expansion of parameter entities, like %nell;, in DTDs. There is a special parser feature flag (*lexical-handler/parameter-entities*) that determines whether parsers report such events. As with general entity references, not all parameter entity expansions can be meaningfully reported. Parameter entities that expand as part of markup declarations or conditional section markers won't be seen, since markup declarations are reported only in their entirety.

Exposing DTD Information

SAX2 exposes DTD information through three different interfaces. Part of it is exposed through the *LexicalHandler* extension interface: the DTD's root element type declaration and boundaries of the various entities. The rest is exposed through two DTD-specific interfaces, presented here.

When you're working with streams of SAX event data, remember that all DTD event data is seen before the document data it describes. This means that if you need it inside the document, you'll need to plan ahead to save the DTD data. It also means that if you need to merge streams of event data, such DTD data may create a problem. Unless you know the DTD data in advance, you'd need to dam up the event stream until all data that needs to go into downstream DTD events is in hand. Only then can you send the events downstream (with the DTD first). Luckily, merging event streams with unknown DTD data isn't common.

DTD information is automatically used inside XML parsers when they parse XML documents. That includes expansion of conditional sections and parameter entities in DTDs, expanding general entities, and normalizing or defaulting attributes. Most DTD validation can be cleanly layered on top of SAX2 since these declaration callbacks provide all the most important information.* SAX2 enables application-level processing of DTD constraints; the only internal support it provides for DTDs is a feature flag to expose parser support for validation. When applications need to construct valid documents, they can use DTD information as they make changes, instead of needing to save the document and reparse the whole thing.

The support for working with DTDs provided by most XML tools is not as good as the support provided by SAX2. For example, DOM Level 2 provides weaker support, and the TRAX support for SAX (*java.xml.transform.sax*) doesn't support *DeclHandler* at all.

Note that while a fully featured SAX2 parser will let you re-create the internal subset, it will not let you round-trip any external parameter entities. That's because parameter entities will be expanded. You will not see

---

* The exceptions relate to lexical constraints that should arguably be well-formedness constraints. Entity nesting is supposed to match nesting of grammatical constructs within DTDs; that's a validity constraint. However, the analogous constraint in a document body affects well-formedness instead.

conditional sections in external PEs, or declarations being built up from parameter entities. Instead, you'll see the actual declarations that apply to your documents. This may help you to understand exactly what a complex DTD is doing.

The DeclHandler Interface

This extension interface is new in SAX2. It's in the *org.xml.sax.ext* package, which means among other things that it is optional and not all SAX APIs support it. (*DefaultHandler* is one example of an API that does not.) However, any SAX2 parser that can be bootstrapped with JAXP must support this interface. There is no setDeclHandler() method; bind these handlers to parsers like this:

```
XMLReader       producer = ...;
DeclHandler     handler = ...;

producer.setProperty ("http://xml.org/sax/properties/
        declaration-handler",handler);
// throws SAXNotSupportedException if parameter isn't a DeclHandler.
// throws SAXNotRecognizedException if parser doesn't support it.
```

Parsers that support *DeclHandler* are essential for applications that need to work with declarations of elements and attributes or with parsed entities. DOM requires such support for parsed entities, although even Level 2 hides or ignores element and attribute type data. This interface is the most common way SAX2 exposes type constraints (the primary role of a Document Type Declaration) from DTDs, so if you need to see those constraints, you'll use this handler. It has four API callbacks:

void attributeDecl(eName,aName,type,mode,value)
    This callback reports <!ATTLIST ... > declarations in a DTD. A given declaration produces one callback for each attribute in the declaration. Much of this information will also be provided through *Attributes* methods if an instance of that element appears in a document.

  String *eName*
    This is the name of the element whose attribute is being declared.

  String *aName*
    This is the name of the attribute associated with that element.

  String *type*
    This is one of the strings CDATA, ID, IDREF, IDREFS, NMTOKEN, NMTOKENS, ENTITY, or ENTITIES, or two types of enumerated values. Enumerated values are encoded with parenthesized strings such

as (a|b|c) to indicate that strings a, b, or c are permissible. If the string is an enumeration of notation names, "NOTATION " (which includes one space) precedes that parenthesized string.

This type information is more complete than information you get through the *Attributes* object provided with `startElement()`, because *Attributes* reports only enumerations as being either NOTATION or NMTOKEN. However, at this time several widely available SAX2 parsers conform to a beta test version of this API and don't correctly report enumerations. You may need to get a bug-fixed version of your parser if you're depending on this support.

String mode

This describes the kind of default value applied to this attribute: #IMPLIED (the application determines the value), #REQUIRED (the value must be given; defaulting is not permitted), #FIXED (only one value is permitted), or null indicating that *value* is the default.

Unless the document provided a value, you won't see #IMPLIED attributes in the `Attributes` object provided with `startElement()`; if you need to know this information, save it when you get this callback.

String value

This parameter is either null or a string with the default value for this attribute. That might be the only permitted value if the attribute mode is #FIXED. The value will be reported exactly as applications will see it: normalized and with character and entity references replaced.

XML structure editors can use this information to constrain the choices presented to document authors so that only valid documents can be created. Other tools that construct documents will also benefit from having this information. When you're mostly reading documents rather than creating them, the most important data here tends to be declaration of ID, IDREF, and IDREFS attributes, which are used to build links within and between XML documents.

If more than one declaration for an attribute is provided, only the first one will be used. (The second one will be ignored; unlike the analogous case for element declarations, attribute redeclaration is not a validity error.) Normally code to implement this callback would first retrieve any existing per-element data structure, or it would create one (with a null content model) if none is yet known. Then if there is no record of an attribute with this name for that element, a per-attribute data structure instance would be created and saved in the element data structure, keyed by attribute name.

`void elementDecl(name,model)`
This method reports `<!ELEMENT ... >` declarations in a DTD.

> `String name`
> This is the element name.
>
> `String model`
> This is the element content model, with all whitespace removed. For example, element content models like `(a,(b|c)+,d?)`, mixed content models like `(#PCDATA|one|two|three)*`, and simple models like `ANY` and `EMPTY` may all be found in the same document. Note that parsers may do more than just remove the whitespace, as long as an equivalent content model is reported.

Because the content model is provided as a string, applications using it must always parse it themselves. Similarly, if applications want to validate against that model, they must provide code to do that. Except for the case of element content, such work is straightforward. Validating element content models requires constructing and using some sort of finite state automaton, and it takes a bit of work to parse the model. Mixed content models are easier to handle since they can be parsed with a *java.util.StringTokenizer* and because the validation logic is simpler.

If more than one declaration for an element is provided, only the first one will be used. (The second one will be considered a validity error; element type redeclaration is not allowed.) Normally the code implementing this callback would create a new per-element data structure to save the name and content model and store it in data structure (hash table or other map) keyed by element name. Such a data structure might already exist if an element attribute was declared before the element. In this case, this callback just provides the content model, which was previously unknown.

`void externalEntityDecl(name,publicId,systemId)`
This callback reports `<!ENTITY ... >` declarations in a DTD for parsed external entities. These may be either general or parameter entities.

> `String name`
> This is the entity name; it is always provided. Names that start with % are parameter entities; all others are general entities.

String *publicId*
: This is the public ID for the entity and can be omitted (provided as null). If public IDs are provided, any embedded whitespace is normalized, so these strings may be directly compared. They may be used to determine a location for the entity, for example, by using an SGML Formal Public Identifier with some sort of catalog.

String *systemId*
: This is the system ID for the entity and is always provided. It is an absolute URI, which parsers normally use to retrieve the entity before parsing it. However, some SAX2 parsers have a bug, and won't report the absolute URI here.

Applications usually ignore all parameter entity declarations and use the *org.xml.sax.EntityResolver* when they want to provide local copies of these entities to a parser. If applications don't ignore these declarations, redeclaration should be ignored (it is not an error). XML editors may want to offer menus of external (and internal) entities when editing element content. And in some cases you may want to track external entities by name so that you can tell when LexicalHandler.startEntity() is reporting the start of one; this is useful for applications that use xml:base attributes to change applications' views of the actual URI that contains an element, using the Locator.getSystemId() method. (Perhaps the actual location was not known, or should for some reason be ignored.)

void internalEntityDecl(name,value)
: This callback reports <!ENTITY ... > declarations in a DTD for (parsed) internal entities. These may be either general or parameter entities.

String *name*
: This is the entity name. Names that start with % are parameter entities, all others are general entities.

String *value*
: This is the entity value, which contains arbitrary XML content (including elements and nested entity references) that will be reparsed when this entity is expanded.

Applications normally ignore all parameter entity declarations. If applications don't ignore these declarations, redeclaration for a name should be be ignored (it is not an error). XML editors may want to offer menus of internal entities when they edit attribute values or element content. However, SAX2 does not report entity references inside the attribute values it parses. This means that you won't be able to re-create such text without heuristics.

The DTDHandler Interface

The *DTDHandler* interface was carried unchanged from SAX1 into SAX2 and is primarily useful for applications that work with two specific SGML notions: notations and unparsed entities. Some DTDs, such as XML DocBook, use notations in such traditional roles. DOM also requires such support. Use XMLReader.setDTDHandler() to bind this handler to a parser. You probably won't ever need to use it for new code. On the Web, those SGML notions correspond roughly to MIME types and URIs respectively, web concepts that are much more widely understood and supported. The interface has only two API callbacks, provided to meet specific requirements in the XML 1.0 specification:

void notationDecl(name,publicId,systemId)
    This callback reports a <!NOTATION ...> declaration in a DTD.

    String *name*
        This is the notation name; it is always provided. These names are used explicitly in unparsed entity declarations and in some kinds of attribute declaration (elements can have one such attribute, used to associate type with the element). Also, some applications follow a convention that they may be used to identify processing instruction targets.

    String *publicId*
        This is the public ID for the notation and may be omitted (provided as null). If public IDs are supplied, then any embedded whitespace is normalized, so these strings may be directly compared. These may be used to assign a meaning to the notation, for example, by using an SGML Formal Public Identifier in a role much like a MIME type.

    String *systemId*
        This is the system ID for the notation and may be omitted (provided as null). When provided, it is an absolute URI. However, some SAX2 parsers have a bug, and won't report the absolute URI here. These may be used to assign a meaning to the notation, for example, by using a URI to identify a type or command.

    In addition to assigning types to unparsed entities, a NOTATION attribute may also associate a type with an element or processing instruction.

Some DTDs provide extensive catalogs of notation declarations specifically for such uses.

Note that notation declarations are the one place in XML syntax where you can provide a public ID without a system ID, and that at least one identifier (public or system) must always be provided. If applications don't ignore these declarations, redeclaration should be ignored (it is not an error).

void unparsedEntityDecl(name,publicId,systemId,notation)
>   This callback reports <!ENTITY ... > declarations with NDATA annotations to associate them with a notation (such as *jpeg* or *png*). Unparsed entities are used only in attributes that are declared to be of type ENTITY or ENTITIES.
>
>   String *name*
>   > This is the name of the unparsed entity; it is always provided.
>
>   String *publicId*
>   > This is the public ID for the notation and may be omitted (provided as null). If public IDs are provided, any embedded whitespace is normalized, so these strings may be directly compared. These may be used to assign a location to the entity, for example, by using an SGML Formal Public Identifier in a role much like a URN.
>
>   String *systemId*
>   > This is the system ID for the notation and is always provided. It is normally an absolute URI. However, some SAX2 parsers have a bug, and won't report the absolute URI here. These may be used to assign a location to the entity.
>
>   String *notation*
>   > This is the name of the notation associated with the entity; it is always provided. The role of these names is much like that of an external MIME type annotation for the entity.
>
>   In XML, unparsed entities are declared to parsers but pass through them without being parsed. Classic examples of unparsed entities include JPEG or PNG image files. Such entities may also be used for XML text that just doesn't need to be parsed in a given processing stage. If applications don't ignore these declarations, redeclaration should be be ignored (it is not an error).

Most XML applications that care about unparsed entities and notations do so because they interface with SGML systems that use them or are migrating such systems to use the XML generation of tools. XML editors supporting this functionality might use these event callbacks to create menus of notations or unparsed entities when they are editing attributes that hold such values.

Applications that use this interface will normally use the callbacks to create two tables, keyed by entity or notation name respectively, that are used to interpret element attributes. More rarely, notations will be used to determine the operation corresponding to a given processing instruction target name. Secure applications will never use notations to directly encode system commands, but will always redirect through application controlled tables. For example, it would be foolish to rely on system IDs found in a document. System IDs such as `rm -rf /`, when run through a Unix or Linux shell, would remove all files accessible through the local system.

Turning SAX Events into Data Structures

As described earlier, one of the great strengths of SAX is that it lets applications use appropriate data structures, instead of forcing the use of generic data structures. In the section "Push Mode Event Production" in Chapter 3, we looked at the problem of producing SAX events from data structures. Here we look at the reverse process: producing data structures from SAX events. This is a process that most SAX applications handle to one degree or another. One of the most traditional names for this process is *unmarshaling*; it's also sometimes called *deserializing*. (I tend to avoid using the latter term with Java except when talking about RMI.)

We'll first look at how to turn SAX into generic DOM (and DOM-like) data structures. If you're working with such data structures, you may find it's advantageous to build them using SAX. With SAX, you can easily discard data you don't need, filtering it out so you don't need to pay its costs. Afterward we'll look briefly at some of the concerns associated with working with data structures that are more specialized to your application.

SAX-to-DOM Consumers

It's easy to turn a SAX event stream into a complete DOM document tree, or into a DOM-like data structure such as DOM4J or JDOM. Most open source DOM parsers build those data structures directly from SAX event streams. (Xerces has the only such DOM I know that doesn't work that way.) Building a DOM document from a SAX2 event stream requires implementing all four event consumer interfaces: *ContentHandler*, of course; *LexicalHandler* to report boundaries of entity references and CDATA sections as well as comments; and both *DeclHandler* and *DTDHandler* to provide the subset of DTD information that DOM requires. The implementations of those interfaces must use nonstandard DOM functions, because key functionality is missing from public DOM APIs. This means that if you're using generic code to construct a DOM tree, you won't be able to implement every behavior DOM specifies. If that doesn't seem like a feature to you, you'll need builder code that's specialized to a particular DOM implementation.

Table 4-1 shows the classes that various DOM implementations provide for turning a SAX2 event stream into a DOM tree.* Most classes have configuration options to let you discard some of the minimally useful data, instead saving it and making your application code ignore it later. Except as noted, they implement all four consumer interfaces. Each one has a way to present the DOM data it produces, usually with a `getDocument()` method; consult documentation (or source code) for full information.

Table 4-1. SAX-to-DOM consumer classes

Implementation	Class name	Comment
Crimson	org.apache.crimson.tree.XmlDocumentBuilder	Implements all the event consumer handlers.
DOM4J	org.dom4j.io.SAXContentHandler	Extends *DefaultHandler*; does not implement *DeclHandler*.
GNUJAXP	gnu.xml.dom.Consumer	Uses the *gnu.xml.pipeline* framework.
JDOM	org.jdom.input.SAXHandler	Extends *DefaultHandler*.

Example 4-1 uses the DOM implementation from Crimson to illustrate how easy it is to construct a DOM tree from SAX events.

---

* As presented in Chapter 3, in the section "DOM-to-SAX Event Production (and DOM4J, JDOM)," most of these packages also support DOM-to-SAX event producers.

Example 4-1. Converting SAX events to a DOM document (Crimson)

```
public Document SAX2DOM (String uri)
throws SAXException, IOException
{
    XmlDocumentBuilder    consumer;
    XMLReader             producer;

    consumer = new XmlDocumentBuilder ();

    producer = XMLReaderFactory.createXMLReader ();
    producer.setContentHandler (consumer);
    producer.setDTDHandler (consumer);
    producer.setProperty
        ("http://xml.org/sax/properties/lexical-handler",
        consumer);
    producer.setProperty
        ("http://xml.org/sax/properties/declaration-handler",
        consumer);

    producer.parse (uri);
    return consumer.getDocument ();
}
```

Pruning Noise Data from a DOM Tree

For various historical reasons, DOM provides much information that just adds overhead to applications. When you build a DOM with SAX2, it's particularly easy to prune that information out of DOM trees: you can simply arrange never to deliver it! Similar techniques are frequently used when feeding SAX event data to a component. It's often easier to let the component see only parts of the Infoset that you care about than to remove the resulting data noise later.

The simplest example of this would be just to hook up the *ContentHandler* to a SAX parser and ignore the other three handlers. The resulting DOM will not have DTD information, but that's no loss, because even DOM Level 2 doesn't provide enough of the DTD information to be useful. (You can save more complete DTD information using custom SAX handlers, if you need it.) Because the *LexicalHandler* isn't provided, you won't see comment nodes or entity reference nodes (or their read-only children which really complicate your code). Also, any CDATA text nodes will be transparently merged with any adjacent "normal" text nodes. A DOM without such information is a lot easier to work with; your code won't need to handle special cases that come from storing such data. It will also need somewhat less memory and take less time to construct the DOM tree.

To further streamline your data, override `ignorableWhitespace()` and discard whitespace characters. While such events won't always be available even for documents that include DTDs, discarding "ignorable" characters can save significant amounts of memory. The savings vary widely based on DTDs and documents; documents that use mostly elements with element content models (often, but not always, data-oriented DTDs) have the biggest savings. Space savings of ten percent aren't unreasonable and are coupled with some time savings for DOM tree construction, but such savings are highly data dependent. (You may be able to discard processing instructions, depending on your application.)

Discarding lots of the DOM data is so common that when you use JAXP to build a DOM tree, you can configure it to automatically discard some of the data. (Unfortunately, the default is to include all of that data. You might not even need to strip out the events yourself. That configuration information gets sent directly to the SAX handler code that builds the DOM, and you can usually use it directly without needing to subclass. Example 4-2, a modified version of the previous example, shows this less noisy setup.

Example 4-2. Converting SAX events to DOM, discarding noise (Crimson)

```
public Document SAX2DOM (String uri)
throws SAXException, IOException
{
    XmlDocumentBuilder    consumer;
    XMLReader             producer;

    consumer = new XmlDocumentBuilder ();
    consumer.setIgnoreWhitespace (true);

    producer = XMLReaderFactory.createXMLReader ();
    producer.setContentHandler (consumer);

    producer.parse (uri);
    return consumer.getDocument ();
}
```

Building a Partial DOM

Often an even better solution for working with DOM is not to build an entire *org.w3c.dom.Document* object. You can build just the individual subtrees you need, never paying memory for the rest. Unfortunately, the classes listed earlier are set up to build entire document objects, so they won't help. However, it's easy to use SAX events to assemble trees of DOM nodes.

Here's one way to do it. This example defines an interface that exposes an element type using a namespace URI and a local name. It also exposes an event handler method to call with a DOM subtree that holds only such elements and their children. In effect, DOM subtrees are streamed, rather than SAX events. Such a model could work well with documents that are huge but highly regular, if the subtrees were processed then immediately discarded to save memory. Such structures might represent a series of composite records built from database queries, for example.

Example 4-3 uses JAXP to bootstrap an empty DOM document, which is used as a factory to create DOM elements and text nodes. The factory should be used for attributes too, in a more complete example, and perhaps for processing instructions. Notice how the SAX document traversal exactly matches a walk over the DOM tree being constructed, and how the partial DOM tree serves as only the state that's needed. Also, that DOM handles namespaces slightly differently than SAX does. If you need to build DOM trees with SAX, your code doesn't need to be much more complicated than this (other than passing attributes along) unless you try to implement all the gingerbread ornamenting the data model exposed by DOM.

Example 4-3. Using SAX to stream DOM subtrees

```
import javax.xml.parsers.DocumentBuilderFactory;
import org.w3c.dom.*;
import org.xml.sax.*;
import org.xml.sax.helpers.DefaultHandler;

// a kind of event handler
interface DomListener
{
    public String getURI ();
    public String getLocalName ();
    public void processTree (Element tree) throws SAXException;
}

public class DomFilter extends DefaultHandler
{
    private Document    factory;
    private Element     current;
    private DomListener listener;

    public DomFilter (DomListener l)
        { listener = l; }

    public void startDocument ()
    throws SAXException
    {
```

Example 4-3. Using SAX to stream DOM subtrees (continued)

```
        // all this just to get an empty document;
        // we need one to use as a factory
        try {
            factory = DocumentBuilderFactory
                .newInstance ()
                .newDocumentBuilder ()
                .newDocument ();
        } catch (Exception e) {
            throw new SAXException ("can't get DOM factory", e);
        }
    }

    public void startElement (String uri, String local,
        String qName, Attributes atts)
    throws SAXException
    {
        // start a new subtree, or ignore
        if (current == null) {
            if (!listener.getURI ().equals (uri))
                return;
            if (!listener.getLocalName ().equals (local))
                return;
            current = factory.createElementNS (uri, qName);

        // Add to current subtree, descend.
        } else {
            Element     e;

            if ("".equals (uri))
                e = factory.createElement (qName);
            else
                e = factory.createElementNS (uri, qName);
            current.appendChild (e);
            current = e;
        }
        // NOTE:  this example discards all attributes!
        // They ought to be saved to the current element.
    }

    public void endElement (String uri, String local, String qName)
    throws SAXException
    {
        Node    parent;

        // ignore?
        if (current == null)
            return;
        parent = current.getParentNode ();

        // end subtree?
        if (parent == null) {
            current.normalize ();
```

Example 4-3. Using SAX to stream DOM subtrees (continued)

```
            listener.processTree (current);
            current = null;

        // else climb up one level
        } else
            current = (Element) current.getParentNode ();
    }

    // if saving, append and continue
    public void characters (char buf [], int offset, int length)
    throws SAXException
    {
        if (current != null)
            current.appendChild (factory.createTextNode (
                new String (buf, offset, length)));
    }
}
```

You can use similar techniques to construct other kinds of data structures and to perform more interesting filter functions. For example, perhaps more than one element type is interesting, or some types of elements should be reported through different event handler callbacks. It's also easy to transform the data as you read it; the DOM trees you construct don't need to match the document structure that the parser reports.

Turning SAX Events into Custom Data Structures

If your application data structure or interchange syntax is already defined, you may not be able to unmarshal it using software based on the numerous schema-oriented tools. However, lots of software uses SAX to do this efficiently. Once you understand how SAX models data in XML documents, you can treat unmarshaling much like any other parsing problem. It's closely associated with marshaling your data structures to XML. Here we'll look at some of the issues you may want to consider when transforming XML into your data structures.

You may find that some individual data items, such as integers and dates, use the low-level encoding rules that are specified in Part 2 of the W3C XML Schema specification (*http://www.w3c.org/TR/xmlschema-2/*). Those encodings are low-level policy decisions, and they're conceptually independent of the rest of the W3C Schema; you can use them even if you don't buy the W3C approach to those schemas. Some other schema systems, such as Relax-NG, incorporate those low-level encoding policies without adopting more problematic parts of the W3C XML Schema specification. Your application might likewise want to use these policies.

One basic high-level encoding issue is how closely the XML structures and application structures should match. For example, an element will be easier to unmarshal by mapping its attributes (or child elements) directly to properties of a single application object rather than by mapping them to properties of several different objects. The latter design is more complex, and for many purposes it could be much more appropriate, but such unmarshaling code needs more complex state.

Regularity of the various structures is another issue. It's usually less work to handle regular structures, since it's easy to create general methods and reuse them. Bugs are less frequent and more easily found than when every transformation involves yet another special case.

You'll need to figure out how much state you need to track and what techniques you will use. You might be able to use extremely simple parsing state machines; one of these is shown later, in Example 6-2. Sometimes it might easier to unmarshal fragments into an intermediate form (as in the DOM subtrees example earlier), and map that form to your application structure before discarding them.

Often some sort of recursive-descent parsing algorithm that explicitly tracks the state of your parsing activities will be useful. It will often be helpful to keep a stack of pending elements and attributes, as shown later (in Example 5-1). But since the XML structures might not map directly to your application structures, you might also need to stack objects you're in various stages of unmarshaling.

The worst scenario is when neither the XML text nor the application data structures are very regular. Software to work with that kind of system quickly gets fragile as it grows, and you'll probably want to change some of your application constraints.

XML Pipelines

In Chapter 2, the section "XMLWriter: an Event Consumer" briefly discussed the concept of an XML pipeline. In that simple case, it involved reading, transforming, and then writing XML text. This concept is a powerful model for working with SAX; it is the natural framework for developing SAX components. These components won't usually be JavaBeans-style components, intended for use with graphical code builder tools, but they will still be specialized and easily reusable.

Exactly what is a SAX event pipeline? It's a series of components, each a *pipeline stage* connected so consumers act as producers for the next stage, as shown in Figure 4-1. The components pass events through, perhaps changing them on the fly to filter, reorganize, augment, or otherwise transform the data as it streams through. (The term *filter* is sometimes used to mean the same thing as a *stage*, though it's only one type of role for a stage.) The first producer could be a parser, or some other program component. The last consumer will probably have some defined output, such as XML text (*XMLWriter*), a DOM document (using the classes shown earlier), or an application-specific data structure. Intermediate stages in the pipeline have at least one pipeline stage as output, and they might produce other outputs such as data structures. Or they might only be used to analyze or condition the inputs to later stages.

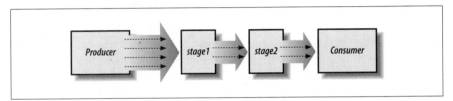

Figure 4-1. SAX2 event pipeline

Pipeline stages can be used to create functional layers, or they can simply be used to define clean module boundaries. Some stages may work well with fragments of XML, while others may expect to process entire documents. The order in which processing tasks occur could be critically important or largely incidental. Stages can be application specific or general purpose. In addition to reading and writing XML, examples of such general-purpose stages include:

- Cleaning up namespace information to re-create prefix declarations and references, replace old URIs with current ones, or give unqualified names a namespace.
- Performing XSLT transformations.
- Validating against an appropriate DTD or schema.
- Transforming input text to eliminate problematic character representations. (Several recent W3C specifications require using Unicode Normalization Format C.)
- Supporting the xml:base model for determining base URIs.

XML Pipelines

- Passing data through pipeline stages on remote servers.
- Implementing XInclude or similar replacements for DTD-based external entity processing.
- Performing well-formedness tests to guard against sloppy producers (parsers won't need this).

More application-specific pipeline stages might include:

- Performing validation using procedural logic with access to system state.
- Collecting links, to support tasks such as verifying they all work.
- Unmarshaling application-specific data structures.
- Stripping out data that later processing must never see. For example, SOAP 1.1 messages must never include processing instructions or DTDs, and some kinds of XHTML rendering engines must not see <font> tweaks.

This process is different from how a work flow is managed in a data structure API such as DOM. In both cases you can assemble work-flow components, with intermediate work products represented as data structures. With SAX, those work-flow components would be pipelines; pipeline stages wouldn't necessarily correspond to individual work-flow components, although they might. With a data structure API, the intermediate work products must always use that API; with SAX they can use whatever representation is convenient, including XML text or a specialized application data structure.

Beyond defining the event consumer interfaces and how to hook them up to XML parsers, SAX includes only limited support for pipelines. That is primarily through the *XMLFilterImpl* class. The support is limited in part because *XMLFilterImpl* doesn't provide full support for the two extension handlers so that by default it won't pass enough of the XML Infoset to support some interesting tasks (including several in the previous lists).

In the rest of this section we talk about that class, XSLT and the *javax.xml.transform* package, and about a more complete framework (the *gnu.xml.pipeline* package), to illustrate one alternative approach.

You might also be interested in the pipeline framework used in the Apache Cocoon v2 project. Cocoon is designed for managing large web sites based on XML. One difference between the current Cocoon pipeline framework and the GNU pipeline framework is that Cocoon excludes the two SAX DTD-handling interfaces, making Cocoon pipelines unsuitable for tasks that need such DTD information. (Examples include DTD-based validation and parts of the XML Base URI specification that require detection of external entity boundaries.) At this writing, Cocoon 2.0 has just shipped its first stable release, ending its beta cycle.

The XMLFilterImpl Class

The *XMLFilterImpl* class is new in SAX2, though a similar layer was in use on top of SAX1 parsers. Think of this class as a hybrid between an event consumer and an event producer, which can be used in either mode:

- In its event consumer role, it's a base class that forwards events to another consumer. Callers push events through the filter, which postprocesses them. Subclasses would normally override methods for those events and invoke the superclass methods when they choose to pass them on (after postprocessing the data to be reported).

- In its event producer role, it's a specialized *XMLReader* that registers itself as the consumer for a parent reader and delegates parsing to that parent. Callers pull data through the filter by calling parse(); it looks like a SAX parser that preprocesses Infoset data before reporting it.

When you subclass *XMLFilterImpl*, you'll primarily be concerned with its role as an event consumer because you'll be writing event handler code. The bulk of the work in a filter is event handling. When you need to filter *DeclHandler* or *LexicalHandler* events, it won't know how to handle them. You'll have to add code to handle those events; get the code to that SAX class, and follow the model used for *ContentHandler* support. The following code snippet shows how this is set up. It supports the producer side (parsing a document and automatically filtering its events). It also shows the consumer-side infrastructure, meaning events are normally passed through untouched, but subclasses will override methods to intercept events and change how they get handled:

```
public class ExtendedFilter extends XMLFilterImpl
    implements LexicalHandler, DeclHandler
{
    DeclHandler         declHandler;
    LexicalHandler      lexicalHandler;

    private static String declID =
            "http://xml.org/sax/properties/declaration-handler";
    private static String lexicalID =
            "http://xml.org/sax/properties/lexical-handler";

    public void setProperty (String uri, Object handler)
    throws SAXNotRecognizedException, SAXNotSupportedException
```

```
        {
            if (declID.equals (uri))
                declHandler = (DeclHandler) handler;
            else if (lexicalID.equals (uri))
                lexicalHandler = (LexicalHandler) handler;
            else
                super.setProperty (uri, handler);
        }

        // support producer mode operations
        public void parse (InputSource in)
        throws SAXException, IOException
        {
            XMLReader       parent = getParent ();

            if (parent != null) {
                parent.setProperty (declID, this);
                parent.setProperty (lexicalID, this);
            }
            super.parse (in);
        }

        // support consumer mode operations
        public void comment (char buf [], int offset, int length)
        throws SAXException
        {
            if (lexicalHandler != null)
                lexicalHandler.comment (buf, offset, length);
        }

        // ... likewise for other LexicalHandler and DeclHandler methods
    }
```

When you're using such a filter just as a consumer, you'll have to register it as a handler for the event classes you're interested in, using methods like setContentHandler() as you would for any other event consumer. In such a case there's never any confusion about which *XMLReader* to use to parse since any filter component is only postprocessing.

When you use an *XMLFilterImpl* to produce events, you need to provide a parent parser, probably by using XMLFilter.setParent(). When you invoke parse(), the filter sets itself up to proxy all of the SAX core event handler methods (as shown earlier for one of the extension methods) as well as *EntityResolver* and *ErrorHandler*. You'll need to pay particular attention that you invoke the filter, instead of that "real" parser. It's easy to run into bugs that way, particularly if you're chaining multiple filters together. Although every filter stage has a parse() method, you only want to invoke it on the last postprocessing stage. It's easy to get confused about that.

Some *XMLFilter* implementations only operate in producer mode. That is unfortunate since it means that they only accept input like a parser; they can't be used to postprocess SAX events.

XMLFilter Examples

This book includes some examples that use *XMLFilterImpl* as a base class, supporting both filter modes:

- Example 6-3 shows a custom handler interface, delivering application-specific unmarshaled data. This interface can be used either to postprocess or to preprocess SAX events, without additional setup.

- Example 6-9 replaces processing instructions with the content of an included document so that downstream stages won't know about the substitution. When used to postprocess events, the handler may need to be set up with appropriate *EntityHandler* and *ErrorHandler* objects.

Sun is developing a "Multi-Schema Validator" engine, which uses SAX filters to implement validators for schema systems including RELAX (also called ISO RELAX), TREX, RELAX-NG (combining the best of RELAX and TREX), and W3C XML schemas. This work ties in to the *org.iso_relax.verifier* framework for validator APIs (at *http://iso-relax.sourceforge.net*), which also supports using SAX objects (such as filters and content handlers) that validate schemas.

If you're using RDDL (*http://www.rddl.org*) as a convention for associating resources with XML namespaces, you may find the *org.rddl.sax.RDDLFilter* class to be useful. It parses RDDL documents and lets you determine the various resources associated with namespaces, such as a DTD, a preferred CSS or XSLT stylesheet, or the schema using any of several schema languages. This is another "producer-mode only" filter.

The javax.xml.transform.sax Package

The *javax.xml.transform* APIs provide ways to apply XSLT transforms to XML data. The top level APIs work with the "pull" model, and map one XML representation into another one with a Transformer.transform(source,result) call. Those representations can include XML text, DOM trees, or some kinds of SAX event streams. Except for that SAX support, you can look at the package as supporting three-stage pipelines, with the middle stage always XSLT (or else a null transform). The

XML Pipelines

javax.xml.transform.sax APIs let you integrate XSLT into longer SAX pipelines in several ways, including one flexible pure "push" mode.

The *SAXTransformerFactory* class is important for most such pipeline usage. You could use code like this to set up to get a factory matching the code fragments shown later:

```
import javax.xml.transform.TransformerFactory;
import javax.xml.transform.sax.*;

String                   stylesheetURI = ...;
String                   documentURI = ...;
ContentHandler           contentHandler = ...;
LexicalHandler           lexicalHandler = ...;
TransformerFactory       tf
SAXTransformerFactory    stf;
SAXSource                stylesheet;

tf = TransformerFactory.newInstance ();
if (!tf.getFeature (SAXTransformerFactory.FEATURE)
        || !tf.getFeature (SAXSource.FEATURE))
    throw new Exception ("not enough API support");
stylesheet = new SAXSource (new InputSource (stylesheetURI));
stf = (SAXTransformerFactory) tf;
```

Most Java XSLT engines, such as SAXON (available at *http://saxon.sourceforge.net*) and Xalan (available at *http://xml.apache.org/xalan-j*) fully support the additional SAX-oriented APIs, although that is not required.

SAX in Push-Mode with XSLT

The approach that's most flexible involves a *TransformerHandler* initialized to apply a specific XSLT transform. These are event consumer stages, set up to push their results through to other stages. They support only the *ContentHandler*, *LexicalHandler* and *DTDHandler* interfaces, but not *DeclHandler*. This is best used in conjunction with the *SAXResult* class, which packages both non-DTD SAX handlers so they can collect the output of a transform. After getting the factory as shown in the preceding code, make sure it supports *SAXResult*, then get and use the handler in a manner such as the following:

```
XMLReader            producer;
SAXResult            out;
TransformerHandler   handler;

if (!tf.getFeature (SAXResult.FEATURE))
    throw new Exception ("not enough API support");

handler = stf.newTransformerHandler (stylesheet);
```

```
out = new SAXResult ();
out.setContentHandler (contentHandler);
out.setLexicalHandler (lexicalHandler);
// no DTD support from the SAXResult class!!
handler.setResult (out);

producer = XMLReaderFactory.createXMLREader ();
producer.setContentHandler (handler);
producer.setDTDHandler (handler);
producer.setProperty ("http://xml.org/sax/properties/lexical-handler",
        handler);

producer.parse (inputURI);
```

This style of usage is particularly well suited to XML pipelines. It's just a DTD-deprived pipeline stage, except that the output setup needs a non-SAX class. The reason that approach is particularly useful for pipeline processing is that both the input and output to the XSLT transform use SAX event streams, so it can easily be spliced between any two parts of an event pipeline. It also means you can use "push" mode event producers, which invoke SAX callbacks directly.

SAX in Pull-Mode with XSLT

You can also get an pull-style API, using an *XMLFilter* that is initialized to apply a specific XSLT tran form. Such filters may be used as event producers, only at one end of a SAX pipeline. After getting the factory as shown in the previous code listing, you would make sure it supports this functionality, then get and use the filter like this.

```
XMLFilter        producer;

if (!tf.getFeature (SAXTransformerFactory.FEATURE_XMLFILTER))
    throw new Exception ("not enough API support");

producer = stf.newXMLFilter (stylesheet);
producer.setContentHandler (contentHandler);
producer.setProperty ("http://xml.org/sax/properties/lexical-handler",
        lexicalHandler);

producer.parse (inputURI);
```

Such a call would use the XSLT stylesheet to preprocess input to the handlers you provide. The *SAXResult* class, shown here, supports a similar processing model. If your transformer can accept one of those, a pull-mode `Transformer.transform()` call pushes preprocessed results into a *ContentHandler* and *LexicalHandler*, like the `XMLFilter.parse()` call.

You can also use SAX in a pull-mode `Transformer.transform()` call by using a *SAXSource* object. That lets you provide an *InputSource* (as shown earlier) as well as an *XMLReader*, which may be set up with a particular *ErrorHandler* and *EntityResolver* (not shown). To use that in a SAX event pipeline, you can make that reader be an *XMLFilter* that preprocesses the input to the XSLT transform.

You can combine both *SAXSource* and *SAXResult* objects to get a kind of "pull" mode pipeline including one XSLT transform stage, without even needing to use the *SAXTransformerFactory* class. To get multiple XSLT transform stages without needing intermediate storage (XML text, a DOM tree, or so on), use the *TransformerHandler* class as shown earlier, post-processing results through in a *SAXResult*. Or if you prefer, package an *XMLFilter* from a *SAXTransformerFactory* to preprocess data through a *SAXSource* that you provide to the `Transformer.transform()` call. (I recommend sticking to the pure *TransformerHandler* approach, since it's not as confusing.)

The gnu.xml.pipeline Framework

This framework takes a different approach to building pipelines than *XML-FilterImpl* or *XMLFilter*. Two key characteristics are its built-in support for all the SAX2 handlers, including the extension handlers, and its exclusive focus on the postprocessing model. In addition, it has several utility filters and some factory methods that can automate construction and initialization of pipelines. The core interface is *EventConsumer*:

```
public interface EventConsumer
{
    public ContentHandler getContentHandler ();
    public DTDHandler getDTDHandler ();

    public Object getProperty (String id)
    throws SAXNotRecognizedException;

    public void setErrorHandler (ErrorHandler handler);
}
```

With that interface, pipelines are normally set up beginning with the last consumer and then working toward the first consumer. There is a formal convention that states pipeline stages have a constructor that takes an *EventConsumer* parameter, which is used to construct pipelines from simple textual descriptions (which look like Unix-style command pipelines). That convention makes it easy to construct a pipeline by hand, as shown in the following code. Stages are strongly expected to share the same error handling; the error handler is normally established after the pipeline is set up, when a pipeline is bound to an event producer.

There is a class that corresponds to the pure consumer mode *XMLFilterImpl*, except that it implements all the SAX2 event consumer interfaces, not just the ones in the core API. *LexicalHandler* and *DeclHandler* are fully supported. This class also adds convenience methods such as the following:

```
public class EventFilter
    implements EventConsumer, ContentHandler, DTDHandler,
        LexicalHandler, DeclHandler
{
    ... lots omitted ...

    // hook up all event consumer interfaces to the producer
    // map some known EventFilters into XMLReader feature settings
    public static void bind (XMLReader producer, EventConsumer consumer)
        { /* code omitted */ }

    // wrap a "consumer mode" XMLFilterImpl
    public void chainTo (XMLFilterImpl next)
        { /* code omitted */ }

    ... lots omitted ...
}
```

Example 4-4 shows how one simple event pipeline works using the GNU pipeline framework. It looks like it has three pipeline components (in addition to the parser), but in this case it's likely that two of them will be optimized away into parser feature flag settings: *NSFilter* restores namespace-related information that is discarded by SAX2 parser defaults (bind() sets *namespace-prefixes* to true and discards that filter), and *ValidationFilter* is a layered validator that may not be necessary if the underlying parser can support validation (in which case the *validation* flag is set to true and the filter is discarded). Apart from arranging that validation errors are reported and using the GNU DOM implementation instead of Crimson's, this code does exactly what the first SAX-to-DOM example above does.*

---

* There is a generic *DomConsumer* class that bootstraps using whatever JAXP sets up as the default DOM. Such a generic consumer can't know the implementation-specific back doors needed to implement all the bells and whistles DOM demands.

Example 4-4. SAX events to DOM document (using GNU DOM)

```
import gnu.xml.pipeline.*;

public Document SAX2DOM (String uri)
throws SAXException, IOException
{
    DomConsumer   consumer;
    XMLReader     producer;

    consumer = new gnu.xml.dom.Consumer ();
    consumer = new ValidationConsumer (consumer);
    consumer = new NSFilter (consumer);

    producer = XMLReaderFactory.createXMLReader ();
    producer.setErrorHandler (new DefaultHandler () {
        public void error (SAXParseException e)
        throws SAXException
            { throw e; }
    });
    EventFilter.bind (producer, consumer);

    producer.parse (uri);
    return consumer.getDocument ();
}
```

There are some interesting notions lurking in this example. For instance, when validation is a postprocessing stage, it can be initialized with a particular DTD and hooked up to an *XMLReader* that walks DOM nodes. That way, that DOM content can be incrementally validated as applications change it. Similarly, application code can produce a SAX event stream and validate content without saving it to a file. This same postprocessing approach could be taken with validators based on any of the various schema systems.

There are a variety of other utility pipeline stages and support classes in the *gnu.xml.pipeline* package. One is briefly shown later (in Example 6-7). Others include XInclude and XSLT support, as well as a *TeeConsumer* to send events down two pipelines (like a tee joint used in plumbing). This can be useful to save output for debugging; you can write XML text to a file, or save it as a DOM tree, and watch the events that come out of a particular pipeline stage to find problematic areas.

Even if you don't use that GNU framework, you should keep in mind that SAX pipeline stages can be used to package significant and reusable XML processing components.

> *In this chapter:*
> - *Helper Classes*
> - *SAX1 Support*

Other SAX Classes

The preceding chapters have addressed all of the most important SAX2 classes and interfaces. You may need to use a handful of other classes, including simple implementations of a few more interfaces and SAX1 support. This chapter briefly presents those remaining classes and interfaces.

Your parser distribution should have SAX2 support, with complete javadoc for these classes. Consult that documentation if you need more information than found in this book. The API summary in Appendix A should also be helpful.

Helper Classes

There are several classes in the *org.xml.sax.helpers* package that you will probably find useful from time to time.

The AttributesImpl Class

This is a general-purpose implementation of the SAX2 *Attributes* interface. As well as reading attribute information (as defined in the interface), you can write and modify it. This class is quite handy when your application code is producing SAX2 events, perhaps because it is converting data structures to a SAX event stream.

Remember the attributes provided to the `ContentHandler.startElement()` event callback are only valid for the duration of that call. If you need a copy of those attributes for later use, it's simplest to use this class; just create a new instance using the copy constructor. That copy constructor is one of the most widely used APIs in this class, other than the *Attributes* methods.

It's often handy to keep a stack around to track the currently open elements and attributes. If you support xml:base, you'll also want to track base URIs for the document and for any external parsed entities. This is easy to implement using another key method provided by this class, addAttribute(). Example 5-1 shows how to maintain such a stack with xml:base support. It shows full support for XML namespaces, unlike Example 2-2, which is simple and attribute-free (shown in Chapter 2 in the section "Basic ContentHandler Events").

Example 5-1. Maintaining an element and attribute stack

```
import java.io.IOException;
import java.net.URL;
import java.util.Hashtable;
import org.xml.sax.*;
import org.xml.sax.ext.*;
import org.xml.sax.helpers.AttributesImpl;
import org.xml.sax.helpers.DefaultHandler;

public class XStack extends DefaultHandler
    implements LexicalHandler, DeclHandler
{
    static class StackEntry
    {
        final String     nsURI, localName;
        final String     qName;
        final Attributes atts;
        final StackEntry parent;

        StackEntry (
            String namespace, String local,
            String name,
            Attributes    attrs,
            StackEntry    next
        ) {
            this.nsURI = namespace;
            this.localName = local;
            this.qName = name;
            this.atts = new AttributesImpl (attrs);
            this.parent = next;
        }
    }

    private Locator              locator;
    private StackEntry           current;
    private Hashtable            extEntities = new Hashtable ();

    private static final String  xmlNamespace
        = "http://www.w3.org/XML/1998/namespace";

    private void addMarker (String label, String uri)
```

Example 5-1. Maintaining an element and attribute stack (continued)

```
    throws SAXException
    {
        AttributesImpl    atts = new AttributesImpl ();

        if (locator != null && locator.getSystemId () != null)
            uri = locator.getSystemId ();

        // guard against InputSource objects without system IDs
        if (uri == null)
            throw new SAXParseException ("Entity URI is unknown", locator);

        // guard against illegal relative URIs (Xerces)
        try { new URL (uri); }
        catch (IOException e) {
            throw new SAXParseException ("parser bug: relative URI",
                    locator);
        }

        atts.addAttribute (xmlNamespace, "base", "xml:base", "CDATA", uri);
        current = new StackEntry ("", "", label, atts, current);
    }

    // walk up stack to get values for xml:space, xml:lang, and so on
    public String getInheritedAttribute (String uri, String name)
    {
        String          retval = null;
        boolean         useNS = (uri != null && uri.length () != 0);

        for (StackEntry here = current;
                retval == null && here != null;
                here = here.parent) {
            if (useNS)
                retval = here.atts.getValue (uri, name);
            else
                retval = here.atts.getValue (name);
        }
        return retval;
    }

    // knows about XML Base recommendation, and xml:base attributes
    // can be used in callbacks for elements, PIs, comments,
    // characters, ignorable whitespace, and so on.
    public URL getBaseURI ()
    throws IOException
    {
        return getBaseURI (current);
    }

    private URL getBaseURI (StackEntry here)
    throws IOException
    {
        String          uri = null;
```

Example 5-1. Maintaining an element and attribute stack (continued)

```
            while (uri == null && here != null) {
                uri = here.atts.getValue (xmlNamespace, "base");
                if (uri != null)
                    break;
                here = here.parent;
            }

            // marker for document or entity boundary?  absolute.
            if (here.qName.charAt (0) == '#')
                return new URL (uri);

            // else it might be a relative uri.
            int             offset = uri.indexOf (":/");

            if (offset == -1 || uri.indexOf (':') < offset)
                return new URL (getBaseURI (here.parent), uri);
            else
                return new URL (uri);
    }

    // from ContentHandler interface
    public void startElement (
        String          namespace,
        String          local,
        String          name,
        Attributes      attrs
    ) throws SAXException
        { current = new StackEntry (namespace, local, name, attrs,
                current); }

    public void endElement (String namespace, String local, String name)
    throws SAXException
        { current = current.parent; }

    public void setDocumentLocator (Locator l)
        { locator = l; }

    public void startDocument ()
    throws SAXException
        { addMarker ("#DOCUMENT", null); }

    public void endDocument ()
        { current = null; }

    // DeclHandler interface

    public void externalEntityDecl (String name, String publicId,
            String systemId)
    throws SAXException
    {
        if (name.charAt (0) == '%')
            return;
```

Example 5-1. Maintaining an element and attribute stack (continued)

```
        // absolutize URL
        try {
            URL url = new URL (locator.getSystemId ());
            systemId = new URL (url, systemId).toString ();
        } catch (IOException e) {
            // what could we do?
        }
        extEntities.put (name, systemId);
    }

    public void elementDecl (String name, String model) { }
    public void attributeDecl (String element, String name,
                String type, String mode, String defaultValue) {}
    public void internalEntityDecl (String name, String value) { }

    // LexicalHandler interface
    public void startEntity (String name)
    throws SAXException
    {
        String  uri = (String) extEntities.get (name);
        if (uri != null)
            addMarker ("#ENTITY", uri);
    }

    public void endEntity (String name)
    throws SAXException
        { current = current.parent; }

    public void startDTD (String root, String publicId, String systemId) {}
    public void endDTD () {}
    public void startCDATA () {}
    public void endCDATA () {}
    public void comment (char buf[], int off, int len) {}
}
```

With such a stack of attributes, it's easy to find the current values of inherited attributes like `xml:space`, `xml:lang`, `xml:base`, and their application-specific friends. For example, an application might have a policy that all unspecified attributes with `#IMPLIED` default values are inherited from some ancestor element's value or are calculated using data found in such a context stack.

Notice how this code added marker entries on the stack with synthetic `xml:base` attributes holding the true base URIs for the the document and external general entities. That information is needed to correctly implement the recommendation, and lets the `getBaseURI()` work entirely from this stack. If you need such functionality very often, you might want to provide a more general API, not packaged as internal to one handler implementation.

The LocatorImpl Class

This is a general-purpose implementation of the *Locator* interface. As well as reading location properties (as defined in the interface), you can write and modify them. It's part of SAX1 and is still useful in SAX2.

The locator provided by the ContentHandler.setDocumentLocator() can be used during any event callback, but the values it returns will change over time. If you need a copy of those values for later use, it's simplest to use this class; just create a new instance using the copy constructor. More typically, you will pass the locator to the constructor for some kind of *SAXException*, or just save the current base URI to use with relative URIs you find in document (or attribute) content.

The NamespaceSupport Class

When your code needs to track namespaces or their prefixes, use this SAX2 class. One audience for this class is authors of XML parsers; that's probably not you. More likely you're writing code that, like XPath or W3C's XML schemas, needs to parse prefixed names when they're found in attribute values or element content; this class can help. Or you may be writing code to select or generate element or attribute name prefixes for output. (If you only need to put those names in element or attribute names, you should be able to package that work in an event filter component that postprocesses your output and ensures that its namespace content matches XML 1.0 rules.)

What this class does is maintain a stack of namespace contexts, in which each context holds a set of prefix-to-URI mappings; the contexts normally correspond to an element. This is the right model to use when you're writing an XML parser. If you try to use this class in a layer on top of a SAX2 parser, you'll notice a slight mismatch: all the prefix-mapping events for an element's namespace context *precede* the startElement() events for that element. That is, you'll need to create and populate new contexts before you see the element that signifies a new context.* One simple way to work around this is with a Boolean flag indicating whether a new context is active yet.

To use this class with a SAX2 parser that's set to report namespace prefix mappings, you have to modify some of your *ContentHandler* callbacks to

---

* This is true unless xmlns* attributes get reported with startElement(), and you only use that form of the prefix-mapping events.

maintain that stack of contexts. This is done in much the same way as you produce those callbacks yourself:

1. Instantiate a *NamespaceSupport* object using its default constructor (the only one). A good time to do this is when you start your event stream, at the `ContentHandler.startDocument()` event callback. When you do this, set a Boolean *contextActive* flag to false, so that you'll create a new context for the root element.

2. When you get (or make) a `ContentHandler.startPrefixMapping(prefix,uri)` event, see if *contextActive* is true. If not, call `pushContext()` and set that flag to true. Then call `declarePrefix(prefix,uri)`. (It returns false if you give it illegal inputs.)

3. At the end of any `ContentHandler.startElement()` event, see if *contextActive* is true. If not, call `pushContext()`. Then set that flag to false, forcing any child elements' namespace declarations to create a new context.

4. Finally, at the end of any `ContentHandler.endElement()` event, call `popContext()`.

5. Call `reset()` to forcibly reset all state before you reuse the class. Doing this at the end of the `ContentHandler.endDocument()` callback should work.

If you follow these rules, you can use `processName()` to interpret element and attribute names that you find according to the current prefix bindings, or you can use `getPrefix()` to choose a prefix given a particular namespace URI:

String [] processName(qName,parts,isAttribute)
> Use this method to find the namespace name corresponding to a qualified element or attribute name (perhaps as found inside an attribute value or element content). Parameters are:
>
> String *qName*
>> This is the qualified name, such as units:currency or fare, that is being examined.
>
> String *parts[3]*
>> This is a three-element array. If this method succeeds in processing the name, the first array element will hold the namespace URI, the second will hold the local (unprefixed) name, and the third will hold the *qName* you passed in. The first and second string may also be empty strings, if the *qName* has no prefix and if no default namespace URI is applicable.

`String isAttribute`
: Pass this value as `true` if the *qName* parameter identifies an attribute; otherwise, pass this as `false`. This information is needed because unprefixed element names are interpreted using any default namespace URI, but attribute names are not.

  If this method succeeds, the *parts* parameter is filled out and returned. Otherwise the name includes a reference to an undeclared prefix, and `null` will be returned.

`String getPrefix(String uri)`
: Use this method to choose a prefix to use when constructing a qualified name. This returns a currently defined prefix associated with the specified namespace URI or null if no such prefix is defined. When no such prefix is defined, the default namespace URI (associated with element names that have no prefixes) might still be appropriate. If so, then `getURI("")` will return this URI.

Consult the class documentation (javadoc) for full details about the methods on this class.

SAX1 Support

This section provides a brief overview of the SAX1 classes and migration support and of differences between SAX1 and SAX2. SAX1 is a subset of SAX2, so SAX2 is backward compatible. The only reason you might not want to have the SAX2 classes and interfaces in your class path is to avoid compiler warnings telling you when you're using now-deprecated APIs.

You shouldn't be using SAX1 APIs to write new code, but you may need to maintain or migrate older code written using these classes. As soon as possible, plan a maintenance step that involves switching to the new SAX2 versions of the APIs. This may include getting rid of some "home-brew" solutions for namespace support. (Some applications have found previously unsuspected bugs when they've made such changes; be alert!) This section has been written to highlight those changes.

If your parser supplier hasn't provided SAX2 support by now, it's probably also time to switch suppliers; however, you can use the *ParserAdapter* class to make these changes without changing parsers. In fact, if you're using *ParserFactory* to get the system default parser and haven't set a SAX2 *XMLReader* default, the reference *XMLReaderFactory* distribution will automatically wrap the SAX1 parser you've probably already identified using the *org.xml.sax.parser* system property. That is, just putting the

SAX2 classes in your class path normally lets you start using SAX2 without needing to change your application configuration. (You can go the other way around with an *XMLReaderAdapter* if you want to use a more current parser while letting the application code continue to use older SAX1 APIs.)

You'll most likely be interested in these classes if you're working with an older, SAX1-based application or tool, such as the XT 0.5 XSLT engine. This includes applications written to the JAXP 1.0 API specification, which doesn't include SAX2 support. If so, the main difference you'll see is that SAX1 has a much simpler way of naming elements and attributes: it only needs to support the *qName* (qualified name) access style, not the namespace-aware style. This eliminates some opportunities for confusion, unless you're writing namespace-aware applications.

The following classes provide SAX1 support:

org.xml.sax.Parser
> This interface corresponds to the SAX2 *XMLReader*. It uses the *DocumentHandler* interface (instead of *ContentHandler*) and has no "getter" methods for handlers or the entity resolver. The SAX2 feature and property management methods are not available. There is a setLocale() method to control the locale used with diagnostics, which was dropped in SAX2.
>
> With SAX1, there was no standard way to indicate whether a parser validated or not. SAX1 applications had to be written to not rely on having validity errors reported, unless either a configuration mechanism enforced the use of a validating parser (specifying validating or nonvalidating classes) or use of some specific implementation's alternative configuration mechanism was hardwired.
>
> Similarly, SAX1 had no standard way to provide the additional infoset data that SAX2 shows using the *DeclHandler* and *LexicalHandler* interfaces. Applications needing such support needed to use implementation-specific APIs.

org.xml.sax.DocumentHandler
> This interface corresponds to the SAX2 *ContentHandler* interface. Namespace information is not available on the element callbacks, and startElement() uses *AttributeList*. Prefix-mapping scopes are not reported. In SAX2, skipped entities are reported; this was an XML 1.0 conformance requirement that was not met by the SAX1 API. SAX1 will not report skipped entities even if you were to wire it into a SAX2 environment.

org.xml.sax.HandlerBase
: This class corresponds to the SAX2 *DefaultHandler* class, except that it's a core class, not a helper class. (Consider that an evolutionary accident.) It supports the older *DocumentHandler* interface.

org.xml.sax.AttributeList
: This interface corresponds to the SAX2 *Attributes* interface. It doesn't include namespace information and is accordingly much simpler. The only name for an attribute is what the namespace specification called the "qName." (In SAX2, providing the qName is optional unless the *namespace-prefixes* property has been set, but most parsers provide it at all times.)

org.xml.sax.helpers.AttributeListImpl
: This class corresponds to the SAX2 *AttributesImpl* class. It doesn't include namespace information and is accordingly much simpler.

org.xml.sax.helpers.ParserAdapter
: This class is intended to help migrate SAX1 parser implementations to the SAX2 namespace-aware API. If you have a SAX1 parser (perhaps it turns some non-XML data into a SAX1 event stream), you can use this class to bring it into the SAX2 world.

org.xml.sax.helpers.ParserFactory
: This class corresponds to the SAX2 *XMLReaderFactory* class. It returns a SAX1 *Parser* and it is controlled only using the *org.xml.sax.parser* system property. It throws many more exceptions than its SAX2 analogue.

org.xml.sax.helpers.XMLReaderAdapter
: This class supports backward migration of SAX2 parsers into SAX1-based applications. You probably won't ever need to use it.

If your environment supports SAX1 but not SAX2, you can just add the SAX2 version of *sax.jar* to your class path, somewhere before the older SAX1 files. (Otherwise, you might get package-sealing violations, because the JVM might mix versions of the package. It may be best if you remove older copies of the SAX1 classes from your class path.) If you set the SAX1 *org.xml.sax.parser* system property to point to a SAX1 parser so that applications can rely on *org.xml.sax.helpers.ParserFactory* bootstrapping, you'll be glad that the SAX2 *org.xml.sax.helpers.XMLReaderFactory* knows how to use this property as a backup in case no default SAX2 parser has been configured.

In this chapter:
- *Rich Site Summary: RSS*
- *XML and Messaging*
- *Including Subdocuments*

Putting It All Together

The preceding chapters have shown most of what you'll need to know to use SAX2 effectively, but as individual techniques, in small bits and pieces. In this chapter, we'll look at more substantial examples, which tie those techniques together. The examples here should help you to understand the kinds of modules you'll need to put together similar SAX2-based applications. You'll also see some of the options you have for building larger processing tasks from SAX components.

Rich Site Summary: RSS

One of the first popular XML document standards is hidden in the guts of web site management toolsets. It dates to back when XML wasn't fully crystallized. Back then, there was a lot of interest in using XML to address a widespread problem: how to tell users about updates to web sites so they didn't need to read the site several times a day. A "channel" based model was widely accepted, building on the broadcast publishers' analogy of a web site as a TV channel. Microsoft shipped an XML-like format called Channel Definition Format (CDF), and other update formats were also available, but the solution that caught on was from Netscape. It is called RSS. This originally stood for "RDF Site Summary,"* but it was simplified and renamed the "Rich Site Summary" format before it saw any wide adoption.

---

* RDF stands for Resource Description Framework. For more information, see *http://www.w3.org/RDF/*.

Rich Site Summary: RSS

RSS 0.91 was the mechanism used to populate one of the earliest customizable web portals, My Netscape. The mechanism is simple: RSS presents a list of recently updated items from the web site, with summaries, as an XML file that could be fetched across the Web. Sites could update static summary files along with their content or generate them on the fly; site management tools could do either task automatically. It was easy for sites to create individualized views that aggregated the latest news from any of the numerous web sites providing RSS feeds.

There's essentially been a fork in the development of RSS. In recent surveys, about two thirds of the RSS sites use "RSS Classic," based on the 0.91 DTD and often with 0.92 extensions. (Mostly, the 0.92 spec removed limits from the non-DTD parts of the 0.91 spec.) Relatively recently, "New RSS" was created. Also called "RSS 1.0" (though not with the support of all the developers who had been enhancing RSS), this version is more complex. It uses RDF and XML namespaces and includes a framework with extension modules to address the complex content syndication and aggregation requirements of larger web sites. RSS toolkits tend to support both formats, but RDF itself is still not widely adopted. This is what part of one "RSS Classic" feed looks like, from the URL *http://xmlhack.com/rss.php*:

```xml
<?xml version="1.0" encoding="ISO-8859-1"?>
<!DOCTYPE rss PUBLIC "-//Netscape Communications//DTD RSS 0.91//EN"
    "http://my.netscape.com/publish/formats/rss-0.91.dtd">
<rss version="0.91">
<channel>
    <title>xmlhack</title>
    <link>http://www.xmlhack.com</link>
    <description>Developer news from the XML community</description>
    <language>en-us</language>
    <managingEditor>editor@xmlhack.com</managingEditor>
    <webMaster>webmaster@xmlhack.com</webMaster>
    <item>
       <title>BEEP implementation for .NET/C#</title>
       <link>http://www.xmlhack.com/read.php?item=1470</link>
    </item>
    <item>
       <title>MinML-RPC, Sandstorm XML-RPC framework</title>
       <link>http://www.xmlhack.com/read.php?item=1469</link>
    </item>
    <item>
       <title>XSLT as query language</title>
       <link>http://www.xmlhack.com/read.php?item=1467</link>
    </item>
    <item>
       <title>Exclusive XML Canonicalization in Last Call</title>
       <link>http://www.xmlhack.com/read.php?item=1466</link>
    </item>
```

```
    <!--many items were deleted for this example-->
</channel>
</rss>
```

In this section we use some of the techniques we've seen earlier and will look at both sides (client and server) of some simple RSS tools for RSS Classic. A full RSS toolset would need to handle New RSS, and would likely need an RDF engine to work with RDF metadata. Such RDF infrastructure should let applications work more with the semantics of the data, and would need RDF schema support. That's all much too complex to show here.*

First we'll build a simple custom data model, then write the code to marshal and unmarshal it, and finally see how those components fit into common types of RSS applications. In a microcosm, this is what lots of XML applications do: read XML into custom data structures, process them, and then write out more XML.

Data Model for RSS Classic

Here are the key parts of the RSS 0.91 DTD; it also incorporates the HTML 4.0 ISO Latin/1 character entities, which aren't shown here, and various other integrity rules that aren't expressed by this DTD:

```
<!ELEMENT rss (channel)>
<!ATTLIST rss
          version    CDATA #REQUIRED> <!-- must be "0.91"> -->

<!ELEMENT channel (title | description | link | language | item+
                  | rating? | image? | textinput? | copyright?
                  | pubDate? | lastBuildDate? | docs? | managingEditor?
                  | webMaster? | skipHours? | skipDays?)*>

<!ELEMENT image (title | url | link | width? | height? | description?)*>

<!ELEMENT item (title | link | description)*>

<!ELEMENT textinput (title | description | name | link)*>

<!ELEMENT title (#PCDATA)>
<!ELEMENT description (#PCDATA)>
<!ELEMENT link (#PCDATA)>
<!ELEMENT url (#PCDATA)>
<!ELEMENT name (#PCDATA)>
<!ELEMENT rating (#PCDATA)>
<!ELEMENT language (#PCDATA)>
```

---

* If you're interested the RDF approach, look at sites like the Open Directory Project, at *http://www.dmoz.org/*, to see one way of using RDF.

Rich Site Summary: RSS

```
<!ELEMENT width (#PCDATA)>
<!ELEMENT height (#PCDATA)>
<!ELEMENT copyright (#PCDATA)>
<!ELEMENT pubDate (#PCDATA)>
<!ELEMENT lastBuildDate (#PCDATA)>
<!ELEMENT docs (#PCDATA)>
<!ELEMENT managingEditor (#PCDATA)>
<!ELEMENT webMaster (#PCDATA)>
<!ELEMENT hour (#PCDATA)>
<!ELEMENT day (#PCDATA)>
<!ELEMENT skipHours (hour+)>
<!ELEMENT skipDays (day+)>
```

In short, the DTD includes a wrapper that gives the version, one channel with some descriptive data, and a bunch of items. RSS 0.92 changes it slightly. Data length limits (which a DTD can't describe) are removed, and a bit more. If you're working with RSS, you should know that most RSS feeds incorporate at least a few of those 0.92 extensions and have your code handle the issues. And if you're generating an RSS feed for your web site, you'll want to know that many aggregators present the image as the channel's icon, along with the newest items and the text input box, to provide quick access to your site.

When you work with XML-based systems and SAX, one of the first things you'll want to do is decide on the data structures you'll use. Sometimes you'll have a pre-existing data structure that must be matched; in cases like this RSS code, you have the luxury of a blank slate to write on. I'm a big believer in designing appropriate data structures, rather than expecting some development tool to come up with a good answer; as a rule, a good "manual" design beats code generator output in any maintainable system. In the case of RSS Classic, simple structures like those shown in Example 6-1 can do the job:

Example 6-1. RSS data structures

```
import java.util.Vector;

public class RssChannel {

    // (optional, not part of RSS) URI for the RSS file
    public StringsourceUri;

    // Five required items
    public Stringdescription = "";
    public Vectoritems = new Vector ();
    public Stringlanguage = "";
    public Stringlink = "";
    public Stringtitle = "";
```

Example 6-1. RSS data structures (continued)

```
    // Lots of optional items
    public String    copyright = "";
    public String    docs = "";
    public RssImage          image;
    public String    lastBuildDate = "";
    public String    managingEditor = "";
    public String    pubDate = "";
    public String    rating = "";
    // public Days              skipDays;
    // public Hours             skipHours;
    public RssTextInput      textinput;
    public String    webMaster = "";

    // channels have a bunch of items
    static public class RssItem
    {
        public String    description = "";
        public String    link = "";
        public String    title = "";
    }

    // Text input is used to query the channel
    static public class RssTextInput
    {
        public String    description = "";
        public String    link = "";
        public String    name = "";
        public String    title = "";
    }

    // Image used for the channel
    static public class RssImage
    {
        public String    link = "";
        public String    title = "";
        public String    url = "";

        // optional
        public String    description = "";
        public String    height = "";
        public String    width = "";
    }
}
```

Note that these classes didn't include any methods; methods can be added later, as application code determines what's really necessary. There are a variety of features that would be good to constrain this way, which you'll see if you look at the RSS specifications. Even pure "value objects" benefit from such internal consistency checks. For example, you may prefer to use beans-style accessor functions, but they would only complicate this example. (So would the class and field documentation, which has been deleted for simplicity.)

There's one type of code that is certainly needed but was intentionally put into different classes: marshaling data to RSS and unmarshaling it from RSS. Such choices are design policies; while it's good to keep marshaling code in one place, that place doesn't need to be the data structure class itself. It's good to separate marshaling code and data structure code because it's easier to support several different kinds of input and output syntax. Examples include different versions of RSS, as well as transfers to and from databases with JDBC. To display RSS in a web browser, different versions of HTML may be appropriate. Sometimes, embedding a stylesheet processing instruction into the XML text may be the way to go. Separate marshaling code needs attention when data structures change, but good software maintenance procedures will ensure that's never a problem.

Consuming and Producing RSS Parsing Events

Earlier chapters have touched on ways to marshal and unmarshal data with SAX. This section shows these techniques more completely, for a real-world application data model.

Example 6-2 shows what SAX-based unmarshaling code can look like, without the parser hookup. In this case it's set up to be the endpoint on a pipeline. This just turns infoset "atoms" into RSS "molecules" and stops. Note that it isn't particularly thorough in how it handles all the various types of illegal, or just unexpected, RSS that's found on the Web, although it handles many RSS Classic sites perfectly well. For example, the controls to skip fetches on particular days (perhaps weekends) or hours (nonbusiness hours) aren't usually supported, so they're just ignored here. With a more complex DTD, unmarshaling might not be able to rely on such a simple element stacking scheme; you might need to stack the objects you're unmarshaling and use a more complex notion of context to determine the appropriate actions to take.

Example 6-2. Unmarshaling SAX events into RSS data

```
import java.util.Stack;

import RssChannel.RssItem;
import RssChannel.RssImage;
import RssChannel.RssTextInput;

public class RssConsumer extends DefaultHandler {
    private RssChannel       channel;
    private RssItem          item;
```

Example 6-2. Unmarshaling SAX events into RSS data (continued)

```java
    private RssImage          image;
    private RssTextInput      input;

    private Stack             stack;
    private Locator           locator;

    public RssChannel getChannel ()
        { return channel; }

    private String getCurrentElementName ()
        { return (String) stack.peek (); }

    // only need a handful of ContentHandler methods

    public void setDocumentLocator (Locator l)
        { locator = l; }

    public void startDocument () throws SAXException
    {
        channel = new RssChannel ();
        if (locator != null)
            channel.sourceUri = locator.getSystemId ();
        stack = new Stack ();
    }

    public void startElement (
        String          namespace,
        String          local,
        String          name,
        Attributes      attrs
    ) throws SAXException
    {
        stack.push (name);

        if ("item".equals (name))
            item = new RssItem ();
        else if ("image".equals (name))
            image = new RssImage ();
        else if ("textinput".equals (name))
            input = new RssTextInput ();
        // parser misconfigured?
        else if (name.length () == 0)
            throw new SAXParseException ("XML names not available", locator);
    }

    public void characters (char buf [], int off, int len)
    throws SAXException
    {
        String  top = getCurrentElementName ();
        String  value = new String (buf, off, len);

        if ("title".equals (top)) {
```

Example 6-2. Unmarshaling SAX events into RSS data (continued)

```
                    if (item != null)
                        item.title += value;
                    else if (image != null)
                        image.title += value;
                    else if (input != null)
                        input.title += value;
                    else
                        channel.title += value;
                } else if ("description".equals (top)) {
                    if (item != null)
                        item.description += value;
                    else if (image != null)
                        image.description += value;
                    else if (input != null)
                        input.description += value;
                    else
                        channel.description += value;
                } else if ("link".equals (top)) {
                    if (item != null)
                        item.link += value;
                    else if (image != null)
                        image.link += value;
                    else if (input != null)
                        input.link += value;
                    else
                        channel.link += value;

                } else if ("url".equals (top)) {
                    image.url += value;

                } else if ("name".equals (top)) {
                    input.name += value;

                } else if ("language".equals (top)) {
                    channel.language += value;
                } else if ("managingEditor".equals (top)) {
                    channel.managingEditor += value;
                } else if ("webMaster".equals (top)) {
                    channel.webMaster += value;

                } else if ("copyright".equals (top)) {
                    channel.copyright += value;
                } else if ("lastBuildDate".equals (top)) {
                    channel.lastBuildDate += value;
                } else if ("pubDate".equals (top)) {
                    channel.pubDate += value;
                } else if ("docs".equals (top)) {
                    channel.docs += value;
                } else if ("rating".equals (top)) {
                    channel.rating += value;

                } // else ignore ... skipDays and so on.
```

Example 6-2. Unmarshaling SAX events into RSS data (continued)

```
    }

    public void endElement (
        String              namespace,
        String              local,
        String              name
    ) throws SAXException
    {
        if ("item".equals (name)) {
            // patch item.link
            channel.items.addElement (item);
            item = null;
        } else if ("image".equals (name)) {
            // patch image.link
            // (patch image.url)
            channel.image = image;
            image = null;
        } else if ("textinput".equals (name)) {
            // patch input.link
            channel.textinput = input;
            input = null;
        } else if ("channel".equals (name)) {
            // patch channel.link
        }
    }
}
```

If you think in terms of higher-level parsing events, rather than in terms of data structures, you might want to define an application-level event handler interface and package your code as an *XMLFilterImpl*, as shown in Example 6-3. This is the "atoms into molecules" pattern for handlers, as sketched in Chapter 3. In the case of RSS, both item and channel might reasonably be expected to be "molecules" that get reported individually as application-level events. If you report finer grained structures (like item) it might be it easier to assemble higher-level data structures, but we won't show that here.

Example 6-3. Building SAX events into an RSS event handler

```
public interface RssHandler {
    void channelUpdate (RssChannel c) throws SAXException;
}

public class RssConsumer extends XMLFilterImpl {
    // ... as above (notice different base class!) but also:

    private RssHandler          handler;

    public static String        RssHandlerURI =
```

Example 6-3. Building SAX events into an RSS event handler (continued)

```
        "http://www.example.com/properties/rss-handler";

    public void setProperty (String uri, Object value)
    throws SAXNotSupportedException, SAXNotRecognizedException
    {
        if (RssHandlerURI.equals (uri)) {
            if (value instanceof RssHandler) {
                handler = (RssHandler) value;
                return;
            }
            throw new SAXNotSupportedException ("not an RssHandler");
        }
        super.setProperty (uri, value);
    }

    public Object getProperty (String uri)
    throws SAXNotSupportedException, SAXNotRecognizedException
    {
        if (RssHandlerURI.equals (uri))
            return handler;
        return super.getProperty (uri);
    }

    public void endDocument ()
    throws SAXException
    {
        if (handler == null)
            return;
        handler.channelUpdate (getChannel ());
    }
}
```

A filter written in that particular way can be used almost interchangeably with the handler-only class shown earlier in Example 6-2. In fact it's just a bit more flexible than that, though it may not be a good pipeline-style component. That's because it doesn't pass the low-level events through consistently; the *ContentHandler* methods this implements don't pass their events through to the superclass, but all the other methods do. That's easily fixed, but it's likely that you'd either want all the XML atoms to be visible (extending the XML Infoset with RSS-specific data abstractions) or none of them (and use an RSS-only infoset).

Example 6-4 shows what the core marshaling code can look like, without the hookup to an *XMLWriter* or the *XMLWriter* setup. For simplicity, this example takes a few shortcuts: it doesn't marshal the channel's icon description or most of the other optional fields. But notice that it does take care to write out the DTD and provide some whitespace to indent the text. (It uses only newlines for end-of-line; output code is responsible for mapping those to CRLF or CR when needed.) Also, notice that it just generates SAX2 events; this data could be fed to an *XMLWriter*, or to the *RssConsumer* class, or to any other SAX-processing component.

Example 6-4. Marshaling RSS data to SAX events

```
import java.util.Enumeration;
import org.xml.sax.*;
import org.xml.sax.ext.LexicalHandler;
import org.xml.sax.helpers.AttributesImpl;
import RssChannel.RssItem;

public class RssProducer implements RssHandler
{
    private static char         lineEnd [] = { '\n', '\t', '\t', '\t' };
    private ContentHandler      content;
    private LexicalHandler      lexical;

    public RssProducer (ContentHandler n)
        { content = n; }

    public void setLexicalHandler (LexicalHandler l)
        { lexical = l; }

    private void doIndent (int n)
    throws SAXException
    {
        n++;    // NL
        if (n > lineEnd.length)
            n = lineEnd.length;
        content.ignorableWhitespace (lineEnd, 0, n);
    }

    private void element (int indent, String name, String val, Attributes
            atts)
    throws SAXException
    {
        char    contents [] = val.toCharArray ();

        doIndent (indent);
        content.startElement ("", "", name, atts);
        content.characters (contents, 0, contents.length);
        content.endElement ("", "", name);
    }

    public void channelUpdate (RssChannel channel)
    throws SAXException
    {
        AttributesImpl          atts = new AttributesImpl ();

        content.startDocument ();
        if (lexical != null) {
            lexical.startDTD ("rss",
```

Example 6-4. Marshaling RSS data to SAX events (continued)

```
                "-//Netscape Communications//DTD RSS 0.91//EN",
                "http://my.netscape.com/publish/formats/rss-0.91.dtd");
            lexical.endDTD ();
        }

        atts.addAttribute ("", "", "version", "CDATA", "0.91");
        content.startElement ("", "", "rss", atts);
        atts.clear ();
        doIndent (0);
        content.startElement ("", "", "channel", atts);

        // describe the channel
        // four required elements
        element (1, "title", channel.title, atts);
        element (1, "link", channel.link, atts);
        element (1, "description", channel.description, atts);
        element (1, "language", channel.language, atts);

        // optional elements
        if ("" != channel.managingEditor)
            element (1, "managingEditor", channel.managingEditor, atts);
        if ("" != channel.webMaster)
            element (1, "webMaster", channel.webMaster, atts);
        // ... and many others, notably image/icon and text input


        // channel contents: at least one item
        for (Enumeration e = channel.items.elements ();
                e.hasMoreElements ();
                /**/) {
            RssItem     item = (RssItem) e.nextElement ();
            doIndent (1);
            content.startElement ("", "", "item", atts);
            if ("" != item.title)
                element (2, "title", item.title, atts);
            if ("" != item.link)
                element (2, "link", item.link, atts);
            if ("" != item.description)
                element (2, "description", item.description, atts);
            doIndent (1);
            content.endElement ("", "", "item");
        }

        content.endElement ("", "", "channel");
        content.endElement ("", "", "rss");
        content.endDocument ();
    }
}
```

Since this code implements the *RssHandler* interface shown earlier, an instance of this class could be assigned as the RSS handler for the

XMLFilter shown here. That could be useful if you wanted to round-trip RSS data. Round-tripping data can be a good way to test marshaling and unmarshaling code. You can create collections of input documents, and automatically unmarshal or remarshal their data. If you compare inputs and outputs, you can ensure that you haven't discarded any important information or added inappropriate text.

Building Applications with RSS

One of the most fundamental things you can do in an RSS application is act as a client: fetch a site's summary data and present it in some useful format. Often, your personal view of a web site is decorated with pages or sidebars that summarize the latest news as provided by other sites; they fetch RSS data, cache it, and reformat it as HTML or XHTML so your web browser shows it. That is, the web server acts as a client to RSS feeds and generates individualized pages that you can read on and click on the latest headlines.

Example 6-5 is a simple client that dumps its output as text. It's simple to write a servlet or JSP that does this for a set of RSS feeds, formatting them as nice XHTML sidebar tables so that a site's pages will be more useful.*

One extremely important point shown here is this code uses a resolver to force the use of a local copy of the RSS DTD. Servers should always use local copies of DTDs. Some RSS applications got a rude reminder of that fact in April 2001, when Netscape accidentally removed the DTD when it reorganized its web site. Suddenly, those badly written applications stopped working on many RSS feeds! Of course, those that were properly set up with local copies of that DTD had no problems at all.

Example 6-5. An RSS data dump

```
import gnu.xml.util.Resolver;
import java.io.File;
import java.util.Hashtable;
import org.xml.sax.*;
import org.xml.sax.helpers.XMLReaderFactory;
import RssChannel.RssItem;
```

---

* If you do this in a server, you should handle one very important task that's not shown here: cache the RSS data! Do not make servers fetch the summary before each page view. That makes for a very slow user experience and can overload remote RSS feeds.

There are two basic techniques to use to create such a cache. One is to put a caching proxy between your server and all the RSS feeds. The other is to write a page cache module, preferably one that uses HTTP "conditional GET" (the If-Modified-Since HTTP header field) to avoid excess cache updates. You can save *RssChannel* data or store channel information in a local database, as variants of the page cache technique.

Example 6-5. An RSS data dump (continued)

```java
public class RssMain
{
    private static String featurePrefix =
        "http://xml.org/sax/features/";

    // Invoke with one argument, a URI or filename
    public static void main (String argv [])
    {
        if (argv.length != 1) {
            System.err.println ("Usage: RssMain [file|URL]");
            System.exit (1);
        }

        try {
            XMLReader          reader;
            RssConsumer        consumer;
            Hashtable          hashtable;
            Resolver           resolver;

            reader = XMLReaderFactory.createXMLReader ();

            consumer = new RssConsumer ();
            reader.setContentHandler (consumer);

            // handle the "official" DTD server being offline
            hashtable = new Hashtable (5);
            hashtable.put (
                "-//Netscape Communications//DTD RSS 0.91//EN",
                Resolver.fileNameToURL ("rss-0_91.dtd"));
            resolver = new Resolver (hashtable);
            reader.setEntityResolver (resolver);

            // we rely on qNames, and 0.91 doesn't use namespaces
            reader.setFeature (featurePrefix + "namespace-prefixes", true);
            reader.setFeature (featurePrefix + "namespaces", false);

            argv [0] = Resolver.getURL (argv [0]);
            reader.parse (argv [0]);

            RssChannel            channel = consumer.getChannel ();

            System.out.println ("Partial RSS 0.91 channel info");
            System.out.println ("SOURCE = " + channel.sourceUri);
            System.out.println ();

            System.out.println ("         Title: " + channel.title);
            System.out.println ("   Description: " + channel.description);
            System.out.println ("          Link: " + channel.link);
            System.out.println ("      Language: " + channel.language);
            System.out.println ("     WebMaster: " + channel.webMaster);
            System.out.println ("ManagingEditor: "
                + channel.managingEditor);
```

Example 6-5. An RSS data dump (continued)

```
            System.out.println ();

            System.out.println ("    Item Count: " + channel.items.size ());
            for (int i = 0; i < channel.items.size (); i++) {
                RssItem        item = (RssItem)
                                   channel.items.elementAt (i);
                System.out.println ("ITEM # " + i);
                if (item != null) {
                    System.out.println ("       Title: " + item.title);
                    System.out.println ("    Description: "
                            + item.description);
                    System.out.println ("        Link: " + item.link);
                }
            }

        // Good error handling is not shown here, for simplicity
        } catch (Exception e) {
            System.err.println ("Whoa: " + e.getMessage ());
            System.exit (1);
        }
        System.exit (0);
    }
}
```

Besides servlets that present RSS data in HTML form to a web site's clients, another kind of servlet is important in the world of RSS applications: servlets that deliver a site's own RSS feed as XML. Servers often arrange that the current channel data is always ready to serve at a moment's notice. You've probably worked with sites that give you HTML forms to publish either short articles (web log entries or discussion follow-ups) or long ones (perhaps XML DocBook source that's then formatted). When such forms post data through a servlet, it's easy to ensure the servlet updates the site's RSS channel data when it updates other site data for those articles.

While the mechanics of such a servlet would be specific to the procedures used at a given web site, almost any site could use code like that in Example 6-6 to actually deliver the RSS feed. Notice the XML text is delivered with an encoding that any XML parser is guaranteed to handle, using CRLF-style line ends (part of the MIME standard for *text/** content types), and this sets the Last-Modified HTTP timestamp so it supports HTTP caches based on either "conditional GET" or on explicit timestamp checks with the HEAD request.

Example 6-6. Servlet generating RSS data

```
import gnu.xml.util.XMLWriter;
import javax.servlet.http.*;

// a "Globals" class is used here to access channel and related data

public class RssGenServlet extend HttpServlet
{
    public void doGet (HttpServletRequest request,
            HttpServletResponse response)
    throws IOException, ServletException
    {
        RssProducer         producer;
        XMLWriter           consumer;

        response.addDateHeader ("Last-Modified", Globals.channelModified);

        response.setContentType ("text/xml;charset=UTF-8");
        consumer = new XMLWriter (response.getWriter ());
        consumer.setEOL ("\r\n");

        try {
            producer = new RssProducer (consumer);
            producer.setLexicalHandler (consumer);
            producer.channelUpdate (Globals.channel);
        } catch (SAXException e) {
            throw new ServletException (e);
        }
    }
}
```

As RSS 1.0 starts to become more widely supported and more RSS/RDF modules are defined, more clever RSS-based services will become available. For example, RSS aggregator services may begin to be able to dynamically create new channels with information filtered from many other channels. That is, you could be able to define a channel that the aggregator will fill with new articles on a particular topic, listed in any of several hundred RSS feeds. Today, you'd have to scan each feed yourself to do that. Such smarter services would also have better reasons to cache information. Today, such a service would have a hard time knowing which articles to remember while you were away on vacation, since there would be far too many articles to remember them all.

XML and Messaging

Most technologies that fueled the "Internet Revolution" of the past few years have been around in one form or another for decades; they were just inaccessible to the volumes of people that were able to use them with mass market web browsers. Some of those technologies are now being re-created: they are updated to work better in today's Internet, which is a larger and more varied world than the earlier versions they were born into. In this section we will look at why XML is an important part of the re-creation of messaging technologies and at some of the roles Java plays in this process. We also look at how lightweight SAX2-based infrastructure supports XML messaging over the Web without requiring developers to master new toolkits.

XML/Internet Versus Older Technologies

Many more developers work with web servers than have ever worked with Remote Procedure Call (RPC) or message-queuing technologies. However, the problem is largely unchanged: the core issue is still how to exchange messages reliably and securely with services operated by other organizations. The combination of XML and web-based messaging has several basic technical benefits compared to those earlier technology generations, especially most forms of RPC:

HTTP-based protocols have truly global reach
> HTTP is in essence a text-based RPC protocol: clients issue requests to objects identified by web server URIs, and those servers dynamically compute the responses. Because it's text-based, HTTP can be (and is) easily supported by almost all programming languages. Because of HTTPS (HTTP over SSL, a security protocol), HTTP security has been at least as good as any available with commercial RPC services. HTTP/HTTPS is now the most ubiquitous and functional RPC transport in the world.

XML is a more accessible and extensible message-encoding technology
> Previous technologies generally focused on binary-oriented technologies, which often rigidly defined the set of possible messages. In practice, most technologies were restricted to particular programming environments because developers needed an API toolkit to generate the correct binary data. XML has a clear win here since essentially every such environment supports text input and output. And unlike other encodings, XML doesn't impose any inherent policy on what such text means, which makes it more flexible. SAX is able to leverage that flexibility because it is data-structure agnostic. Much of the work in XML messaging is to establish and promote particular policies; SAX can support all the important ones.

The Internet biases toward larger, coarse-grained messages
   Before the Internet, applications were optimized for private local area networks (LANs) or for low-speed, application-specific wide area networks (WANs). Neither optimization point is a good match for today's typical Internet link (56 kbps modem, or megabit links for some home use and most enterprises). Two key Internet issues are network latency and reliability. Using HTTP with XML provides an opportunity to develop newer systems using a design policy that works with the Internet rather than against it: use bigger messages, less often. This is the antithesis of many RPC systems, which bias toward constant exchange of small messages just like they were local procedure calls.

XML favors loose coupling
   RPC-based systems were often developed to assume that clients and servers are in the same organization. Some even assumed only one vendor's product would be used. That is, developers often aimed for a monoculture and tended to characterize diversity as either a commercial threat, an inefficiency, a security problem, or just a support headache. Actually, diversity is a source of strength: human groups that are diverse are more adaptable and more resilient because they have more resources to draw on. Because XML messaging focuses on protocols and message formats, rather than vendor-specific implementations or APIs, it promotes diversity. That reduces inappropriate coupling and makes systems less vulnerable to the problems of any particular implementation.

In short, as the limitations of earlier messaging infrastructures became well known, organizations of all sizes were investing in new, web-based technology. Internet-savvy applications were developed with HTTP technology, and the flexibility of XML as well as its introduction to the web developer community, made it the inevitable choice for the most widely deployed messaging technologies.

While much of the current work is focused on business applications, notably business-to-business integration, that's hardly the only type of application it benefits. There's also interest in peer-to-peer (P2P) protocols built with XML. P2P is usefully viewed as just messaging policies for applications that have finally escaped from the "client or server" straitjacket. Now, essentially anyone can run a server and act as a publisher for information they have produced. These new publishing systems are most naturally built with the same XML and HTTP technologies adopted elsewhere.

Another interesting way to compare these models is that while the RPC model moves computations to where the data lives, the Web model moves the data to where the computation lives. That has been called the "representational state transfer" (REST) model. When code is downloaded, a third model can be said to come into effect. The design of distributed systems needs to balance among all these alternatives and not focus exclusively on any single model.

Roles for Java in XML Messaging

Since Java was the first true "Internet-integrated" programming environment and had XML support very early, it's no surprise that a huge amount of XML messaging work is done in Java. There are a variety of higher-level XML APIs and tools, all of which define particular messaging policies and frameworks. This book may seem somewhat iconoclastic in its perspective on such tools: many of them are overkill. Most applications will be fine without any of the heavier-weight items on the API smorgasbord (for any language!); a lighter meal will often be the healthier solution, even on an expense account budget. There's plenty of scope for innovative applications written without such toolkits, and it's easier to spread them if they don't depend on first deploying lots of complex new infrastructure.

From an interoperability perspective, the most interesting work is language-neutral development of protocols. Some such initiatives hide or limit use of XML, such as XML-RPC. Others, notably BEEP and SOAP, let applications provide their own payloads, although SOAP is usually coupled with synchronous RPC-style messaging and payloads using W3C XML schema and precluding full use of XML, such as DTDs. BEEP is a standards-track peer-to-peer Internet protocol, building on decades of community experience and supporting both synchronous and asynchronous messaging models. *http://www.beepcore.org* has a wealth of relevant information, including protocol specifications and toolkits in many languages including Java. And as presented in various parts of this book, it's easy to use HTTP/HTTPS directly with SAX; that approach is very lightweight. Many applications can define XML messages and pass them using HTTP without needing additional policies or APIs; it's only a small stretch to use SMTP and email queues if you need asynchronous queuing.

To develop lightweight XML-based applications, get a JDK, an HTTP/HTTPS servlet engine, an XML toolset with SAX2 support, and probably a relational database that you can access through JDBC. That's enough for quite a lot of web services. When you need to get beyond HTTP-centric models, look at protocol frameworks like BEEP, which has long had Java support. Remember to carefully document and review your XML messages and protocols and to keep that documentation current. That is important

XML and Messaging

for maintaining your software, and such good practices will help uncover design bugs early in system life cycles, when they're easy to fix.

XML Messaging over HTTP with SAX2

HTTP is a request/response protocol, loosely called an "RPC transport." Strictly speaking, RPC touches on APIs in some programming language and makes them location transparent, but here we use the term in a broader request/response sense. HTTP has several operations, sent to a particular server port (typically 80 for nonencrypted HTTP) and directed to a particular URI. For the purposes of XML messaging, the most important HTTP operations are GET and POST.

HTTP's GET request asks the server to return the data associated with the request's URI, as modified by various header fields. Other than the request itself, this is a one-way data transfer, from server to client; the data is returned using MIME as a typed envelope. For the purposes of this book, that data is most interesting when it's XML text. Web browsers normally issue GET to retrieve documents, and in Java when you read data from a *java.net.URL* you are normally issuing a GET. In particular, when a client passes a URI to the SAX XMLReader.parse(uri) call, the call uses GET underneath. It's easy to dynamically generate XML content from Java servlets, as shown in the section "Building Applications with RSS" earlier in this chapter.

HTTP's POST request is more interesting. POST is very similar in structure to GET, but it provides something that GET doesn't have: the request includes MIME-encoded data. (Again, that's most interesting when it's XML text.) That is, unlike GET, POST is a two-way data transfer; XML can be sent to the server as part of the request, as well as returned in the response. Another key difference is that GET is idempotent: clients are expected to reissue GET calls, which must not change significant server state. If you wanted to transfer money between bank accounts, POST is the call to use since it's expected to execute exactly once.

It's a bit messy to issue XML-in/XML-out POST requests from Java clients. We'll discuss how to do this in relatively pure SAX, but first let's look at this process using a SAX-friendly API library. No matter how you actually transfer this data, the real work of your application will be to turn the SAX events into application work. You'll likely connect code resembling this example to application-specific code that marshals and unmarshals custom data structures needed to do its work.

The *gnu.xml.pipeline.CallFilter* class packages the entire process as a pipeline stage, sending its input events as a POST request and parsing the POST response to produce output events. That makes it easy to use POST as a generic processing component. For example, in a batch processing scenario you might want to POST an XML file to a server and print its response. Such a server might schedule work as described in the particular document, and it could easily have access to resources or privileges unavailable to your client. This request can be issued programmatically or in some cases using a standard command-line tool.

Example 6-7 shows one way to send an XML file to a server and save its XML response as another file. As mentioned, the *NSFilter* class can be (and in this case, is) optimized away. It's just making sure the namespace prefix information in the event stream isn't missing anything important.

Example 6-7. Exchanging XML with a server (GNU pipeline version)

```
import gnu.xml.pipeline.*;
import gnu.xml.util.Resolver;
import org.xml.sax.*;
import org.xml.sax.helpers.XMLReaderFactory;

public class CallFile
{
    // argv [0] == in.xml (filename)
    // argv [1] == url for posting service
    public static void main (String argv [])
    {
        try {
            EventConsumer    out;
            XMLReader        in;

            out = new TextConsumer (System.out);
            out = new NSFilter (out);
            out = new CallFilter (argv [1], out);
            out = new NSFilter (out);

            in = XMLReaderFactory.createXMLReader ();
            EventFilter.bind (in, out);

            in.parse (Resolver.fileNameToURL (argv [0]));

        } catch (Exception  e) {
            e.printStackTrace ();
            System.exit (1);
        }
    }
}
```

XML and Messaging

If you want to do the same thing without using that pipeline framework, you have more work to do. You'll be driving the *java.net.URLConnection* directly, ensuring the text encodings are correct. And you won't have a generic way to group all SAX handlers together; you'd need to create an analogue of *gnu.xml.pipeline.EventConsumer* or, as shown in Example 6-8, write code that knows the specific output class it's talking to.

Example 6-8. Exchanging XML with a server (SAX-only version)

```java
import java.io.*;
import java.net.*;
import gnu.xml.util.Resolver;
import gnu.xml.util.XMLWriter;
import org.xml.sax.*;
import org.xml.sax.helpers.XMLReaderFactory;

public class CallFile
{
    // argv [0] == in.xml (filename)
    // argv [1] == url for posting service
    public static void main (String argv [])
    {
        try {
            XMLReader           in;
            Caller              caller;
            XMLWriter           out;

            out = new XMLWriter (System.out);
            caller = new CallWriter (new URL (argv [1]), out);

            in = XMLReaderFactory.createXMLReader ();
            in.setFeature (featurePrefix + "namespace-prefixes", true);
            bindAll (in, caller);

            in.parse (Resolver.fileNameToURL (argv [0]));

        } catch (Exception e) {
            e.printStackTrace ();
            System.exit (1);
        }
    }

    private static void bindAll (XMLReader in, Object out)
    throws SAXException
    {
        if (out instanceof ContentHandler)
            in.setContentHandler ((ContentHandler) out);
        if (out instanceof DTDHandler)
            in.setDTDHandler ((DTDHandler) out);
        try {
            if (out instanceof DeclHandler)
```

Example 6-8. Exchanging XML with a server (SAX-only version) (continued)

```
            in.setProperty
                ("http://xml.org/sax/properties/
                declaration-handler", out);
    } catch (SAXNotRecognizedException e) { /* IGNORE */ }
    try {
        if (out instanceof LexicalHandler)
            in.setProperty
                ("http://xml.org/sax/properties/
                lexical-handler", out);
    } catch (SAXNotRecognizedException e) { /* IGNORE */ }
}

// print input to server
// block till response
// print output as XML text to stdout
private static class CallWriter extends XMLWriter
{
    private URL              target;
    private URLConnection    conn;
    private XMLWriter next;

    CallWriter (URL url, XMLWriter out)
    {
        super ((Writer)null);
        target = url;
        next = out;
    }

    // Connect to remote object and set up to send it XML text
    public synchronized void startDocument () throws SAXException
    {
        try {
            conn = target.openConnection ();
            conn.setDoOutput (true);

            // "text/*" expects DOS-style EOL
            next.setEOL ("\r\n");
            conn.setRequestProperty ("Content-Type",
                    "text/xml;charset=UTF-8");

            setWriter (new OutputStreamWriter (
                    conn.getOutputStream (),
                    "UTF8"), "UTF-8");

        } catch (IOException e) {
            fatal ("can't write (POST) to URI: " + target, e);
        }
        super.startDocument ();
    }

    // finish sending request
    // receive the POST response
```

Example 6-8. Exchanging XML with a server (SAX-only version) (continued)

```
        public void endDocument () throws SAXException
        {
            super.endDocument ();

            try {
                InputSource source = new InputSource
                        (conn.getInputStream ());
                XMLReader   producer = XMLReaderFactory.createXMLReader ();
                String      encoding;

                producer.setFeature (featurePrefix +
                        "namespace-prefixes", true);
                encoding = Resolver.getEncoding (conn.getContentType ());
                if (encoding != null)
                    source.setEncoding (encoding);
                bindAll (producer, next);
                producer.parse (source);

            } catch (IOException e) {
                fatal ("I/O Exception reading response, "
                        + e.getMessage (), e);
            }
        }
    }
}
```

In that example scenario, you might also be able to just use binary file I/O and trust that the inputs and outputs are actually XML. But in general, inputs won't be sitting in files, and output processing will involve more than creating a new file. Both the *CallFilter* and *CallWriter* classes shown here are structured to be reusable.

On the server side, it's also easy to handle POST. In fact, you've seen all you need to know already! We saw how to pull XML data out of the POST request using the `XmlReader.parse(InputSource)` method in Chapter 3, in the section "Providing entity text." Writing XML data in the response works exactly like it does for a GET, as shown earlier in this chapter in the section "Building Applications with RSS." The main XML-specific issue is to handle the character encoding correctly, as shown in both of those examples. (UTF-8 is the safest over-the-wire encoding.) It's safe to use the *application/xml* MIME content type whenever you pass XML using HTTP, since there are fewer things that can (and will!) go wrong. You should also make sure to use CRLF-style line ends whenever you use a *text/** MIME content type. You might want to pay attention to some servlet-specific issues, such as structuring your code to support connection keepalives or (less commonly) on-the-fly compression of response data.

In many cases it's probably good to have servlets' `doPost()` methods save input to persistent storage, so that some other thread can pick it up as work item, and then just use the response data to acknowledge the request. The client would collect any additional requests later, either when it polled or when the server called back to the client (with another POST). That approach avoids tying up connections for a long time and creates a framework whereby many component failures will be transparently recovered from. Using such an atomic transaction model correctly can let you avoid the need for transactional roll-back mechanisms to recover from common system failure modes.

Including Subdocuments

In XML, external parsed entities are used to merge one file into another. This mechanism is used to partition larger XML documents (such as this book) into smaller ones (such as this chapter). Such external entities aren't quite the same as actual XML documents. They do not have DTDs; they have zero or more top-level elements instead of exactly one; and they have text declarations at the top instead of XML declarations.*

Those entities are in some ways awkward to use. Some people don't like to use DTDs, and their tools might not let them declare and create references to such entities. In any case, DTDs add the requirement that such entities be declared in advance. When you're building big documents out of little ones, widely spreading such knowledge can be undesirable. It's often easier to keep a local reference accurate than to update the remote declarations it depends on. Also, documents nest inside others, and small changes nested inside one document could force updates to many DTDs if the document is included in several others. In short, external parsed entities aren't as easy or natural to use as the `#include "filename"` syntax widely known to C/C++ developers. This is often viewed as a problem.

The response is obvious: use some other part of XML syntax to define a more natural inclusion construct. There's a W3C draft called *XInclude*, which doesn't quite do this (in the most current draft). XInclude uses element syntax, which is fine, but it doesn't just define a simple and familiar

---

* These might show only the text encoding `<?xml encoding='Big5'?>` is a legal text declaration. To be an XML declaration, it would need to include a version first, like `version='1.0'`; it's good practice is to include both. Documents that use encoding declarations with no version number cannot be opened as XML directly. They can only be included in XML documents by way of an entity.

inclusion mechanism. XInclude supports the XPointer superset of XPath to embed almost arbitrary fragments of XML text. In effect, W3C's XInclude is a generalized linking model, and one which depends on significant infrastructure. The model hasn't met with widespread acceptance, and in any case is too complex to use for an example here. That's really too bad; normal inclusion is a strict streaming model, ideal for implementing with SAX, and the model of including fragments is exotic pretty much everywhere except within the linking community.

Here we show how to implement a variant of XInclude, which can replace many uses of external entities because it doesn't use XPointer. To emphasize the difference, we'll use a different syntax:

```
<?XInclude http://www.example.com/data/included.xml?>
    <!-- instead of what XInclude uses: -->
<xi:include
      xmlns:xi="http://www.w3.org/2001/XInclude"
      href="http://www.example.com/data/included.xml"
      parse='xml'
      encoding='euc-jp'
      >
    content of xi:include is ignored,
    the whole element gets replaced
</xi:include>
```

This example highlights several different SAX2 mechanisms. It uses the *XMLFilterImpl* class in two different modes and pays careful attention to the data it passes through. The different modes are as follows:

- The outer filter must be used as a mixed event producer and consumer, with access to the full stream of event data as well as any *ErrorHandler* and *EntityResolver* objects in use. If it's not used this way, it won't be correct; it's hard to know such things about a SAX Filter unless they are discussed in the class documentation.

  The outer filter proxies the *Locator* so that applications see the right event locations and base URIs. It usually forwards the events to the true recipient of the event stream, but it will also handle nested inclusions when they are sent from the inner filter.

- The inner filter is used as a pure event consumer. It cooperates with the outer filter to keep the proxy working correctly, and is set up to strip out DTD-related events and forward the rest to the outer filter.

The code in Example 6-9 takes a few shortcuts but implements the essential inclusion functionality.

Example 6-9. XInclude processing instruction

```java
import java.io.IOException;
import java.net.URL;
import java.util.Vector;
import org.xml.sax.*;
import org.xml.sax.ext.*;
import org.xml.sax.helpers.XMLFilterImpl;
import org.xml.sax.helpers.XMLReaderFactory;

public final class XI extends XMLFilterImpl
    implements LexicalHandler, Locator
{
    // Act as a proxy for whatever the current locator is.
    private Locator            locator;

    // to avoid circular inclusion
    private Vector             pending = new Vector (5, 5);

    private LexicalHandler     lexicalHandler;

    private static String lexicalID =
            "http://xml.org/sax/properties/lexical-handler";

    public void setDocumentLocator (Locator l)
    {
        locator = l;
        super.setDocumentLocator (this);
    }

    public String getSystemId ()
        { return (locator == null) ? null : locator.getSystemId (); }
    public String getPublicId ()
        { return (locator == null) ? null : locator.getPublicId (); }
    public int getLineNumber ()
        { return (locator == null) ? -1 : locator.getLineNumber (); }
    public int getColumnNumber ()
        { return (locator == null) ? -1 : locator.getColumnNumber (); }

    // Inner Filter Class: manage the current locator,
    // and filter out events that would be incorrect to report
    private class Scrubber extends XMLFilterImpl implements LexicalHandler
    {
        Locator         savedLocator;
        LexicalHandler  next;

        Scrubber (Locator l, LexicalHandler n)
            { savedLocator = l; next = n; }

        // maintain proxy locator
        // only one startDocument()/endDocument() pair per event stream
        public void setDocumentLocator (Locator l)
            { locator = l; }
        public void startDocument ()
```

Example 6-9. XInclude processing instruction (continued)

```
            { }
        public void endDocument ()
            { locator = savedLocator; }

        private void reject (String message) throws SAXException
            { throw new SAXParseException (message, locator); }

        // only the DTD from the base document gets reported
        public void startDTD (String root, String publicId, String systemId)
        throws SAXException
            { reject ("DTD: " + systemId); }
        public void endDTD ()
        throws SAXException
            { reject ("DTD"); }
        // ... so this should never happen
        public void skippedEntity (String name) throws SAXException
            { reject ("entity: " + name); }

        // since we rejected DTDs, only built-in entities can be reported
        public void startEntity (String name)
        throws SAXException
            { next.startEntity (name); }
        public void endEntity (String name)
        throws SAXException
            { next.endEntity (name); }

        // other lexical events cause no worries
        public void startCDATA () throws SAXException
            { next.startCDATA (); }
        public void endCDATA () throws SAXException
            { next.endCDATA (); }
        public void comment (char buf[], int off, int len)
                throws SAXException
            { next.comment (buf, off, len); }
    }

    // count is zero in the document prologue and epilogue
    private int          count;

    public void startElement (String u, String l, String q, Attributes a)
    throws SAXException
        { count++; super.startElement (u, l, q, a); }

    public void endElement (String u, String l, String q)
    throws SAXException
        { --count; super.endElement (u, l, q); }

    public void startDocument () throws SAXException
        { pending.addElement (locator.getSystemId ());
                super.startDocument (); }
```

Example 6-9. XInclude processing instruction (continued)

```
    public void endDocument () throws SAXException
        { pending.clear (); super.endDocument (); }

    // handle <?XInclude URI> processing instructions
    public void processingInstruction (String target, String data)
    throws SAXException
    {
        if ("XInclude".equals (target)) {
            // this should do full XML base processing
            // instead we just handle relative and absolute URLs
            try {
                URL             url = new URL (getSystemId ());

                url = new URL (url, data.trim ());
                data = url.toString ();
            } catch (Exception e) {
                throw new SAXParseException (
                    "XInclude, can't use URI: " + data, locator, e);
            }
            xinclude (data);
        } else
            super.processingInstruction (target, data);
    }

    // this might be called from startElement too
    private void xinclude (String uri)
    throws SAXException
    {
        XMLReader       helper;
        Scrubber scrubber;

        if (count == 0)
            throw new SAXParseException (
                    "XInclude, illegal location", locator);
        if (pending.contains (uri))
            throw new SAXParseException (
                    "XInclude, circular inclusion", locator);

        // start with another parser acting just like us
        helper = XMLReaderFactory.createXMLReader ();
        helper.setEntityResolver (this);
        helper.setErrorHandler (this);

        // Set up the proxy locator and inner filter.
        scrubber = new Scrubber (locator, this);
        locator = null;
        scrubber.setContentHandler (this);
        helper.setContentHandler (scrubber);
        helper.setProperty (lexicalID, scrubber);

        // we INTEND to discard DTDHandler and DeclHandler events
```

Example 6-9. XInclude processing instruction (continued)

```java
            // Merge the included document, except its DTD
            try {
                pending.addElement (uri);
                helper.parse (uri);
            } catch (java.io.IOException e) {
                SAXParseException    err;
                ErrorHandler handler;

                err = new SAXParseException (uri, locator, e);
                handler = getErrorHandler ();
                if (handler != null)
                    handler.fatalError (err);
                throw err;
            } finally {
                pending.removeElement (uri);
            }
    }

    // LexicalHandler interface
    public void startEntity (String name)
    throws SAXException
        { if (lexicalHandler != null) lexicalHandler.startEntity (name); }

    public void endEntity (String name)
    throws SAXException
        { if (lexicalHandler != null) lexicalHandler.endEntity (name); }

    public void startDTD (String root, String publicId, String systemId)
    throws SAXException
        { if (lexicalHandler != null) lexicalHandler.startDTD (root, publicId,
            systemId); }

    public void endDTD () throws SAXException
        { if (lexicalHandler != null) lexicalHandler.endDTD (); }
    public void startCDATA () throws SAXException
        { if (lexicalHandler != null) lexicalHandler.startCDATA (); }
    public void endCDATA () throws SAXException
        { if (lexicalHandler != null) lexicalHandler.endCDATA (); }
    public void comment (char buf[], int off, int len) throws SAXException
        { if (lexicalHandler != null) lexicalHandler.comment (buf, off, len); }

    // so this works as a "consumer"
    public void setProperty (String uri, Object handler)
    throws SAXNotRecognizedException, SAXNotSupportedException
    {
        if (lexicalID.equals (uri))
            lexicalHandler = (LexicalHandler) handler;
        else
            super.setProperty (uri, handler);
    }

    // so this works as a "producer"
```

Example 6-9. XInclude processing instruction (continued)

```
public void parse (InputSource in)
throws SAXException, IOException
{
    XMLReader       parent = getParent ();

    if (parent != null)
        parent.setProperty (lexicalID, this);
    super.parse (in);
    }
}
```

The most significant shortcut in this code is that, to simplify the example, XML Base isn't supported. That's easily fixed using the technique shown earlier, in Example 5-1. Similarly, the namespace reporting and validation modes of the default parser are assumed to be OK; they should be copied or specified as part of this event consumer's API.

Merging SAX event streams from two different sources is quite simple, except for DTD-related information. One basic problem is structural: DTD events may be reported only at the beginning of a SAX event stream, and the chance to do that has been lost by the time an included document is processed. Another basic problem is semantic: the events from the two sources could easily conflict with each other. Neither of those problems can be solved with a pure stream processing model, unless the included documents use the same DTD as the base document. Accordingly, this example treats DTD events from included streams as errors.

The best way to use XML inclusions is with XML text that doesn't use DTDs, perhaps using "XML 1.0 plus Namespaces" rules to help assign meaning to individual elements and attributes. Eliminating DTDs means some important bits of the XML Infoset will be unavailable, such as the attribute-typing information that tells you which elements are used as IDs. If all the files in question are themselves well-formed XML documents with both version and encoding in any XML declarations (and without a DTD), they can easily be included without significant restrictions. Such an inclusion facility can be convenient in a variety of application contexts, such as template-driven document processing and other cases where it's important to build larger documents from smaller ones.

SAX2 API Summary

This appendix provides a quick reference to each of the SAX2 APIs presented in this book. It shows API signatures and provides a brief overview for each interface, class, and exception in alphabetical order.

Full documentation for these APIs is available for you to download or browse online at the SAX web site (*http://sax.sourceforge.net/*), and it should also be available with documentation for your SAX parser.

The org.xml.sax Package

The *org.xml.sax* package holds the interfaces and exceptions that are at the core of SAX, including some deprecated SAX1 APIs.

The AttributeList Interface

This SAX1 interface is not used in SAX2; the *Attributes* interface, which supports namespace identifiers, is used instead.

For more information, refer to the section "SAX1 Support" in Chapter 5.

```
public interface AttributeList
{
    public int getLength();
    public String getType(int index);
    public String getValue(int index);
    // access to name info
    public String getName(int index);
```

181

```
    // access by XML 1.0-style names
        public String getType(String qName);
        public String getValue(String qName);
}
```

The Attributes Interface

This interface groups all the attributes associated with a given element in the `ContentHandler.startElement()` call. Attribute characteristics are frequently accessed using an indexed access model, though you can also determine the index, type, or value of an attribute given XML 1.0–style (qName) or namespace-style (uri, localName) versions of its name.

For more information, refer to the section "The Attributes Interface" in Chapter 2.

```
public interface Attributes
{
    public int getLength();
    public String getType(int index);
    public String getValue(int index);
    // access to name info
    public String getQName(int index);
    public String getLocalName(int index);
    public String getURI(int index);
    // access by XML Namespace-style names
    public int getIndex(String uri, String localName);
    public String getType(String uri, String localName);
    public String getValue(String uri, String localName);
    // access by XML 1.0-style names
    public int getIndex(String qName);
    public String getType(String qName);
    public String getValue(String qName);
}
```

The ContentHandler Interface

This is the primary SAX2 handler interface, which is used in almost all applications.

For more information, refer to the section "Essential ContentHandler Callbacks," and the section "ContentHandler and Prefix Mappings," both in Chapter 2, as well as the section "Other ContentHandler Methods" in Chapter 4.

```
public interface ContentHandler
{
    // bookkeeping
```

```
    public void setDocumentLocator(Locator locator);
    public void startDocument() throws SAXException;
    public void endDocument() throws SAXException;
    // content events
    public void startElement(String uri, String localName, String qName,
            Attributes attributes)
        throws SAXException;
    public void endElement(String uri, String localName, String qName)
        throws SAXException;
    public void characters(char buf[], int offset, int length)
        throws SAXException;
    public void processingInstruction(String target, String data)
        throws SAXException;
    // extra info
    public void ignorableWhitespace(char buf[], int offset, int length)
        throws SAXException;
    public void startPrefixMapping(String prefix, String uri)
        throws SAXException;
    public void endPrefixMapping(String prefix) throws SAXException;
    public void skippedEntity(String name) throws SAXException;
}
```

The DocumentHandler Interface

This SAX1 interface is not used in SAX2; the *ContentHandler* interface, which reports namespace identifiers and scopes as well as skipped entities, is used instead.

For more information, refer to the section "SAX1 Support" in Chapter 5.

```
public interface DocumentHandler
{
    // bookkeeping
    public void setDocumentLocator(Locator locator);
    public void startDocument() throws SAXException;
    public void endDocument() throws SAXException;
    // content events
    public void startElement(String qName, AttributeList attributes)
        throws SAXException;
    public void endElement(String qName) throws SAXException;
    public void characters(char buf[], int offset, int length)
        throws SAXException;
    public void processingInstruction(String target, String data)
        throws SAXException;
    // extra info
    public void ignorableWhitespace(char buf[], int offset, int length)
        throws SAXException;
}
```

The DTDHandler Interface

This interface is used to report information that is useful to some SGML-derived applications.

For more information, refer to the section "The DTDHandler Interface" in Chapter 4.

```
public interface DTDHandler
{
    public void notationDecl(String notationName,
            String publicId, String systemId)
        throws SAXException;
    public void unparsedEntityDecl(String entityName,
            String publicId, String systemId, String notationName)
        throws SAXException;
}
```

The EntityResolver Interface

This interface encapsulates a strategy for resolving public or system identifiers for parsed entities into data that a parser will read. It is commonly used to ensure that local copies of DTDs are used, instead of DTDs accessed across a network link that may be saturated or unavailable. It can resolve general entities, used to store non-DTD parts of a document in separate storage units.

For more information, refer to the section "The EntityResolver Interface" in Chapter 3.

```
public interface EntityResolver
{
    public InputSource resolveEntity(String publicId,
            String systemId)
        throws SAXException, java.io.IOException;
}
```

The ErrorHandler Interface

This interface encapsulates a strategy for handling different kinds of errors. Parsers use its methods when reporting errors, and have default policies that are used if the application's strategy doesn't result in throwing an exception. Applications can benefit from sharing the same mechanism to report their own errors. Implementations typically use the problem's severity to choose first whether to emit a diagnostic, and then whether to throw the parameter (to terminate processing) or return (to continue processing).

For more information, refer to the section "ErrorHandler Interface" in Chapter 2.

```
public interface ErrorHandler
{
    public void error(SAXParseException x) throws SAXException;
    public void fatalError(SAXParseException x) throws SAXException;
    public void warning(SAXParseException x) throws SAXException;
}
```

The HandlerBase Interface

This SAX1 class is not used in SAX2; the *org.xml.sax.helpers.Defaulthandler* class, which supports SAX2 features, is used instead.

For more information, refer to the section "SAX1 Support" in Chapter 5.

```
public class HandlerBase
        implements EntityResolver, DTDHandler,
            DocumentHandler, ErrorHandler
{
    public HandlerBase();
    // DocumentHandler (SAX1)
    public void setDocumentLocator(Locator locator);
    public void startDocument() throws SAXException;
    public void endDocument() throws SAXException;
    public void startElement(String qName,
        AttributeList attributes)
        throws SAXException;
    public void endElement(String qName) throws SAXException;
    public void characters(char buf[], int offset, length)
        throws SAXException;
    public void ignorableWhitespace(char buf[], int offset,
        length)
        throws SAXException;
    public void processingInstruction(String target,
        String data)
        throws SAXException;
    // DTDHandler ... NOTE: no "throws SAXException"!
    public void notationDecl(String notationName,
        String publicId, String publicId);
    public void unparsedEntityDecl(String entityName,
        String publicId, String publicId, notationName);
    // EntityResolver
    public InputSource resolveEntity(String publicId,
        String publicId);
        throws SAXException;
```

```
// ErrorHandler
    public void error(SAXParseException x) throws SAXException;
    public void fatalError(SAXParseException x) throws SAXException;
    public void warning(SAXParseException x) throws SAXException;
}
```

The InputSource Class

This class is used to encapsulate entities for consumption by an *XMLReader* (or a SAX1 *Parser*). Applications should make every effort to provide a usable system identifier (an absolute URI, rather than null). This will ensure that relative URIs can be properly resolved so that diagnostics are meaningful. Given that identifier, SAX parsers can do the rest, possibly with assistance from an *EntityResolver*.

For more information, refer to the section "The InputSource Class" in Chapter 3.

```
public class InputSource {
    public InputSource();
    public InputSource(String systemId);
    public InputSource(java.io.InputStream in);
    public InputSource(java.io.Reader in);
    // getters
    public String getPublicId();
    public String getSystemId();
    public java.io.InputStream getByteStream();
    public String getEncoding();
    public java.io.Reader getCharacterStream();
    // setters
    public void setPublicId(String publicId);
    public void setSystemId(String systemId);
    public void setByteStream(java.io.InputStream in);
    public void setEncoding(String encodingName);
    public void setCharacterStream(java.io.Reader in);
}
```

The Locator Interface

An event producer may invoke the `ContentHandler.setDocumentLocator()` call to provide one of these objects. It may then be used inside event callbacks, until the final `ContentHandler.endDocument()` call, to determine the location of the data that triggered the event. A common use is to figure out the base URI used to resolve relative URIs found in document content.

This is true even when `xml:base` attributes have been used to override the real base URI of the document. Another common use is to construct *SAXParseException* objects to construct application-level diagnostics.

For more information, refer to the section "The Locator Interface" in Chapter 4.

```
public interface Locator
{
    public String getPublicId();
    public String getSystemId();
    public int getLineNumber();
    public int getColumnNumber();
}
```

The Parser Interface

This SAX1 interface is no longer used in SAX2; the *XMLReader* is used instead.

For more information, refer to the section "SAX1 Support" in Chapter 5.

```
public interface Parser
{
    // setters
    public void setLocale(java.util.Locale locale)
        throws SAXException;
    public void setEntityResolver(EntityResolver resolver);
    public void setDTDHandler(DTDHandler dtdHandler);
    public void setDocumentHandler(DocumentHandler docHandler);
    public void setErrorHandler(ErrorHandler errHandler);
    // parsing
    public void parse(InputSource in) throws SAXException,
        java.io.IOException;
    public void parse(String uri) throws SAXException,
        java.io.IOException;
}
```

SAXException

This is the base SAX exception class. It can wrap another exception, and (like most exceptions) a descriptive message.

For more information, refer to the section "SAX2 Exception Classes" in Chapter 2.

```
public class SAXException extends Exception {
    public SAXException(String message);
    public SAXException(Exception cause);
    public SAXException(String message, Exception cause);
    // getters
    public Exception getException();
    public String getMessage();
}
```

SAXNotRecognizedException

This exception is used to report that the identifier for a feature flag, or parser property, is not recognized. When this doesn't indicate a mistyped identifier, it means that the parser isn't exposing that particular information.

For more information, refer to the section "SAX2 Exception Classes" in Chapter 2.

```
public class SAXNotRecognizedException extends SAXException {
    public SAXNotRecognizedException(String message);
}
```

SAXNotSupportedException

This exception is used to report that while the identifier for a feature flag, or parser property, was recognized, setting the value was not practical. For example, read-only values can't be changed to nondefault values, handler properties need to implement the appropriate interface, and some values can't be changed while parsing, or accessed except while parsing.

For more information, refer to the section "SAX2 Exception Classes" in Chapter 2.

```
public class SAXNotSupportedException extends SAXException {
    public SAXNotSupportedException(String message);
}
```

SAXParseException

This type of *SAXException* is reported to the *ErrorHandler*, and adds information that is useful for locating (and hence fixing) problems in input text. That information may include the line and character offset in the entity being parsed, the entity's URL, and any public identifier associated with the entity. When used to report application-level errors, any exception caused by problematic data can be encapsulated, and associated with such *Locator* information to help pinpoint problematic input data. It's safe to provide null *Locator* or *Exception* objects.

For more information, refer to the section "SAX2 Exception Classes" as well as the section "Errors and Diagnostics," which are both located in Chapter 2.

```
public class SAXParseException extends SAXException {
    public SAXParseException(String message, Locator where);
    public SAXParseException(String message, Locator where,
        Exception cause);
    public SAXParseException(String message,
        String publicId, String systemId, int line, int column);
    public SAXParseException(String message,
        String publicId, String systemId, int line, int column,
        Exception cause);
    // getters
    public String getPublicId();
    public String getSystemId();
    public int getLineNumber();
    public int getColumnNumber();
}
```

The XMLFilter Interface

This interface encapsulates the notion that one *XMLReader* may process the output of another one before delivering it. The *XMLFilterImpl* helper class is substantially more interesting, since it does the real work and can be used in a postprocessing mode as well.

For more information, refer to the section "The XMLFilter Interface" in Chapter 3.

```
public interface XMLFilter extends XMLReader
{
    public void setParent(XMLReader parent);
    public XMLReader getParent();
}
```

The XMLReader Interface

A SAX2 "parser" will normally be packaged as an implementation of this interface. Such a parser often takes XML text as input, though it need not.

Some parsers need a DOM Document as input, and others parse non-XML text and report it as if it were XML, to leverage the SAX event processing model.

For more information, refer to the section "The XMLReader Interface" in Chapter 3. For quick reference to the standard SAX2 feature and property identifiers, refer to the section "XMLReader Feature Flags" and the section "XMLReader Properties," both in Chapter 3.

```
public interface XMLReader
{
    // getters
    public ContentHandler getContentHandler();
    public DTDHandler getDTDHandler();
    public EntityResolver getEntityResolver();
    public ErrorHandler getErrorHandler();
    public boolean getFeature(String uri)
        throws SAXNotRecognizedException,
        SAXNotSupportedException;
    public Object getProperty(String uri)
        throws SAXNotRecognizedException,
        SAXNotSupportedException;
    // setters
    public void setContentHandler(ContentHandler contentHandelr);
    public void setDTDHandler(DTDHandler dtdHandler);
    public void setEntityResolver(EntityResolver resolver);
    public void setErrorHandler(ErrorHandler errHandler);
    public void setFeature(String uri, boolean value)
        throws SAXNotRecognizedException,
        SAXNotSupportedException;
    public void setProperty(String uri, Object value)
        throws SAXNotRecognizedException,
        SAXNotSupportedException;
    // parsing
    public void parse(InputSource in)
        throws java.io.IOException, SAXException;
    public void parse(String uri)
        throws java.io.IOException, SAXException;
}
```

The org.xml.sax.helpers Package

The *org.xml.sax.helpers* package holds support classes, including vendor-neutral bootstrapping support and some support for the original SAX1 APIs. These classes are in a sense optional but are provided by all widely available implementations. They're also required for conformance with Sun's JAXP API.

The AttributeListImpl Interface

This SAX1 class is not used in SAX2; the *AttributesImpl* class is used instead.

For more information, refer to the section "SAX1 Support" in Chapter 5.

```
public class AttributeListImpl implements AttributeList {
    public AttributeListImpl();
    public AttributeListImpl(AttributeList original);
    // AttributeList (accessors only)
    public int getLength();
    public String getName(int index);
    public String getType(int index);
    public String getValue(int index);
    public String getType(String qName);
    public String getValue(String qName);
    // mutators
    public void setAttributeList(AttributeList original);
    public void addAttribute(String qName, String type, String value);
    public void removeAttribute(String qName);
    public void clear();
}
```

The AttributesImpl Class

This class can be a convenient way to snapshot attribute information using the copy constructor. Since the attributes provided by an event producer are only valid during the particular ContentHandler.startElement() call that provides them, applications may need such snapshots. The class also supports construction of arbitrary attribute sets for filtering or event production.

For more information, refer to the section "The AttributesImpl Class" in Chapter 5.

```
public class AttributesImpl implements Attributes {
    public AttributesImpl();
    public AttributesImpl(Attributes original);
    // Attributes (accessors only)
    public int getLength();
    public String getURI(int index);
    public String getLocalName(int index);
    public String getQName(int index);
    public String getType(int index);
    public String getValue(int index);
    public int getIndex(String uri, String localName);
    public int getIndex(String qName);
    public String getType(String uri, String localName);
    public String getType(String qName);
```

```
            public String getValue(String uri, String localName);
            public String getValue(String qName);
            // setters
            public void setLocalName(int index, String localName);
            public void setQName(int index, String qName);
            public void setType(int index, String type);
            public void setURI(int index, String uri);
            public void setValue(int index, String value);
            // mutators
            public void addAttribute(String uri, String localName,
                String qName,
                    String type, String value);
            public void clear();
            public void removeAttribute(int index);
            public void setAttribute(int index, String, String,
                String, String, String);
            public void setAttributes(Attributes original);
    }
```

The DefaultHandler Class

This class provides stub implementations of all the standard SAX2 handlers, including *ErrorHandler*, and the *EntityResolver*. Those stub implementations do nothing, except that `ErrorHandler.fatalError()` throws its argument. Extension handler callbacks are not supported; if you need *DeclHandler* or *LexicalHandler* stubs you'll need to provide them yourself (perhaps by subclassing).

For more information, refer to the section "The DefaultHandler Class" in Chapter 2.

```
    public class DefaultHandler
        implements EntityResolver, DTDHandler, ContentHandler,
            ErrorHandler
    {
        public DefaultHandler();
        // ContentHandler
        public void setDocumentLocator(Locator locator);
        public void startDocument() throws SAXException;
        public void endDocument() throws SAXException;
        public void startElement(String uri, String localName,
                String qName, Attributes)
            throws SAXException;
        public void endElement(String uri, String localName,
            String qName)
            throws SAXException;
        public void characters(char buf[], int offset, int length)
            throws SAXException;
        public void ignorableWhitespace(char buf[], int offset,
            int length)
```

```
            throws SAXException;
    public void processingInstruction(String target, String data)
            throws SAXException;
    public void startPrefixMapping(String prefix, String uri)
            throws SAXException;
    public void endPrefixMapping(String prefix) throws
            SAXException;
    public void skippedEntity(String name) throws SAXException;
    // DTDHandler
    public void notationDecl(String notationName,
            String publicId, String systemId)
        throws SAXException;
    public void unparsedEntityDecl(String entityName,
            String publicId, String systemId, String
        notationName)
        throws SAXException;
    // EntityResolver
    public InputSource resolveEntity(String publicId,
        String publicId);
        throws SAXException;
    // ErrorHandler
    public void error(SAXParseException x) throws SAXException;
    public void fatalError(SAXParseException x) throws
        SAXException;
    public void warning(SAXParseException x) throws SAXException;
}
```

The LocatorImpl Class

This class can provide a convenient way to snapshot locator information. Since the locator provided by an event producer may report different values during each event callback, applications may need such snapshots.

For more information, refer to the section "The LocatorImpl Class" in Chapter 5.

```
    public class LocatorImpl implements Locator {
        public LocatorImpl();
        public LocatorImpl(Locator);
        // Locator
        public String getPublicId();
        public String getSystemId();
        public int getLineNumber();
        public int getColumnNumber();
        // setters
        public void setPublicId(String publicId);
        public void setSystemId(String systemId);
        public void setLineNumber(int line);
        public void setColumnNumber(int column);
    }
```

The NamespaceSupport Class

This class helps implement stacks of XML namespace context data. It's mostly useful for applications that need to handle element or attribute names within document content (including attributes) or for parser writers.

For more information, refer to the section "The NamespaceSupport Class" in Chapter 5.

```
public class NamespaceSupport {
    // fixed uri for the "xml" prefix
    public static final String XMLNS;
    public NamespaceSupport();
    // manipulate binding stack
    public void reset();
    public void pushContext();
    public void popContext();
    public boolean declarePrefix(String prefix, String uri);
    public String [] processName(String qName, String parts[],
        boolean isAttribute);
    // access currently visible prefix bindings
    public String getURI(String prefix);
    public java.util.Enumeration getPrefixes();
    public String getPrefix(String uri);
    public java.util.Enumeration getPrefixes(String uri);
    public java.util.Enumeration getDeclaredPrefixes();
}
```

The ParserAdapter Class

This class is used to convert SAX1 *Parser* objects into *XMLReader* objects by converting SAX1 event callbacks into SAX2 callbacks. It uses the *NamespaceSupport* class internally to track namespaces so it can report them for elements and attributes, as required by SAX2. If you need to make a SAX1 parser report handling of validation or external entities though feature flags, you can subclass *ParserAdapter* and override the appropriate methods.

For more information, refer to the section "SAX1 Support" in Chapter 5.

```
public class ParserAdapter implements XMLReader,
        DocumentHandler {
    public helpers.ParserAdapter() throws SAXException;
    public helpers.ParserAdapter(Parser sax1);
    // XMLReader getters
    public boolean getFeature(String uri)
        throws SAXNotRecognizedException,
        SAXNotSupportedException;
    public ContentHandler getContentHandler();
```

```
            public DTDHandler getDTDHandler();
            public EntityResolver getEntityResolver();
            public ErrorHandler getErrorHandler();
            public Object getProperty(String uri)
                throws SAXNotRecognizedException,
                SAXNotSupportedException;
        // XMLReader setters
            public void setContentHandler(ContentHandler contentHandler);
            public void setDTDHandler(DTDHandler dtdHandler);
            public void setEntityResolver(EntityResolver resolver);
            public void setErrorHandler(ErrorHandler errHandler);
            public void setFeature(String uri, boolean value)
                throws SAXNotRecognizedException,
                SAXNotSupportedException;
            public void setProperty(String uri, Object value)
                throws SAXNotRecognizedException,
                SAXNotSupportedException;
        // XMLReader parsing
            public void parse(String uri) throws java.io.IOException,
                SAXException;
            public void parse(InputSource in) throws java.io.IOException,
                SAXException;
        // DocumentHandler (internals -- don't use)
            public void setDocumentLocator(Locator locator);
            public void startDocument() throws SAXException;
            public void endDocument() throws SAXException;
            public void startElement(String qName, AttributeList
                attributes)
                throws SAXException;
            public void endElement(String qName) throws SAXException;
            public void characters(char buf[], int offset, int length)
                throws SAXException;
            public void ignorableWhitespace(char buf[], int offset,
                int length)
                throws SAXException;
            public void processingInstruction(String target,
                String data)
                throws SAXException;
        }
```

The ParserFactory Class

This SAX1 interface is not used in SAX2; the *XMLReaderFactory* is used instead. The *org.xml.sax.parser* system property was used to configure the default SAX1 parser.

For more information, refer to the section "SAX1 Support" in Chapter 5.

```
            public class ParserFactory {
                public static Parser makeParser()
                    throws ClassNotFoundException, IllegalAccessException,
                        InstantiationException, NullPointerException,
```

```
        ClassCastException;
    public static Parser makeParser(String classname)
        throws ClassNotFoundException, IllegalAccessException,
            InstantiationException, ClassCastException;
}
```

The XMLFilterImpl Class

This class implements all the standard SAX2 events received from its parent *XMLReader* by passing them on to the handlers (or EntityResolver) registered with it. It only supports filtering core events, because it ignores the two extension handlers for declaration and lexical events.

This means you can use it in two modes. First, it can be a base class for simple consumer pipelines, unless you need information that's provided using extension handlers. Second, you can package a filter with a parser, so it can produce events like an *XMLReader* that just happens to do a bit of extra work (such as cleaning up input data).

For more information, refer to the section "The XMLFilterImpl Class" in Chapter 4.

```
public class XMLFilterImpl
    implements XMLFilter, EntityResolver, DTDHandler,
        ContentHandler, ErrorHandler
{
    public XMLFilterImpl();
    public XMLFilterImpl(XMLReader parent);
    public void setParent(XMLReader parent);
    // EntityResolver
    public InputSource resolveEntity(String publicId,
            String publicId);
        throws SAXException;
    // DTDHandler
    public void notationDecl(String notationName,
            String publicId, String systemId)
        throws SAXException;
    public void unparsedEntityDecl(String entityName,
            String publicId, String systemId,
        String notationName)
        throws SAXException;
    // ContentHandler
    public void setDocumentLocator(Locator locator);
    public void startDocument() throws SAXException;
    public void endDocument() throws SAXException;
    public void startElement(String uri, String localName,
```

Appendix A: SAX2 API Summary

```
            String qName,
                    Attributes attributes)
                throws SAXException;
            public void endElement(String uri, String localName,
                String qName)
                throws SAXException;
            public void characters(char buf[], int offset, int length)
                throws SAXException;
            public void ignorableWhitespace(char buf[], int offset,
                int length)
                throws SAXException;
            public void processingInstruction(String target, String data)
                throws SAXException;
            public void startPrefixMapping(String prefix, String uri)
                throws SAXException;
            public void endPrefixMapping(String prefix) throws
                SAXException;
            public void skippedEntity(String name) throws SAXException;
            // ErrorHandler
            public void error(SAXParseException x) throws SAXException;
            public void fatalError(SAXParseException x) throws
                SAXException;
            public void warning(SAXParseException x) throws SAXException;
            // XMLFilter
            public XMLReader getParent();
            // XMLReader
            public ContentHandler getContentHandler();
            public DTDHandler getDTDHandler();
            public EntityResolver getEntityResolver();
            public ErrorHandler getErrorHandler();
            public boolean getFeature(String uri)
                throws SAXNotRecognizedException,
                SAXNotSupportedException;
            public Object getProperty(String uri)
                throws SAXNotRecognizedException,
                SAXNotSupportedException;
            public void setContentHandler(ContentHandler contentHandler);
            public void setDTDHandler(DTDHandler dtdHandler);
            public void setEntityResolver(EntityResolver resolver);
            public void setErrorHandler(ErrorHandler errHandler);
            public void setFeature(String uri, boolean value)
                throws SAXNotRecognizedException,
                SAXNotSupportedException;
            public void setProperty(String uri, Object value)
                throws SAXNotRecognizedException,
                SAXNotSupportedException;
            public void parse(InputSource in)
                throws java.io.IOException, SAXException;
            public void parse(String uri)
                throws java.io.IOException, SAXException;
        }
```

The XMLReaderAdapter Class

This class is used to convert SAX2 *XMLReader* objects into *Parser* objects by converting SAX2 event callbacks into SAX1 callbacks.

For more information, refer to the section "SAX1 Support" in Chapter 5.

```
public class XMLReaderAdapter implements Parser,
        ContentHandler {
    public XMLReaderAdapter() throws SAXException;
    public XMLReaderAdapter(XMLReader reader);
    // Parser
    public void setLocale(java.util.Locale locale) throws
        SAXException;
    public void setEntityResolver(EntityResolver resolver);
    public void setDTDHandler(DTDHandler dtdHandler);
    public void setDocumentHandler(DocumentHandler docHandler);
    public void setErrorHandler(ErrorHandler errHandler);
    public void parse(String uri) throws java.io.IOException,
        SAXException;
    public void parse(InputSource in) throws java.io.IOException,
        SAXException;
    // ContentHandler (internals -- don't use)
    public void setDocumentLocator(Locator locator);
    public void startDocument() throws SAXException;
    public void endDocument() throws SAXException;
    public void startElement(String uri, String localName,
        String qName,
            Attributes attributes)
        throws SAXException;
    public void endElement(String uri, String localName,
        String qName)
        throws SAXException;
    public void characters(char buf[], int offset, int length)
        throws SAXException;
    public void ignorableWhitespace(char buf[], int offset,
        int length)
        throws SAXException;
    public void processingInstruction(String target,
        String data)
        throws SAXException;
    public void startPrefixMapping(String prefix, String uri);
    public void endPrefixMapping(String prefix);
    public void skippedEntity(String name) throws SAXException;
}
```

The XMLReaderFactory Class

This factory is the parser-independent bootstrapping API for SAX2. The reference implementation uses the *org.xml.sax.driver* system property (or *META-INF/services/org.xml.sax.driver* resource in the class path) to determine the package-qualified name of the environment's default implementation for the no-parameters call. Most implementations maintain that behavior, but some resource-constrained environments can use simpler policies with less configurability.

For more information, refer to the section "The XMLReaderFactory Class" in Chapter 3.

```
public final class XMLReaderFactory {
    public static XMLReader createXMLReader() throws
        SAXException;
    public static XMLReader createXMLReader(String classname)
        throws SAXException;
}
```

The org.xml.sax.ext Package

The *org.xml.sax.ext* package holds extension interfaces that not all SAX2 parsers are expected to implement. These classes are in a sense optional but are provided by all widely used implementations and are required by Sun's JAXP API.

Unlike the handlers in the SAX core, these handlers do not have type-safe routines to bind them to *XMLReader* objects. They are identified using URIs, and bindings are accessed using the getProperty() and setProperty() methods.

The DeclHandler class

This is the primary way SAX2 exposes typing constraints from an XML Document Type Declaration. It also reports entity declarations.

For more information, refer to the section "The DeclHandler Interface" in Chapter 4.

```
public interface DeclHandler
{
    // data typing
    public void attributeDecl(String element, String string
        attribute,
            String type, String mode, String defaultValue )
        throws SAXException;
    public void elementDecl(String name, String model) throws
        SAXException;
    // entity info
    public void externalEntityDecl(String name,
            String publicId, String systemId)
        throws SAXException;
    public void internalEntityDecl(String name, String value)
        throws SAXException;
}
```

The LexicalHandler Interface

Many parsers expose certain data even though it is, for most purposes, not part of the information that an XML document intends to convey to applications. This interface exposes some such data.

For more information, refer to the section "The LexicalHandler Interface" in Chapter 4.

```
public interface LexicalHandler
{
    public void startDTD(String root, String publicId,
        String systemId)
        throws SAXException;
    public void endDTD() throws SAXException;
    public void startEntity(String name) throws SAXException;
    public void endEntity(String name) throws SAXException;
    public void startCDATA() throws SAXException;
    public void endCDATA() throws SAXException;
    public void comment(char buf[], int offset, int length)
        throws SAXException;
}
```

B

SAX2 and the XML Infoset

This appendix shows how the various parts of the XML Infoset are made available through the SAX2 event consumer APIs. Think of it as a structural index for concepts in SAX2, or for the underlying XML information structure. Use it when you're trying to develop SAX2-based software that needs access to particular data. It can also be viewed as an Infoset conformance statement for SAX2; it will help you to understand what parts of the XML Infoset aren't supported by SAX2 and to see where SAX2 lets you access information beyond what the Infoset addresses. The Infoset is not a data structure; what's important is that the information be provided, not randomly accessible.

The presentation here is the same as used in the Infoset specification itself; the structure and order are identical. *Information items* are similar to object types, and each is presented in its own section. Information items consist of sets of named *[properties]*, each of which is presented in a table. Properties can have one or more values, sometimes ordered, which are provided in SAX2 using consumer callbacks. You should be able to make sense of this without reading the infoset specification if you know XML, but you'll need it to understand some details.

As of this writing, the XML Infoset (*http://www.w3.org/TR/xml-infoset/*) has recently been finalized. This appendix was written using the 24 October 2001 "Recommendation," which omits almost all declarations found in the DTD. Some other W3C specifications use related data models, like the XPath Data Model. The W3C approach to XML Schemas augments this core Infoset with additional data-typing information items, defining the *Post-Schema-Validation Infoset* (PSVI) items and properties associated with schema-valid XML text. Most of those PSVI properties relate to data-typing models.

Event Producer Issues

Although the focus of this appendix is on how SAX2 event consumers see Infoset data, you may also need to pay attention to some producer-side issues beyond ensuring that the event stream itself is legal (and perhaps valid). As the Infoset specification puts it, "synthetic" infosets might have inconsistencies that real ones (from XML documents) don't. If you produce a synthetic infoset, by writing SAX events directly rather than by using a parser, make sure the event stream is properly constructed.

As noted earlier, you should make sure you always provide the document URI when you invoke XMLReader.parse(). Not only is this needed to correctly absolutize relative URIs found in the document's DTD (for notations and all types of external entities) and to provide accurate diagnostics, but it is essential for computing [base URI] properties in the document entity.

The *namespace-prefixes* feature on *XMLReader* instances has a problematic default; set its value to *true* unless you're comfortable with parsers hiding [namespace attributes] and [prefix] properties. (In this book, this is called *mixed mode* namespace support.) SAX2 parsers aren't required to support setting this feature value to *true*, but most do. If your parser doesn't support this, you can re-create prefixes and declarations, but they normally won't correspond to the original versions. This appendix assumes you kept the default setting (true) for the *namespaces* feature flag.

Some SAX2 *XMLReader* implementations may not produce all of this information. Most of today's widely used SAX2 parsers are fully featured, so in practice this won't be a common problem. However, information provided through the optional SAX2 extension callbacks *DeclHandler* or *LexicalHandler* might not be available. Similarly, reporting of [base URI] ingredients through a *Locator* is also optional.

The SAX2 *ErrorHandler* exposes some data that is not addressed by the XML Infoset: validity and well-formedness errors. Exposing such information is required for parser conformance to the XML 1.0 specification.

Event Consumer Issues

The primary Infoset concern for SAX2 event consumers is to understand how the stream of events represents the information structures used in the Infoset. Applications need to track some state if they need access to some of those structures or random access to anything. It's typical to track only a few items, and ignore the rest as being incidental background noise. Streaming processing discards items as soon as possible.

You really shouldn't care, but since the *String* datatype can't handle more than two gigabytes of data, and strings are used to pass certain document data to applications, there's a chance that some documents could cause trouble by overflowing that limit. If you encounter such a document, consult a pathologist. There really isn't much you can do about this.

Structural Issues

The [children] properties are arbitrarily sized, ordered sequences of information items, which are presented in document order by SAX2 event callbacks. Most other information items are not ordered, such as [notations], [unparsed entities], and [attributes] properties. Only [children] properties would need to be stored in order-preserving data structures.

While most information items are provided through a single callback, some of the more complex ones involve matched, and (except in one case) cleanly nested, pairs of calls to start() and end() the item. Such items include the Document itself, its Document Type Declaration, Elements, and Namespace Information. To track those items, applications implement some kind of context stack tracking.

The [parent] properties of some information items are implicitly encoded through such SAX2 nested event reports. Except for items that can be direct children of the Document or Document Type Information Items, applications often push stack entries when startElement() is called and pop them when endElement() is called.

The children of Document and Document Type Information Items have curious restrictions: they don't always match the actual text structure. For example, information items for notations and unparsed entities are found in the Document Information Item, but they're textually part of the Document Type; and comments are stripped out of DTDs. You can use more natural structures in your applications if the descriptive Infoset structure seems awkward.

Other complex information items are implicitly decoded from DTD declarations. To track such items, applications must save declarations during DTD processing, to ensure that they can be correlated with information in the body of a document. Examples of such items include [notation] properties for Unparsed Entities and processing instructions, most properties for Unexpanded Entity References, and [references] properties of attributes.

Base URIs, xml:base, and Locator Data

Some information items have a [base URI] property that is computed according to `xml:base` rules. Except for two cases, these rules amount to using `Locator.getSystemId()` to find the absolute base URI; the producer needs to provide this information. SAX2 effectively augments *every* information item with this information, as well as line and column location within such entities. (However, applications can cause this information to be lost if they provide *InputSource* objects without including those base URIs as the system IDs.)

The two exceptional cases are for Elements and for processing instructions within the document element. In these instances, the computation is complex because `xml:base` attributes can play a role; it is demonstrated in Example 5-1. Consumers must be able to invoke `Locator.getSystemId()` to get the entity's URI in `LexicalHandler.startEntity()` when the entity is shown to be external using `DeclHandler.externalEntityDecl()`. And they must also maintain a stack of URIs, augmenting it with `xml:base` values.

Application code should use *Locator* information to generate meaningful diagnostics. However, conforming applications will use the URI computed with `xml:base` when absolutizing relative URIs found in attribute values, character data, processing instructions, or (primarily for HTML legacy data models) comments. Except for the `startDTD()` call, all system identifiers reported through SAX are delivered as absolute URIs. An upcoming extension feature flag will probably let that behavior be changed, so you can choose whether the parser or the application absolutizes the URIs. Meanwhile, you should be aware that some SAX parsers have bugs in how they report such identifiers.

Document Information Item

The *Document Information Item* is the root of the information found in an XML document. There is only one such root item.

This information item begins with the `ContentHandler.startDocument()` call and ends with the `ContentHandler.endDocument()` call. Many SAX2 event calls are used to construct its children or constituents.

Property	Callbacks	Explanation
[children]		See the sections for each type of Information Item: Document Type Declaration (one, if present), Element (one), processing instruction (possibly many), Comment (possibly many).
[document element]		This is the element in the [children] property.
[notations]		See the section on Notation Information Items. (Unordered.)
[unparsed entities]		See the section on Unparsed Entity Information Items. (Unordered.)
[base URI]	`Locator.getSystemId()`, or `XMLReader.parse()`	*Locator* may be used during the `startDocument()` callback (and earlier callbacks, unless they were made in the context of an external parameter entity). Alternatively, for any parsers that don't provide a Locator, applications using an *XMLReader* are responsible for providing this information (if it exists) to the `parse()` method. This is passed directly as the string parameter or indirectly as the *systemId* property of an *InputSource*.

Property	Callbacks	Explanation
[character encoding scheme]	unavailable; or `InputSource.getEncoding()`	Normally this property is unavailable; it won't affect the interpretation of character data in Java. However, applications will in rare cases provide this to the parser when they call `XMLReader.parse(InputSource)` to start parsing. It's likely that an upcoming extension API will provide this information.
[standalone]	`XMLReader.getFeature()`	It's likely that an upcoming extension API will provide this information using an *is-standalone* feature flag.
[version]	unavailable	You can probably assume the value of this property is "1.0" for now. It's likely that an upcoming extension API will provide this information.
[all declarations processed]	`ContentHandler.skippedEntity()`: `LexicalHandler.endDTD()`	When `endDTD()` is invoked, the value of this property is known. If no external parameter entities are reported as skipped, then the value is *true*. If the parser doesn't support the lexical handler, then the later call to `startElement()` may be used instead of `endDTD()`.

Because text in Java is always accessed using UTF-16 character strings or arrays, most applications won't need to worry about encoding issues; the SAX2 parser handles that. However, there are cases when encoding may matter:

Input normalization

Some recent XML standards require that text be normalized. For example, XML Canonicalization (as used in digital signature applications) requires the use of Unicode Normalization Form C; some other

W3C specifications have the same requirement. Text originally represented in UTF-8 or UTF-16 might need further normalization to remove some deprecated character codes that can be represented using those encodings.

Such encoding data is required on a per-entity basis, not a per-document basis as implied by the Infoset specification. And for internal entity expansions or defaulted attributes, you'll need to normalize if the encoding associated with the original definition supported denormalized text.

Output encoding

When using an output encoding that is not based on the Unicode character set, you may not be able to represent XML names that use particular characters. For example, ASCII cannot handle element or attribute names using accented characters (used in Europe and Latin America) or using ideographic characters (used in Asia).

The preferred encoding solution is to always use UTF-8 or UTF-16 when outputting XML, so that such problems cannot occur and so that all XML processors can work with such output. Similar logic applies to display systems like window systems: prefer font rendering systems that use Unicode over those tied to some specific encoding.

Element Information Items

An *Element Information Item* holds the most frequently needed data in an XML document. There is one top-level element, associated with the Document Information Item, and all but a handful of information items are its descendants.

This information item starts with a `ContentHandler.startElement()` call, and ends with a `ContentHandler.endElement()` call.

Property	Callbacks	Explanation
[namespace name]	ContentHandler.start-Element(), *namespaceURI* parameter	
[local name]	ContentHandler.start-Element(), *localName* parameter	

Property	Callbacks	Explanation
[prefix]	`ContentHandler.start-Element()`, *qName* parameter (when available)	The QName (namespace-prefixed name) includes any prefix available; for example, a QName `xhtml:a` uses the prefix *xhtml*.
[children]		See the sections for each type of information item: Element, Processing Instruction, Unexpanded Entity Ref, Character, Comment.
[attributes]	`ContentHandler.start-Element()`, *attributes* parameter, `DeclHandler.attributeDecl()`	When the [namespace attributes] property value is accessible, both groups of attributes are intermixed. Values that are `#IMPLIED`, but not specified in the document text, are only visible through the `attributeDecl()` callback. If you need to know about such attributes, record them during DTD processing.
[namespace attributes]	`ContentHandler.start-Element()`, *attributes* parameter (when available)	If the *namespace-prefixes* feature flag is *true*, these attributes are mixed with the [attributes] property. They're the ones with QName values of `xmlns`, or starting with `xmlns:`.[a] Otherwise, this data is unavailable.
[in-scope namespaces]		See the section on Namespace Information Items.
[base URI]	computed using `xml:base`	In the absence of `xml:base` attributes, this is normally the value that *Locator.getSystemId()* exposes during the `startElement()` callback.
[parent]		Applications must keep track of this information item if it is needed.

[a] Manually associate these with the namespace URI *http://www.w3.org/2000/xmlns/*.

Attribute Information Items

The Attribute Information Items are the contents of the [attributes] property in the element information item. Although the attributes are presented in an order through the *Attributes* class, there is no expectation that this order reflects an order in the document or its DTD.

Property	Callbacks	Explanation
[namespace name] [local name] [prefix]	Attributes.getURI() Attributes.getLocalName() Attributes.getQName() (when available)	The QName (namespace-prefixed name) includes any prefix available; for example, a QName xhtml:href uses the prefix *xhtml*.
[normalized value]	Attributes.getValue()	If you're generating a stream of Infoset data programmatically, don't forget to normalize these values correctly. The XML specification explains how to normalize this text; it mostly translates whitespace (but not character references) into space characters and eliminates unneeded spaces for values that aren't CDATA.
[specified]	unavailable	SAX2 does not distinguish between attribute values that were specified in document text and those that have been defaulted from a DTD. It's likely that an upcoming extension API will provide this information.

Property	Callbacks	Explanation
[attribute type]	`Attributes.getType()`, `DeclHandler.attribute-Decl()`	For most types of attribute, `getType()` gives all the type data needed, but you may want to distinguish types that are actual CDATA versus (invalid) ones that just look like CDATA because the attribute was not declared.
		Attribute values that are constrained to an enumerated set are reported with special syntax in `attributeDecl()` callbacks. Enumerations use a parenthesized syntax, like `(true|false)`, to enumerate all possibilities. NOTATION enumerations prepend the string `"NOTATION "` (with a space) to that syntax.
[references]		For NOTATION type values, see the section on Notation Information Items. For ENTITY or ENTITIES type values, see the section on Unparsed Entity Information Items. For IDREF or IDREFS type values, applications must track attributes by using the [attribute type] IDs reported as keys to application-specific representations of elements, and they must be ready to handle forward references. (ENTITIES and IDREFS values must be tokenized by the application.)
[owner element]		Attributes are associated with the element signified by the `startElement()` call providing the *Attributes* object.

Note that DOM extends this information item to expose entities (expanded or not) within attribute values. That is not widely believed to be a useful feature. Since SAX doesn't extend the Infoset in that way, you can't implement that part of DOM using pure SAX.

Processing Instruction Information Items

Processing instructions (PIs) are used within XML documents to capture information that doesn't necessarily fit into the nested structure found elsewhere. Such data doesn't need to relate to processing tasks, although that's one historical use for such constructs.

Property	Callbacks	Explanation
[target]	`ContentHandler.process-ingInstruction()`, *target* parameter	
[content]	`ContentHandler.process-ingInstruction()`, *target* parameter	
[base URI]	computed using `xml:base`	In the absence of `xml:base` attributes, this property is normally the value that *Locator.getSystemId()* exposes during the `processingInstruction()` callback.
[notation]		See the section on Notation Information Items. Tracking notations is the responsibility of applications.
[parent]		When `startElement()` is invoked with no matching `endElement()`, the parent is the current element. Between calls to `LexicalHandler.startDTD()` and `LexicalHandler.endDTD()`, the parent is the Document Type Declaration. Otherwise, the document itself is the parent.

Some applications use a convention that PI target names are matched against notation declarations, and the notations' public (or system) IDs are used to deduce the meaning behind a given PI. For example, such an ID might indicate a particular tool to use on receipt of a document (preferably redirecting through a table to facilitate useful security constraints). This is purely a convention, but it's recognized by the XML specification. It is not an XML error if such notations are undeclared. Moreover, PIs can precede notation declarations in the DTD.

If the SAX2 implementation doesn't support the *LexicalHandler*, then there is no way to determing whether processing instructions are part of the DTD or a part of another section of the document prologue.

Unexpanded Entity Reference Information Items

For any nonvalidating XML parser that doesn't read all external entities—possibly because it was configured not to do so or because it didn't choose to implement that feature—the XML specification says you need to be able to indicate when an entity that would normally be parsed wasn't actually processed. These unexpanded entities are not the same as "unparsed" entities, although neither kind of entity gets parsed.

The XML Infoset describes some information that can be made available in one of those cases: when the entity was an external general entity. For external parameter entities, the Infoset is silent beyond defining a document information item property to expose whether all declarations have been processed; no declarations are exposed.

Property	Callbacks	Explanation
[name]	Content.skippedEntity(), *name* parameter	SAX2 makes this callback for all entities that have been skipped, including parameter and internal entities.
[system identifier]	DeclHandler.externalEntityDecl(), *systemId* parameter	If [all declarations processed] is *false*, this information may be unavailable. Otherwise, the application must have recorded this information for later use. Note that SAX parsers absolutize this property against the appropriate base URI before reporting it. However, some parsers have a bug here, and don't absolutize this URI.
[public identifier]	DeclHandler.externalEntityDecl(), *publicId* parameter	If [all declarations processed] is *false*, this information may be unavailable. Otherwise, the application must have recorded this information for later use.

Property	Callbacks	Explanation
[declaration base URI]	`Locator.getSystemId()`	If [all declarations processed] is *false*, this information may be unavailable. Otherwise, the application must have recorded this information for later use, when this entity was reported through a `DeclHandler.external-EntityDecl()` callback. (`xml:base` does not apply.)
[parent]		Applications must keep track of this information item if it is needed.

SAX2 effectively defines new types of information items for internal and external entities. (So does DOM Level 1.) The XML Infoset doesn't expose such entities except for this one case (for external entities), but applications may use those extension information items for other purposes if appropriate.

Character Information Items

Along with element and attribute information items, characters are one of the core types of information used by XML applications. SAX2 reports characters in groups, rather than one at a time.

Property	Callbacks	Explanation
[character code]	`ContentHandler.characters()`, `ContentHandler.ignorable-Whitespace()`	These calls provide one or more characters in the UTF-16 encoding. Normally, each Java char is a single [character code], but surrogate pairs are used to encode characters from the "Astral Planes," which don't fit into 16 bits. (No whitespace characters need surrogate pairs.)

Property	Callbacks	Explanation
[element content whitespace]		When known, this Boolean property is encoded by using the `ignorableWhitespace()` callback instead of `characters()`. Most SAX parsers report this property even when they aren't validating, though that's not required. (If any external parameter entities are skipped, it is not possible to reliably provide this information.)
[parent]		Applications must keep track of this information item if it is needed.

SAX2 permits reporting of a character property that the XML Infoset doesn't address: whether the characters are in a CDATA section. (DOM requires this information.) Such section boundaries are reported using methods in the *LexicalHandler* class.

Comment Information Items

Comments are intended for human consumption; processing instructions are reserved for application data. The main curiosity here is that the Infoset doesn't believe in comments within DTDs, perhaps on the grounds that they'd need to be associated with the declarations they describe. (Some DTD documentation tools rely on magic comment syntax, much like *javadoc*.)

Property	Callbacks	Explanation
[content]	`LexicalHandler.comment()`	The characters identified in this callback are the contents of the comment.
[parent]		When `startElement()` is invoked with no matching `endElement()`, the parent is the current element. The Infoset ignores comments reported between calls to `LexicalHandler.startDTD()` and `LexicalHandler.endDTD()`. Otherwise, the document itself is the parent.

Some legacy applications use comments to represent the sort of information that processing instructions were designed to hold; an example is wrapping of CSS rendering hints in HTML comments.

Document Type Declaration Information Item

This is a curious item in the Infoset, because it doesn't expose all the DTD information. In particular, it doesn't include any declarations (including the expected root element name) or comments in DTDs.

This information item starts with a `LexicalHandler.startDTD()` call and ends with a `LexicalHandler.endDTD()` call.

Property	Callbacks	Explanation
[system identifier]	`LexicalHandler.startDTD()`, `systemId` parameter	If the DTD includes an external subset, this is its system identifier. Note that this URI is not absolutized.
[public identifier]	`LexicalHandler.startDTD()`, `publicId` parameter	External subsets are not required to have public identifiers. When provided, this value is normalized.
[children]		See the section on Processing Instruction Information Items. Comments within DTDs are not part of the Infoset, and the few declarations that are included (notations and unparsed entities) are separated from the DTD.
[parent]		This is the Document Information Item.

SAX2 exposes more information than the Infoset describes, though somewhat less than XML allows. Comments may be reported using the *LexicalHandler*. Element and attribute declarations, as well as external and internal entity declarations, may be reported using the *DeclHandler*.

Unparsed Entity Information Items

When unparsed entities are used, these information items are normally saved by applications during DTD processing (keyed by entity name) and then accessed on demand. Unparsed entities are used only with attribute values of type ENTITY or ENTITIES.

Property	Callbacks	Explanation
[name]	`DTDHandler.unparsedEntityDecl()`, *name* parameter	
[system identifier]	`DTDHandler.unparsedEntityDecl()`, *systemId* parameter	This ID should be absolutized by the parser. However, some parsers have a bug here and don't absolutize this URI.
[public identifier]	`DTDHandler.unparsedEntityDecl()`, *publicId* parameter	Unparsed entities are not required to have public identifiers. When provided, this value is normalized.
[declaration base URI]	`Locator.getSystemId()`	If a SAX parser provides a *Locator*, it may be used to determine the current base URI during parser callbacks. (`xml:base` does not apply.)
[notation name]	`DTDHandler.unparsedEntityDecl()`, *notationName* parameter	
[notation]		See the section on Notation Information Items. Locating notations is the responsibility of applications. It's best not to try accessing this property until all declarations have been processed.

Notation Information Items

When notations are used, these information items are normally saved by applications during DTD processing (keyed by notation name) and then accessed on demand. Notations are used with NOTATION attributes (at most one per element) or with unparsed entities, and perhaps with processing instruction target names.

Property	Callbacks	Explanation
[name]	`DTDHandler.notationDecl()`, *name* parameter	
[system identifier]	`DTDHandler.notationDecl()`, *systemId* parameter	Notations are not required to have system identifiers if they have a public identifier. This ID should be absolutized by the parser. However, some parsers have a bug here and don't absolutize this URI—although, because of an issue with early versions of the SAX1 and SAX2 specifications, some parsers might absolutize such URIs.
[public identifier]	`DTDHandler.notationDecl()`, *publicId* parameter	Notations are not required to have public identifiers if they have a system identifier. When provided, this value is normalized.
[declaration base URI]	`Locator.getSystemId()`	If a SAX event producer provides a *Locator*, it can be used to determine the current base URI during parser callbacks. (`xml:base` does not apply.)

Namespace Information Items

These information items expose namespace identifiers and the prefixes currently used to associate element or attribute names with those identifiers. With SAX2, applications that track these prefixes need to use a stack to handle the lexical scoping rules: in the context of one element and its children, a prefix may indicate a different namespace than in parent elements because of a locally scoped redefinition. You can use the *NamespaceSupport* helper class to manage this stack or write something of your own.

These information items start with a `ContentHandler.startPrefixMapping()` call and end with a `ContentHandler.endPrefixMapping()` call. These are the only two start/end calls that SAX2 doesn't require to be cleanly nested. Alternatively, if the *namespaces* feature flag is *false*, this information can be reconstructed from the `xmlns` and `xmlns:*` element attributes.

Property	Callbacks	Explanation
[prefix]	`ContentHandler.startPrefixMapping()`, *prefix* parameter	
[namespace name]	`ContentHandler.startPrefixMapping()`, *uri* parameter	Since these values aren't dereferenced, they are exactly as provided in the XML source text. Don't assume dereferencing such URIs lets you do anything useful.

If the *namespaces* feature is set to *false* (its default is *true*) this information is not made available except implicitly through the element [attributes] property, which will implicitly include all [namespace attributes]. (It is illegal to set *namespaces* to *false* without setting *namespace-prefixes* to *true*.)

Index

Symbols

<!-- ... --> (comments), using
    comment() to report characters
    inside, 112
!= (not equal to), testing string
    equality, 86
== (equal to), testing string
    equality, 86
% (percent sign) in parameter
    entities, 85, 118

Numbers

80/20 rule for application
    requirements, 10

A

addAttribute() function, 141
Ælfred Java parser, 9, 15
    XMLReader feature flags and, 85
always validating parsers, 46
Apache
    Cocoon v2 project, 131
    Software License, 17
    XML project, 17
APIs (Application Programming
    Interfaces), 1-22
    consumers and producers, 24
    high-level, flexibility of, 5
    JAXP (Java API for XML
        Processing), 13
    types of XML, 2
Application Programming Interface
    (see API)
Astral Planes, 110
Attribute Information Items, 209
Attribute interface, 182
attributeDecl() callback function, 116
AttributeList interface, 181
AttributeListImpl interface, 191
attributes, 38-41
    indexes, 40
    namespaces and, 56, 58-63
    naming, 38, 57, 61
Attributes atts element, 42
Attributes method, using DeclHandler
    interface, 116
Attributes.getLocalName()
    function, 209
Attributes.getType() function, 41
Attributes.getURI() function, 209
AttributesImpl class, 42, 98, 140-144,
    191

We'd like to hear your suggestions for improving our indexes. Send email to *index@oreilly.com*.

B

base URIs, 204
BEEP, 168
BLOB (Binary Large Object), storing text as, 75
Blueberry, 21, 110
boolean feature flags, 81, 145
boolean values, 84
Bosak, Jon, 10
Bray, Tim, 9
buf[ ] character array in LexicalHandler class, 112
bytes, in XML text, 6

C

C programming language, 13
C++ programming language, 13
callbacks (event), 103-139
CallFilter class, 173
CallWriter class, 173
Canonicalization (XML), 206
CDATA attribute, 116
CDF (Channel Definition Format), 150
char buf[] character array, 43
Character Information Items, 213
characters( ) function, 34
   ignorableWhitespace( ) parameters and, 106
   startCDATA( )/endCDATA( ) functions and, 114
Chemical Markup Language (CML), 9
Clark, James, 9
class paths, installing SAX 2.0, 18
classes, 26
   exception, 50
CML (Chemical Markup Language), 9
Cocoon pipeline framework, 131
command lines, installing SAX 2.0, 18
Comment Information Items, 214
comment( ) function, 112
comments, 11
   using comment( ) to report characters inside, 112
compound objects, 102
consumers, 24
   SAX-to-DOM, 122
   XMLFilterImpl class and, 132

ContentHandler class, 28, 33, 65, 103-111, 182
   callbacks, 41-43, 103-107
   DOM documents, building, 123
   events, 33-43
   example of elements and text, 34
   internationalization and, 110, 111
   push mode with XSLT and, 135
ContentHandler.characters( ) function, 213
ContentHandler.endElement( ) function, 146
ContentHandler.ignorableWhitespace( ) function, 213
ContentHandler.processingInstruction( ), 211
ContentHandler.skippedEntity( ) function, 206
ContentHandler.startDocument( ) function, 146
ContentHandler.startElement( ) function, 207
   AttributesImpl class and, 140
   parameters for element names, 60
ContentHandler.startPrefixMapping( ) function, 146
Content.skippedEntity( ) function, 212
coupling (loose), 167
Crimson parser, 13, 16, 123
   XMLReader feature flags and, 84
CSV (Comma Separated Values) files, turning into SAX events, 95-98
custom data structures, turning SAX event into, 128

D

data modeling, 99
data parameter for processingInstruction( ) function, 106
data structures, 3
   custom, turning events into, 128
   flexibility, 5
   SAX events, turning into, 122-129
DeclHandler interface, 116-120, 199
   DOM documents, building, 123
   push mode with XSLT and, 135

Index

DeclHandler.attributeDecl() function, 41
DeclHandler.externalEntityDexl() function, 212
DefaultHandler class, 27, 34, 69, 192
deserializing, 122
design tools, affecting runtime, 5
diagnostics, 53-56
Document Information Items, 205-207
Document Object Model (see DOM)
Document Type Declarations (see DTDs)
DocumentHandler interface, 148, 183
DOM (Document Object Model), 3
   building partial, 125-128
   consumer classes, 122-129
   event production and, 92-94
   memory consumption with SAX, 6
DOM trees, 122-129
   constructing with SAX 1.0, 10
   pruning noise data from, 124
   SAX events, turning into, 93
DOM4J, 123
   trees, turning into SAX events, 93
DOS
   filenames, turning into URIs, 75
   XML output, writing, 32
DTD-based validation, 44
DTDHandler interface, 29, 69, 120-122, 184
   DOM documents, building, 123
   push mode with XSLT and, 135
DTDHandler.notationDecl() function, 105, 217
DTDHandler.unparsedEntityDexl() function, 216
DTDs (Document Type Declarations), 20, 115-122
   EntityReslover class, using, 89
   Information Items, 215
   producer-side validation and, 44
   subdocuments, including, 174

E

EBCDIC (Extended Binary Coded Decimal Interchange Code) encodings, 73
elementDecl() function, 118

elements, 34-38
   Information Items, 207
   naming, 57-61
      with namespaces, 58-63
endCDATA() function, 114
endDocument() function, 97, 104
endDTD() function, 113
endElement() function, 37, 42, 66
endEntity() function, 114
endPrefixMapping() function, 64, 66, 86
ENTITIES attribute, 116
   unparsedEntityDecl() and, 121
ENTITY attribute, 116
   unparsedEntityDecl() and, 121
EntityResolver interface, 69, 84, 88-91, 184
   InputSource objects, creating with, 75
EntityResolver objects, 175
enumerated values in attributeDecl(), 116
error handling, 5, 44
   diagnostics and, 53-56
   producer-side validation and, 48, 49
error() method, 52
ErrorHandler class, 28, 51-54, 69, 184
   Locator class and, 108
   producer-side validation, handling errors, 48
ErrorHandler object, 175
ErrorHandler.error() function, 64
event pipelines, 32
event producers, 67-76, 202
   defining custom, 5
   DOM-to-SAX, 92-94
   push modes, 94-100
event streams, producing, 100
EventConsumer interface, 137
events, 103-139
   consumer issues, 203
   CSV files, turning into, 95-98
   custom data structures, turning into, 128
   data structures, turning into, 122-129
   DOM trees, turning into, 93
   objects, turning into, 98
   pipelines, 130

events (continued)
    XMLFilterImpl class and, 132
exception handling, 49-56
    classes, 50
Extended Binary Coded Decimal
        Interchange Code (EBCDIC)
        encodings, 73
Extensible Markup Language (see
        XML)
extensions directory, adding to when
    . installing SAX 2.0, 18
external subsets, 113
externalEntityDecl() callback
        function, 118

F

fatal errors, handling, 5
fatalError() method, 52
feature flags, 44-48
    namespaces, 63-65
    XMLReader class, 84-88
file: (scheme), 46
filenames, 75
filters (pipelines), 130
#FIXED attribute, 117
flags, 44-48
    namespaces, 63-65
    XMLReader class, 84-88
flat file text formats, 95
Formal Public Identifiers (FPIs), 89
    SGML, 119
forward-only event streams, 8
FPIs (Formal Public Identifiers), 89
ftp: (scheme), 46

G

GCC Java (GCJ), 16
GCJ (GNU General Public License), 16
GET request, 169
get*() method, 81
getBaseURI() function, 144
getCause() method, 51
getColumnNumber() function, 108
getDTDHandler() function, 69
getEntityResolver() function, 69
getErrorHandler() function, 69
getException() function, 51
getFeature() function, 69

namespace feature flags, 63
getIndex() function, 39
getLength() function, 40
getLineNumber() function, 108
getLocalName() function, naming
        attributes, 61
getPrefix() function, 147
getProperty() function, 69
getPublicId() function, 108
getQName() function, naming
        attributes, 61
getSystemId() function, 108
getType() function, 39
getURI() function, naming
        attributes, 61
getValue() function, 38
GNU Classpath Extensions project, 15
GNU General Public License (GCJ), 16
GNU pipeline framework, 131
GNUJAXP, 123
gnujaxp.jar file, 16
    XMLWriter and, 31
gnu.xml.pipeline framework, 137-139
gnu.xml.pipeline.CallFilter class, 170
gun.xml.dom.Consumer class, 123

H

HandlerBase interface, 185
handlers, 24, 29, 30
    ContentHandler callbacks, 41-43
    errors, 44
        diagnostics and, 53-56
        validity (producer-side), 48, 49
        exception, 49-56
helper classes, 140-149
high surrogate (Java char values), 110
high-level APIs, 2
    flexibility of, 5
HotJava web browser, 16
HTML (HyperText Markup
        Language), 92
HTML Tidy tool, 92
HTTP protocol, 46, 166
    messaging and, 169-174
HyperText Markup Language
        (HTML), 92

Index

I

IANA Internet encoding names, 73
ID attribute, 116
IDREF attribute, 116
IDREFS attribute, 116
IETF (Internet Engineering Task Force), 9
ignorableWhitespace( ) callback function, 106, 125
#IMPLIED attribute, 117, 144
indexes, looking up attributes witg, 40
Infoset (XML), 5, 20, 201-218
input normalization, 206
InputSource class, 70-75, 186
    entity text, providing, 71-75
    EntityResolver interface and, 89
    methods for, 71
Inputsource.getEncoding( ) function, 205
InputStreamReader class, providing entity text, 72
interface facility, working with multiple products, 2
interfaces, 26
    ErrorHandler, 51-53
internal subsets, 113
internalEntityDecl( ) function, 119
International Standards Organization (ISO), 12
internationalization, 110
Internet, 166-168
Internet Engineering Task Force (IETF), 9
Internet xml-dev mailing list, developing SAX 1.0, 9
ISO (International Standards Organization), 12

J

J2EE (Java2 Enterprise Edition), 13
Java in XML messaging, 168
Java parsers, 9
Java Project X, 16
Java2 Enterprise Edition (J2EE), 13
java.io.CharArrayReader method for InputSource class, 72
java.io.InputStream in method for InputStream class, 72
java.io.IOException class, 89
java.io.Reader class, 27, 67
    InputSource class and, 72
    installing SAX 2.0, 19
java.lang.Character class, using surrogate pairs, 110
java.lang.String class, using surrogate pairs, 110
JavaScript language, 13
javax.xml.parsers.SAXParserFactory, using JAXP, 79
javax.xml.transform.sax package, 134-137
JAXP (Java API for XML Processing), 13, 79-81
jaxp.jar file, 17
JDOM, 123
    trees, turning into SAX events, 94
.jpeg files, declaring with NDATA annotations, 121
Jumbo XML browser, 9

L

LANs (local area networks), 167
Lark Java parser, 9
late binding of handlers, 69
LexicalHandler class, 85, 111-114, 200
    DOM documents, building, 123
    DTD data and, 115
    push mode with XSLT and, 135
LexicalHandler.comment( ) function, 214
LexicalHandler.endDTD( ) function, 206
LexicalHandler.startDTD( ) function, 215
LexicalHandler.startEntity( ) function, 119
local area networks (LANs), 167
localName parameter, 207
Locator class, 104, 107-110, 186
locator data, 204
Locator.getSystemId( ) function, 205, 212, 217
LocatorImpl class, 145, 193

M

loose coupling, 167
low surrogate (Java char values), 110

Macintosh
  filenames, turning into URIs, 75
  XML output, writing, 32
marshalling, 99
MathML, 110
Megginson, David, 9
memory
  consuming, with SAX and DOM, 6
  SAX parsers, using, 4
messaging, 165-174
  HTTP with SAX 2.0 and, 169-174
  Java, roles for, 168
methods
  attribute names, accessing, 61
  InputSource class, 71
Microsoft, shipping CDFs, 150
mixed mode, 64
MSXML Java parser, 9
multithreaded applications, using SAX with, 7
My Netscape, using RSS, 151

N

namespace flag, 64
namespace-prefixes feature, 86
namespaces, 20, 46, 56-66
  feature flags, 63-65
  Information Items, 217
  NamespaceSupport class and, 145-147
  naming attributes and elements with, 58-63
  specification of, 11
NamespaceSupport class, 99, 145-147, 194
namespaceURI parameter, 207
naming
  attributes, 38, 61
  elements, 57-61
    with namespaces, 58-63
NDATA attribute, 121
Netscape, shipping RSS, 150
NMTOKEN attribute, 116
NMTOKENS attribute, 116

noise data, pruning from DOM trees, 124
nonvalidating parsers, 46
NOTATION attribute, 120
Notation Information Items, 216
notationDecl( ) callback function, 120
NSFilter class, 170
null, setting handlers, 69
NullPointerException class, 69

O

OASIS group, 10
OASIS SGML/Open Catalog (SOCAT), 91
object tree parsers API, 3
object values, 84
objects, turning into SAX events, 98
Open Directory Project, 152
optionally validating parsers, 44
org.apache.crimson.tree.XmlDocumentBuilder class, 123
org.dom4j.io.SAXContentHandler class, 123
org.dom4j.io.XMLWriter, 31
org.jdom.input.SAXHandler, 123
org.xml.sax package, 10, 14, 181-190
org.xml.sax.AttributeList class, 149
org.xml.sax.ContentHandler, 29
org.xml.sax.DocumentHandler class, 148
org.xml.sax.driver class, 77
org.xml.sax.DTDHandler, 29
org.xml.sax.ErrorHandler, 29
org.xml.sax.ext package, 14, 199
org.xml.sax.ext.DeclHandler, 29
org.xml.sax.ext.LexicalHandler, 30
org.xml.sax.HandlerBase class, 149
org.xml.sax.helpers package, 14, 190-199
org.xml.sax.helpers.AttributeListImpl class, 149
org.xml.sax.helpers.ParserAdapter class, 149
org.xml.sax.helpers.ParserFactory class, 149
org.xml.sax.helpers.XMLReaderAdapter class, 149

Index

org.xml.sax.Parser class, 67, 148
org.xml.sax.SAXException class, 50, 89
org.xml.sax.SAXNotRecognizedException class, 50
org.xml.sax.SAXNotSupportedException class, 50
org.xml.sax.SAXParseException class, 50
org.xml.sax.XMLReader class, 67
output encoding, 207
output, when writing XML text, 32

P

P2P (peer-to-peer), 167
parse( ) function, 50, 67, 68
   EntityResolver class, passing InputSource objects to, 75
   InputSource class and, 70
parser configuration, 44
Parser interface, 187
ParserAdapter class, 147, 194
ParserFactory class, 147, 195
parser-level APIs, 2
parsers, 1
   advantages of SAX, 4
   distributions for SAX 2.0, 14-17
   feature flags and, 44
   SAX 2.0, 11
     installing, 17-19
Pascal language, 13
passive APIs, 2
peer-to-peer (P2P), 167
percent sign (%) in parameter entities, 85, 118
Perl language, 13
PHP, syntax of, 106
pipeline stage, 130
pipelines, 129-139
   events, 32
   using SAX parsers, 4
.png files, declaring with NDATA annotations, 121
popContext( ) function, 146
POST (HTTP) request, 169
Post-Schema-Validation Infoset (PSVI), 44, 201
prefix mapping, 65
procedural logic, 44

Processing Instruction Information Items, 211
processingInstruction( ) function, 105
processName( ) function, 146
producer.parse ( ), 28
producers, 24
producer-side validation, 44-49
   handling errors for, 48, 49
producing events, 67-102
property objects, 81
PSVI (Post-Schema-Validation Infoset), 44, 201
public IDs for entities, 119
publicId parameter, 215
pull mode event producer
   with XMLReader, 67-76
   with XSLT, 136
pull-to-push adapter, 67
push mode event producers, 67, 94-100
   with XSLT, 135
pushContext( ) function, 146
Python language, 13

Q

qualified names, naming attributes and elements, 58

R

random access, providing for XML data, 8
RDF (Resource Description Framework) Site Summary, 150
Remote Procedure Call (RPC), 166
#REQUIRED attribute, 117
reset( ) function, 146
Resource Description Framework (RDF) Site Summary, 150
Rich Site Summary (see RSS)
RPC (Remote Procedure Call), 166
RSS (Rich Site Summary), 150-165
   applications, building with, 162-165
   data model for, 152-155
   parsing events, consuming and producing, 155-162
RssConsumer class, 159
RssHandler interface, 161

rule-based logic, 44

S

SAX 1.0, 9
  support, 147-149
SAX 2.0, 10-13
  extensions, 11
  installing, 17-19
  introducing, 23
  parser distributions for, 14-17
SAX parsers, 67
SAX (Simple API for XML)
  APIs and, 1-9
  history of, 9-14
SAXException class, 49, 51, 68, 187
  error and diagnostics when using, 53
SAXNotRecognizedException, 188
SAXNotSupportedException, 188
SAXON Java XSLT engine, 135
SAXParseException, 188
SAXParseException class, 54
  Locator class and, 108
SAXResult class, 135
SAXTransformerFactory class, 135, 137
schemes, 46
  EntityResolver interface and, 88
serialization, 94
set*() method, 81
setDocumentLocator() callback
    method, 104
setEncoding() function, 72
setFeature() function, 48, 69
  namespace feature flags and, 63
setLocale() function, 148
setProperty() function, 69, 77
setSystemId() function, 72
SGML Formal Public Identifiers, 119
skippedEntity() function, 107
SOAP, 168
SOCAT (OASIS SGML/Open
    Catalog), 91
sockets network API, 13
stages (pipeline), 130
startCDATA() function, 114
startDocument() function, 104
startDTD() function, 113

startElement() function, 35, 37, 40, 42, 66
  attributeDecl() and, 117
  using for elements and naming, 57
  NamespaceSupport class and, 145
  XMLReader feature flags and, 84
startEntity() function, 114
startPrefixMapping() function, 64, 66, 86
stream validator in Ælfred parsers, 16
stream-based processing, 4
streaming parsers API, 2
String class, parsing data with no
    URI, 70
String local element, 42
String qName element, 42
String uri element, 42
StringBuffers, 43
String.equals() function, 86
String.intern() function, 86
StringReader class, 109
subdocuments, including, 174-180
Sun, using JAXP, 13
surrogate pairs (Java char values), 110
system ID for notations, 121
systemId parameter, 70, 215
  EntityResolver interface and, 88
System.setProperty() function, 77

T

target parameter for
    processingInstruction()
    function, 105
text, 34-38
  entity text, providing with
    InputSource, 71-75
  input normalization, 206
  writing XML output, 32
TransformerHandler class, 135
Transformer.transform() function, 134, 136
TRAX API, 13

Index

U

Unexpanded Entity Reference Information Items, 212
Unicode for internationalization, 110
Unicode Normalization Form C, 206
  internationalizing character encodings, 111
universal names for attributes and elements, 58
Universal Resource Identifier (see URI)
Universal Resource Locator (URL), 46
Universal Resource Name (see URN)
UNIX, writing XML output, 32
unknown validation behavior, 46
unmarshaling, 99, 122
unparsed entity information items, 215
unparsedEntityDecl() callback function, 121
URI (Universal Resource Identifier), 46
  base, 204
  defining new handlers and features, 81
  filenames vs., 75
  InputSource class and, 70
  namespaces and, 57
URL (Universal Resource Locator), 46
URNs (Universal Resource Names), 46
  FPIs (Formal Public Identifiers) and, 89
UTF-8/16 character encoding, 33, 73, 206

V

validation (producer-side), 44-49
  handling errors for, 48, 49

W

W3C Character Model, internationalizing character encodings, 111
warning() method, 52
web site for SAX, 9
whitespace, 106
wrapped exceptions, 51

X

Xerces parser, 17
  XMLReader feature flags and, 84, 87
XHTML, 92
XInclude, 20, 174
XML 1.0
  Blueberry (see Blueberry)
XML 1.0 mode, 64
XML Canonicalization, 206
XML (Extensible Markup Language)
  APIs for, 1-22
  Infoset, 5, 20, 201-218
  Internet versus older technologies, 166-168
  Java, roles for in messaging, 168
  JAXP, using for, 13
  messaging and, 165-174
  namespaces (see namespaces)
  piplines, 129-139
  related standards of, 19-22
  SAX parsers and, 4
  validity and, 44
XML Infoset, 20
XML Namespaces, 20
  specification of, 11
XML plus namespace mode, 64
XML Schema Datatypes (XSD), 65
XML4J (XML for Java) parser, 17
xml:base attribute, 21, 141, 144, 204
XMLFilter interface, 101, 189
  pull modes with XSLT and, 136
XMLFilterImpl class, 102, 132-134, 158, 196
  examples of, 134
xml.jar, installing SAX 2.0, 17
xml:lang attribute, 144
xmlns attributes, using XMLReader feature flags, 86
XMLReader class, 26, 189
  configuring behavior, 81-88
  feature flags, 84-88
  functional groups, 68-70
  JAXP, using, 79
  obtaining, 76-81
  properties, 81
  pull mode event production and, 67-76

XMLReaderAdapter class, 198
XMLReaderFactory class, 76-78, 147, 199
XMLReaderFactory.createXMLReader(), 27
XMLReader.getFeature() function, 206
XMLReader.parse() function, 67, 169, 173, 202, 205
  InputSource class and, 70
XMLReader.setDTDHandler() function, binding DTDHandler to parsers, 120
XMLReader.setEntityResolver() method, 89
XML-RPC, 168
xml:space attribute, 144
XMLWriter, 31-33
  event pipelines and, 32, 130
XP Java parser, 9
XPath, 174
XPath data model, reading comments, 112
XPointer, 174
XSD (XML Schema Datatypes), 65
XSLT, 134
  push mode with XSLT, 135

About the Author

David Brownell is a software engineer. He's been involved with SAX since shortly after the XML 1.0 specification went final, and is currently involved in maintaining the SAX APIs and the GNUJAXP implementation. When he worked at Sun, he started the Java XML engineering effort, including SAX support, as a natural follow-up to the servlet-based web software infrastructure.

Colophon

Our look is the result of reader comments, our own experimentation, and feedback from distribution channels. Distinctive covers complement our distinctive approach to technical topics, breathing personality and life into potentially dry subjects.

The animal on the cover of *SAX2* is a pampas cat. Not much is known about this cat, as extensive studies on it have never been done. For instance, the pampas cat is believed to be mainly nocturnal and to live primarily on the ground. However, some pampas cats that reside in zoos have been observed as being somewhat active in daylight, as well as comfortable spending time in trees.

The pampas cat is native to South America. Its natural habitat allows for quite a range, as some species are found in grasslands, some in mountain regions, and some in swampy areas. It is not a large cat, weighing only between 7 and 8 pounds when fully grown. Its features are marked by a wide face and pointed ears. The color and markings on its fur are determined by the area in which it lives. For example, in the Andes Mountains, the cat is found with gray fur and red stripes; Brazilian cats are reddish-brown with black stripes; and cats living in Argentina are a light brown shade and have faint markings. The stripes always appear on the cat's legs and torso, and the cat has very long hair, which can grow up to three inches long. When the cat is frightened, these hairs stand on end, which makes the cat seem larger, as well as more menacing. This no doubt serves as a deterrent to predators.

The pampas cat population was dwindling for a time, as the cat was hunted for its skin. However, in 1980 laws were passed against this, so that particular threat to the species seems to have passed. Now the main danger is the growing human population, which is infringing on the pampas cat's home in the plains and forests.

Mary Brady was the production editor and proofreader and Melanie Wang was the copyeditor for *SAX2*. Colleen Gorman, Matt Hutchinson, and Claire

Cloutier provided quality control. Derek Di Matteo and Philip Dangler provided production support. Joe Wizda wrote the index.

Ellie Volckhausen designed the cover of this book, based on a series design by Edie Freedman. The cover image is a 19th-century engraving from *Mammalia*. Emma Colby produced the cover layout with QuarkXPress 4.1, using Adobe's ITC Garamond font.

Melanie Wang designed the interior layout based on a series design by Nancy Priest. The print version of this book was created by translating the DocBook XML markup of its source files into a set of gtroff macros, using a filter developed at O'Reilly & Associates by Norman Walsh. Steve Talbott designed and wrote the underlying macro set on the basis of the GNU *troff* *–gs* macros; Lenny Muellner adapted them to XML and implemented the book design. The GNU groff text formatter Version 1.11.1 was used to generate PostScript output. The text and heading fonts are ITC Garamond Light and Garamond Book. The illustrations that appear in the book were produced by Robert Romano and Jessamyn Read, using Macromedia FreeHand 9 and Adobe Photoshop 6. This colophon was written by Mary Brady.

Whenever possible, our books use a durable and flexible lay-flat binding.